The Digital Metrics Field Guide

The Definitive Reference for Brands
Using the Web, Social Media,
Mobile Media, or Email

About the Advertising Research Foundation

Founded in 1936 by the Association of National Advertisers and the American Association of Advertising Agencies, the Advertising Research Foundation (ARF) is the preeminent professional organization providing fact-based thought leadership to the advertising, marketing, and media industries. The ARF's membership includes more than 400 companies in four major industries: advertisers, agencies (creative and media), media companies, and research companies. Additionally, the ARF's knowledge and thought leadership are leveraged by industry associations, educational institutions, and international organizations.

The ARF's core activities for advancing knowledge include multiday events such as the annual Re:think Convention + Expo and Audience Measurement Conference; and daylong Industry Leader Forums. The ARF Forum program addresses topics which are central to the industries we serve. Each council presents the latest cases, trends, practices, and insights from A-list brands, companies, and presenters. Additionally, the ARF publishes the *Journal of Advertising Research*, a peer reviewed publication with contributions by leading academics and practitioners.

ARF members enjoy the many benefits of an engaged community: professional networking; opportunities to contribute to industry development; access to advertising, marketing, and media knowledge through state-of-the-art web-based research tools, such as ARF PowerSearch and ARF Morning Coffee; community forums; and personal assistance from the ARF Knowledge Center.

If you are interested in learning more about membership, email membership@thearf.org or visit the membership section of the ARF website: http://thearf.org/member-benefits.php.

BIS Publishers
Building Het Sieraad
Postjesweg 1
1057 DT Amsterdam
The Netherlands
T +31 (0)20 515 02 30
F +31 (0)20 515 02 39
bis@bispublishers.nl
www.bispublishers.nl

ISBN 978 90 6369 377 0

The Digital Metrics Field Guide

The Definitive Reference for Brands
Using the Web, Social Media,
Mobile Media, or Email

by Stephen D. Rappaport

BIS Publishers

Dedication

To everyone discovering the humanity within their metrics.

Contents

Acknowledgements

This work on digital measurement owes enormous debts of gratitude and thanks to the many industry authorities supplying information and their expertise, and to ARF's leadership, staff and interns supporting the research effort. Online publishers, commercial measurement companies and nonprofit media associations contributed content and contributed their valuable time to vet the work as it unfolded; their comments improved the final product immeasurably. We thank the following companies and people within them.

■ **CALIBRE CONSULTING GROUP:** Jay Fischer, Managing Partner. ■ **COMSCORE:** Andrea Vollman, Marketing Director; Andrew Lipsman, VP Industry Analysis; Dan Piech, Senior Product Manager; Gian Fulgoni, Chairman; and Shelly Chiang, Learning Program Manager. ■ **DIGITAS:** Terry Cohen, SVP Strategy and Analysis, and Board Member Digital Analytics Association. ■ **EXPERIAN MARKETING SERVICES:** Alex Schumacher, Sr. Marketing Director, Consumer Insights; Ellen Romer, VP, NA Strategy & Innovation, Consumer Insights; Shelley Kessler, Sr. Email Marketing Analyst; Max Kilger, Ph.D., Chief Behavioral Scientist, Consumer Insights. ■ **FACEBOOK:** Patrick Kemp, Marketing Effectiveness Researcher; Sean Bruich, Head of Measurement Research, Development, and Partnerships. ■ **FORDHAM UNIVERSITY:** Philip Napoli, Ph.D., Professor, Communications and Media Management. ■ **GOOGLE:** Gunnard Johnson, Advertising Research Director; Harry Case, Media Research Scientist; Jeffrey Buchan, Senior Associate, Global Industry Relations. ■ **IAB:** Sherrill Mane, Senior Vice President, Research, Analytics, and Measurement. ■ **INSITES CONSULTING USA:** Niels Schillewaert, Ph.D., Managing Partner; Annelies Verhaeghe, Head of Research Innovation, Managing Partner. ■ **INSTITUTE FOR PUBLIC RELATIONS MEASUREMENT COMMISSION MEMBERS:** David Geddes, Ph.D., Geddes Analytics; David Michaelson, Ph.D., Managing Director, Teneo Strategy. ■ **KAPLAN TEST PREP:** Vincent Santino, Associate Director of Insights and Analytics. ■ **KRAFT FOODS GROUP:** Paul Banas, Director, Consumer Insights & Strategy. ■ **MEDIA BEHAVIOR INSTITUTE:** Kevin Moeller, Executive Director, Research and Analytics; Mike Bloxham, Executive Director, Marketing. ■ **METRIXLAB:** Laurent Flores, Ph.D., Global Director and Professor of Marketing, INSEEC Business School; ■ **MILLWARD BROWN DIGITAL:** Yaakov Kimelfeld, Ph.D., Chief Research Officer. ■ **MOTIVEQUEST:** David Rabjohns, CEO. ■ **NIELSEN:** Bill Moult, former President, Knowledge Collaborations; Linda Tansey, VP Knowledge Management; Megan Clarken, EVP, Global Product Leadership; Mike Hess, EVP Data Integration and Social TV Analytics; Patrick Chang, Client Solutions Associate; Tristan Gaiser, VP Online Analytics. ■ **NORMAN LEAR CENTER AT USC ANNENBERG:** Johanna Blakley, Ph.D., Managing Director, Martin Kaplan, Ph.D., Professor and Founding Director. ■ **OLSON ZALTMAN ASSOCIATES:** Joe Plummer, Ph.D. ■ **PAINE PUBLISHING:** Katie Delahaye Paine, CEO. ■ **RAY, AUGIE:** Fortune 100 Company, Social Media Director. ■ **UNIVERSAL MCCANN:** Graeme Hutton, SVP, Group Partner, Research. ■ **VINTCO:** Gilles Santini, CEO. ■ **THE WHARTON SCHOOL, UNIVERSITY OF PENNSYLVANIA:** Yoram (Jerry) Wind, Ph.D., The Lauder Professor, Professor of Marketing, Director, SEI Center for Advanced Studies in Management.

Advertising Research Foundation's staff provided invaluable support for conceiving and completing the *Digital Metrics Field Guide*. The *Field Guide* was inspired by ARF member **Laurent Flores**, then a Professor of Marketing at Fordham Business School and CRMMetrics' founder, and supported by ARF EVPs **Bob Woodard** and **Ted McConnell** who believed that ARF members and the industry needed a guide to digital metrics for practitioners. **Robert Barocci**, retired ARF President/CEO green-lighted this project. Current President and CEO **Gayle Fuguitt** saw it through. Chief Research Officer **Don Gloeckler** championed the *Field Guide*, furnished guidance, and provided invaluable encouragement when the going got tough. Chief Revenue Officer **Felix Yang** made sure the project had the proper resources. Senior Knowledge Specialist **Mi hui Pak**, Knowledge Specialist **Jessica Letizia**, and Junior Librarian **Cristina Reyes** of ARF's Knowledge Center located references of the highest quality (as they always do) and furnished moral support (as only they can). **Ed Reilley**, Project Coordinator, expertly managed the production from manuscript to published work. Fellow colleagues **Bill Cook**, **David Marans**, **Horst Stipp**, **Peter Orban**, and **Todd Powers** from the Research Department gave helpful feedback and advice. **Gwen LaFantasie**, **Jeremiah Tucker**, **Michael Heitner**, **Rosie Aponte**, and **Sara Gretschel** from Membership Services made sure that ARF members benefit from this *Guide*. **Amaury Besse**, **Christopher Lee Boon**, **Jake Rosenbaum**, and **Jennifer Brodman** from Business Development will do the same for prospective members. **Jacqueline Badler**, **Lauren Rubino**, and **Shanika Gunawardena** ably marketed this work to ARF members and the industry-at-large. **Geoffrey Precourt**, Editor in Chief, and **Nanette Burns**, Managing Editor of the Journal of Advertising Research, provided valuable editorial assistance.

Thanks also to staff not directly involved but whose collegiality meant so much: **Kristin Konis**, Executive Assistant and Board Liaison; **Norman Cordova**, Accounting Manager; **Chris Ducharme**, Graphic Designer; **Rachael Feigenbaum**, Program Director; **Chris Kosar**, Sales Director; **Jo Hogan**, Chief People Officer, **Kelly McSorley**, Director of Events; **Erica Palmisano**, former Human Resources Manager; and **Ronni Umles**, Events Coordinator.

ARF Interns **Bradford Priest** and **Tina Kim** tirelessly performed the digging and tracking down, acquiring the many pieces that were eventually incorporated into this work. Theirs is the unsung work that is critical to the success of a publication like this. Through it all, their enthusiasm and commitment never wavered. Bradford stayed involved even after his internship ended. ARF is proud that both are employed in our industry, Bradford as an Account Manager with Microsoft, and Tina as an Analyst in Digital Ad Sales Research at MTV Networks. We wish them success and long careers. ✦

Foreword

Gayle Fuguitt, President and CEO

Welcome to the world of "humetrics." Stephen Rappaport coined this term to describe the big shift from our industry's age-old preoccupation with media measurement to understanding people by gauging and interpreting their digital lives. This book helps us recognize data points not merely as impersonal dots on a trend line, percentage changes, or ratios. They are, in fact, personal—capturing what people say, do, and feel in real time. Once we view digital metrics as reflecting individuals, they become characters we employ to craft compelling narratives about people and brands that we later share with our colleagues in and outside of our areas. Those narratives fortify brands with a common understanding that increases the potential to act in the best interests of customers and prospects, and to create and execute successful marketing strategies.

The Digital Metrics Field Guide honors a fundamental obligation of the ARF to its membership and industry: to clarify the great research issues of the day and point a way forward. Today, 77 years after ARF's founding, we all marvel at the exploding digital media advertising industry. Yet, our members and industry friends constantly wonder about the meaning of the new measures: how they are calculated, what questions they answer, and how they should be interpreted. The *Field Guide* brings perspective and guidance to brands of all sizes in a changing, uncertain world.

The *Field Guide* is meant to be a tool that supports your current needs, with easy-to-find terms, and metrics listed by category along with pertinent information. For example, if you are interested in learning more about engagement, you'll find the various metrics at a glance and the different media to which they apply, along with answers to relevant, frequently asked questions. There's also a section devoted exclusively to how to choose a metric, and—when you have time and want to think about the future for measurement—twelve essays by our industry's finest authorities.

We hope the *Field Guide* gives you the confidence to select and use those digital metrics that matter most to your brand and enable it to inspire change—a metric's signature test. We hope, too, that it helps you gain deeper insight into the people your brand serves, or intends to serve, by recognizing the humetrics—the humanity within the metrics. ✦

Introduction

"Online is the most measurable medium. But the logical corollary is that it is also the medium with the most measures." So said Josh Chasin, comScore's Chief Research Officer, at an Advertising Research Foundation (ARF) Q&A session in 2012. Almost all of us would agree. We at the ARF definitely do: We winnowed a list of 350 metrics down to 197 for this book. Does any other medium you know come at all close?

Why ARF Prepared The *Digital Metrics Field Guide*

Those hundreds of metrics—the counts, percentages and ratios of just about everything that happens online—figure into conversations and presentations nearly each day in our offices at the ARF, at our conferences, and in member meetings we hold on hot topics called Forums. Those discussions also take place in your workplace, in the coffee shops you patronize, at the airport, in the trade outlets you watch, listen to, or read. Every advertiser, agency, media or research firm that uses digital communication contends with digital metrics daily.

We hear the questions asked by our 400+ corporate members and our non-member colleagues: Which metrics should we use? What does a particular metric, like the new Viewable Impression, mean? Will it affect media buying and selling? Should I care about the hot new metric X? Has any research been done on it? What does it say?

Most of us want answers we can understand and apply to build brands. That is why ARF developed *The Digital Metrics Field Guide*: to fulfill our commitment of clarifying and promoting advertising industry understanding of vital and vexing issues so that brands can better respond, adapt, and confidently move forward in uncertain, changing, and challenging times.

The *Field Guide* Is for Anyone Involved with the Web, Social Media, Mobile Media, or Email

The *Field Guide* is for every enterprise that sends emails, has a website, maintains a social media presence, or uses mobile to communicate with customers or prospects, and for the suppliers, vendors, and consultants who service them. It is for those who are given reports that include metrics, who work with analysts but are not themselves analysts, and who hold some responsibility for planning and evaluating a brand's web, social, mobile, or email communications. The *Field Guide* provides the background, foundation, and authority for everyone in an organization, no matter its size, category, brands, or budget, to speak a common language of metrics while enhancing their ability to manage, make informed and wise decisions, and grow their business. Our specialist colleagues will find this book helpful as a companion to their more technical, detailed books, blogs, or academic resources that explain and discuss the ins and outs of measurement matters.

Key Features of the *Field Guide* that Benefit You

The *Field Guide* will help you understand, appreciate, select, and utilize metrics to your brand's advantage. The *Field Guide* provides:

A comprehensive guide to generally available digital metrics. The *Field Guide*'s 197 metrics source from the four primary digital channels: email, mobile, social, and the web. The *Field Guide* presents metrics that you are likely to come across, such as those cited in trade-related articles; internal documents from your brand's advertising, marketing, media or research departments; dashboards; and reports or files from service vendors, measurement companies, or analytics suppliers. The *Field Guide* steers clear of proprietary metrics that are not generally available.

Authoritative definitions, calculations, and examples. Each metric is referenced to one or more sources. These authorities include: industry standards bodies (such as the Interactive Advertising Bureau or Digital Analytics Association); measurement companies (including such firms as comScore, Experian Marketing Services, Millward Brown Digital, and Nielsen); and measurement experts (Avinash Kaushik or Paul W. Farris and colleagues, for example, who authored important books or actively blog). The *Field Guide* provides a list of all sources used to develop the metrics definitions. When two or more parties define a metric similarly but use different names, the alternatives are listed. And if the definitions vary, those differences are pointed out.

Calculations and relevant examples accompany each metric, to reflect how it is computed and what information goes into calculating it. You will be able to judge if a metric is appropriate or not, and know what additional data to look for and which questions to ask your experts in order to interpret a metric accurately.

During the course of writing, we were repeatedly asked: Which metrics matter? The *Field Guide* answers by identifying core metrics with an asterisk following their names. These metrics were selected because they are essential to advertising practices or are frequently reported email, mobile, social, or web measures. A caveat: Any "best of" list reflects judgment. We do not claim that the starred list is perfect—you need to decide which metrics are best for your brand—but it offers a starting place.

Metrics organized by your industry interest.

Practitioners often think of metrics in different, ways, depending on their point of view. Some are interested in channel metrics, those relating to the web, social media, mobile, and email. Advertisers and agencies concern themselves with, and make distinctions among, paid, owned, and earned media. Marketers like to view their activities through a progression of purchase funnel-like stages. Analysts looking to measure site performance, media usage, or user behavior commonly look at metrics in categories such as traffic, media consumption, engagement, or conversion actions. (A conversion action is something that site owners want people to do, such as downloading a white paper, signing up for a newsletter subscription, or making a purchase.) Lastly, there are those who like their metrics ordered A to Z. Whichever your interest, the *Field Guide* presents the metrics through each of these different lenses. You will be able to look them up in a way that most closely matches your needs or preferences.

We specify those metrics that are unique, those that fit into multiple categories, and those whose meanings depend on their context. One such example is the metric "Bounce," which has different meanings in different channels, such as when Bounce refers to emails or to the web. Additionally, all metrics are cross-referenced to related measures so that you can easily access more information and see connections among metrics.

Research and comments.
Not only do we as practitioners want to know how a metric is defined, we want to learn what research, if it is publicly available, tells us about the metric. Roughly half of the metric entries present ARF Comments that review and summarize findings or expert commentary. Those brief essays separate fact from opinion or guru-speak. They furnish you with results, considerations, or issues surrounding metrics so that you are equipped to evaluate the relevance, utility, and impact of metrics for your brands. Take the Viewable Impression highlighted a few moments ago. ARF Comments explain why the Viewable Impression became important and the progress made to make the Viewable Impression a currency for media buying and selling. The comments also raise counter-arguments about the value of non-viewable impressions. ARF Comments spell out the pros and cons, and offer guidance gleaned from research reports and industry position papers. All research is cited within the metric entry and listed in the Research References section.

Viewpoints on measurement.
A dozen experts contributed essays on measurement in today's environment and in the emerging future. Their contributions range from offering practical advice on creating a metrics strategy, to a lively controversy around the notion that the ad industry needs comparable cross-media metrics, and finally to the need to incorporate behavioral, social, and effectiveness data into metrics. The authors point out the shift underway from metrics that answer legacy questions first posed during the mass media era ("What is my advertising doing to people?") to questions more relevant to today's web, social, and mobile era ("What are people doing with my advertising?"). ✦

How to Choose the Right Metrics

Metrics are the counts, percentages, and ratios that describe events or trends. The *Field Guide* concentrates on metrics for websites, email, social media, and mobile media. The great majority of digital metrics concern activities—the things that people do, such as opening emails, clicking links, reading pages and viewing videos, posting and commenting, sharing, downloading content, installing apps, liking, checking-in, and friending, are merely several of the most common actions. Instead of thinking technically about metrics, think about them in two ways: 1) as measures that reflect business performance that brands can easily understand, control, and use for improvement, and 2) as "humetrics,"measures that represent flesh-and-blood people. Brands that understand metrics can tell compelling stories about their tire-kickers, hand-raisers, prospects, customers, advocates, and even their naysayers and detractors.

Our ARF members often ask: "How do I choose the right metrics? There are sooooo many." In a moment the *Field Guide* offers a set of selection criteria. Sometimes they ask: "Which metrics should I choose?" The unsurprising answer: "It depends." It depends on a brand's goals, objectives, strategies, and tactics. Those vary from brand to brand, but also can vary brand by brand within parent company portfolios. They may also vary for a single brand as that brand learns from its in-market experiences, then adapts, adjusts, or shifts direction to keep pace with its ever-changing consumer.

Six Questions Brands Should Ask to Select Metrics

Choosing the right metrics is pretty straightforward … if you know the right questions to ask. Here they are:

1. What are the metrics we need to measure progress on our strategy? Metrics selection begins by identifying metrics that appear to relate to agreed-upon business outcomes, not with a standard one-size-fits-all set. Kraft's Oscar Mayer unit, for example, initiated a strategy to increase brand advocacy. Their approach was to move people through four steps that began with awareness, then moved to participation, involvement, and concluded with advocacy. The team considered many metrics, eventually winnowing the number down to a concise group of 12 that they felt captured and communicated the actions and behaviors that best reported each step. (More details about this case are presented below in an essay section titled "Impose a Framework on Measurement.")

Public relations measurement authority Katie Delahaye Paine (2013) supports Kraft's approach to settle on a set of keenly relevant metrics. "The role of metrics in any organization," she states, "is to help people focus. No human, no matter how smart or how hardworking, can focus on 20 different metrics." Pick those that "are the most likely to help the business succeed."

2. Is the metric easily understood by everyone on the team and by the people to whom it is reported? Metrics authority Avinash Kaushik (2007a) advocates simplicity—measures should be "uncomplex," meaning that they should be simple, descriptive, and easy to explain. Take this example of Facebook's metric "People Talking About This."

Often abbreviated as PTAT, this measure combined a number of different types of events that create Facebook Stories (see Story) into a single number. But brands using this number found it difficult to interpret, asking: "What actions are driving this number up or down?" It was hard to figure out and harder to act upon. Facebook eventually deprecated the metric and is reporting the individual activities instead. Transparency is key.

3. Is the metric "instantly useful" and actionable? Metrics should quickly and clearly signify what they mean, and indicate what brands should consider doing when their numbers go up, go down, or remain unchanged. Let us repurpose the PTAT example. PTAT sowed much confusion over what it meant and failed to give guidance for what to do. A metric such as Bounce Rate, Kaushik mentions, answers this question. Lower bounce rates typically mean that things are fine; higher bounce rates generally mean that things need attention. The ways that metrics are presented in reports, dashboards, and visualizations can help enhance their ability to communicate by narrowing the focus, contextualizing the numbers, simplifying the presentation, and telling a sharp story. Infographics became popular for these reasons, and have even become a standard reporting format for some companies.

4. Are the underlying metrics data credible and timely for the brand? Data quality is an issue all brands face, whether it comes from their own systems or from third-parties. Even bedrock measures with very precise definitions, such as Unique Visitors, can be over-counted because of cookie deletion. Ad Impression counts often differ because of how and when they are counted at the ad server and in users' browsers. Brands must be confident that they have the cleanest, most accurate data they need or risk the consequences of misleading analyses and the decisions based on them.

The data exhaust spewed by myriad digital media both bless and curse brands with "big data," much of it real-time second-by-second recording of action people take. What sometimes gets lost in big data discussions is how frequent data need to be collected for brands' purposes. Those frequencies will vary depending on the brand and its situation, but it is something brands should take time to decide upon. Right-sizing data enables brands to collect, analyze, and develop metrics from their data in a timely manner. Working with too much or too little data collected at the wrong times works against developing and leveraging meaningful metrics.

5. What experience has the brand had using a particular metric? Even if answers to the four questions above give the green light, consult people who have history with the metrics being selected. Their hard won lessons may reveal that the metric works as expected, or that there are marketing, media or advertising considerations that make it less suitable for a particular purpose.

6. Should we change out our metrics? Analyst Kaushik points out that because business changes all the time, some metrics may need to be dropped or revised or new ones added to keep pace. He makes the excellent suggestion that metrics be reviewed periodically, with the set optimized on the brand's ability to take action on them. Metrics that can't be "actioned" become candidates for dropping and being replaced with metrics that can. Those new metrics would not be mere substitutes but would provide new analytic ability. And, of course, the new ones would be selected by answering the five questions above. ✦

How to Locate Metrics in the *Field Guide*

The *Field Guide* provides three ways to locate metrics you are interested in: alphabetically, by category, and by marketing stage. After you identify the metrics you want to read about in detail, look up the metric in the section **Digital Metrics Field Guide Entries**.

Alphabetical: The alphabetical listing provides the metrics in A to Z order. The metrics category and the questions the metrics answer are included.

Category: The category listing provides the metrics in groups: advertising, audience/traffic, site navigation and site performance, media consumption, engagement and interaction, amplification and endorsement, conversion, e-commerce, and ad effectiveness. The questions the metrics answer are included.

Marketing Stage: The marketing stage index organizes the metrics by the four stages: capture, connect, close, and keep. As with the others, the questions that the metrics answer are included. ✦

Metrics Listed Alphabetically

Metric	Category	Answers Question
Abandonment Rate (Page)*	7. Conversion	On which pages are Visitors abandoning the conversion path?
Abandonment Rate (Shopping Cart)*	7. Conversion	What percent of Visitors abandoned the shopping cart on our site?
Actions Rate (Facebook)	5. Engagement/Interaction	What is the number of actions generated by our paid ad impressions?
Actions (Facebook)	5. Engagement/Interaction	How many actions were taken on our ad, Page, app or event after our ad was served?
Active User Rate (Mobile Apps)*	2. Audience/Traffic	What percentage of people who downloaded our app are using it?
Ad Awareness*	9. Ad Effectiveness	What percentage of our target customers are aware of our brand's advertising?
Ad Impression*	1. Advertising	What is an ad impression and how are they counted?
Average Order Value*	8. E-Commerce	What is the average order value on our site?
Average Time Spent on Page*	4. Media Consumption	How long is a specific page being viewed on average?
Average Time Spent on Site (Session Length)*	5. Engagement/Interaction	How much time did Visitors spend on our site, on average, for a reporting period?
Bounce—Email*	1. Advertising	How many emails bounced because they could not be delivered?
Bounce (Website or Social Network)*	2. Audience/Traffic	How many people came to our site and saw only one page?
Bounce Rate—Email	1. Advertising	What percentage of our emails bounced?
Bounce Rate (Site or Network)*	3. Site Navigation/Site Performance	What is the percentage of times a page bounces?
Brand Advocate*	6. Amplification/Endorsement	What are brand advocates and what impact do they have?

Metrics Listed Alphabetically

Metric	Category	Answers Question
Brand Awareness*	9. Ad Effectiveness	What percentage of our target market is aware of our brand?
Brand Lift*	9. Ad Effectiveness	Did exposure to our advertising campaign have an impact on our brand lift measures?
Brochure Downloads	7. Conversion	How many of our brochures were downloaded over a period of time?
Browse to Buy Ratio	7. Conversion	What percentage of browsers to our site converted to place an order?
Browser	2. Audience/Traffic	What is a Web browser?
Channel	2. Audience/Traffic	Which online media channels are Visitors using to arrive at our site?
Check-Ins—Page (Facebook)	6. Amplification/Endorsement	How many people checked-in to our Place?
Click	5. Engagement/Interaction	What is a click?
Click Stream	3. Site Navigation/Site Performance	What path did Visitors take through our site?
Click-Through	5. Engagement/Interaction	How many times was our ad, or content, clicked on?
Click-Through Rate (CTR)*	5. Engagement/Interaction	How often do people click on our ad or content after they have seen it?
Click-Through Rate after Video Exposure	5. Engagement/Interaction	How many Click-Throughs did our video generate?
Comments*	5. Engagement/Interaction	How many comments did an ad, post, or item of content receive?
Consumers—Page (Facebook)	2. Audience/Traffic	How many unique people clicked on any of our page content?
Consumers—Post (Facebook)	2. Audience/Traffic	How many unique people clicked on anything in our post?
Consumptions—Post (Facebook)	5. Engagement/Interaction	How many clicks did our post receive?

Metrics Listed Alphabetically

Metric	Category	Answers Question
Conversation Relevant Sites	5. Engagement/Interaction	How many sites are there with conversation relevant to our brand?
Conversation*	5. Engagement/Interaction	How many conversations are people having about our brand?
Conversion Funnel*	7. Conversion	What are the steps we expect Visitors to take to complete an action we want?
Conversion Goal*	7. Conversion	What is a conversion goal?
Conversion Rate*	7. Conversion	What is the conversion rate for any conversion action on our site or through our email?
Conversion*	7. Conversion	Which conversion actions were performed on the site or in our email over a reporting period?
Cookie	2. Audience/Traffic	What is a cookie?
Cost Per Action (CPA)*	1. Advertising	What cost per action are we paying?
Cost per Click (CPC)*	1. Advertising	How much are we paying for each click on our ad?
Cost per Lead (CPL)*	1. Advertising	What cost per lead we are paying?
Cost per Order	8. E-Commerce	How much did it cost to generate one sale?
Cost per Sale (CPS)	8. E-Commerce	How much did it cost us to close one sale over a reporting period?
Cost per Targeted Thousand Impressions (CPTM)	1. Advertising	How much are we paying for one thousand targeted ad impressions?
Cost Per Thousand (CPM) Impressions*	1. Advertising	How much are we paying for each thousand impressions?
Cost per Transaction	1. Advertising	What did it cost to generate one sales transaction?
Cost per Unique Visitor	1. Advertising	What is the average cost of our ad placement or app, per Unique Visitor?

Metrics Listed Alphabetically

Metric	Category	Answers Question
Coupon Downloads	7. Conversion	How many coupons were downloaded over a specific time period?
Customers*	8. E-Commerce	How many unique browsers placed an order on our site?
Direct Traffic Visitors	2. Audience/Traffic	How many Visitors came to our site or page directly?
Earned Impression*	1. Advertising	How many earned impressions did our ad generate?
Email Capture Rate	7. Conversion	How many email addresses are we capturing on our website?
Email Click to Open Rate*	5. Engagement/Interaction	How many clicks did our emails generate from messages that were opened?
Email Complaint Rate	6. Amplification/Endorsement	What percentage of people complained about our email?
Email Complaints	6. Amplification/Endorsement	How many people marked our email as spam or junk?
Email Delivered*	1. Advertising	How many of our emails were actually received?
Email Delivery Rate*	1. Advertising	What percentage of our emails were completely received?
Email Forwards*	6. Amplification/Endorsement	How many times was our email forwarded?
Email Inbox Delivered*	1. Advertising	How many emails were delivered to Inboxes?
Email Inbox Delivered Rate	1. Advertising	How many emails were delivered to Inboxes as a percentage of emails delivered?
Email Open Rate*	1. Advertising	What is the percentage of unique subscribers that opened an email message?
Email Opens*	1. Advertising	How many times did a person look at our email?

Metrics Listed Alphabetically

Metric	Category	Answers Question
Email Sent to Open Ratio*	1. Advertising	How many of the unique emails we sent were opened?
Email Unsubscribe Rate*	2. Audience/Traffic	What percentage of unique people unsubscribed from our email?
Engaged Users - Post (Facebook)	5. Engagement/Interaction	How many unique people took any sort of action on our post?
Engagement—Tweet (Twitter)	5. Engagement/Interaction	What percentage of our Tweet impressions generated an action?
Engagement—Video	5. Engagement/Interaction	What percentage of our videos generated some type of engagement?
Engagement*	5. Engagement/Interaction	How are people interacting with our ad, content or app?
Entry Page (Top Entry Pages)*	3. Site Navigation/Site Performance	Which pages did visitors access to enter our site?
Entry Type*	2. Audience/Traffic	How did Visitors arrive at our site?
Episode Completions	5. Engagement/Interaction	How many times was our episode viewed through to the end?"
Episode Starts	5. Engagement/Interaction	How many times was a specific episode in our program started?
Estimated Minutes Watched*	4. Media Consumption	How many minutes was our video watched?
Event	5. Engagement/Interaction	What is an Event?
Event Tracking*	5. Engagement/Interaction	What are the types of interactions people are having with our site?
Exit Page*	3. Site Navigation/Site Performance	At which page did Visitor leave our site or process?
Fan (Facebook)	2. Audience/Traffic	What is a Facebook fan?
First Orders	8. E-Commerce	What is the number of first purchase orders our site received?
Followers / Subscribers*	2. Audience/Traffic	How many people subscribe to our content?

Metrics Listed Alphabetically

Metric	Category	Answers Question
Form Submissions*	7. Conversion	How many forms were submitted on our site?
Frequency*	1. Advertising	How many times did a person see a specific ad or other piece of content?
Friends of Fans (Facebook)	2. Audience/Traffic	What is the maximum number of people we could reach through people who Like our page?
Gross Ratings Points (GRP)*	1. Advertising	How much advertising weight did we purchase?
Hit	2. Audience/Traffic	How many hits did our site receive over a reporting period?
In-unit Click	5. Engagement/Interaction	How many clicks did our ad receive that took a Visitor to another page within our site?
Incoming Links (Backlinks)	2. Audience/Traffic	Which sites are linking to our Website and specific Web pages?
Influencer*	6. Amplification/Endorsement	What are Influencers and how do they work for brands?
Interactions - In ad	5. Engagement/Interaction	How did Visitors interact with our ad or app over a reporting period?
IP Address	2. Audience/Traffic	What is the IP address of a Visitor's device?
Key Content Downloads (Coupons, Recipes, Apps, etc.)*	7. Conversion	Which of our content files were downloaded, and how many times?
Key Performance Indicator (KPI)*	9. Ad Effectiveness	What is a Key Performance Indicator?
Like*	6. Amplification/Endorsement	How many Likes did our ad or content receive?
Likes—Page (Facebook)	5. Engagement/Interaction	How many people Like our brand Page?
Mentions*	6. Amplification/Endorsement	How many mentions did our brand receive in social media?

Metrics Listed Alphabetically

Metric	Category	Answers Question
Mobile App Downloads	7. Conversion	How many times was our app downoaded?
Mobile Browser Version	2. Audience/Traffic	Which mobile browsers were used to visit our mobile Web site?
Mobile Operating System	2. Audience/Traffic	Which mobile operating systems accessed our mobile Web site?
Mouseover	5. Engagement/Interaction	How long did visitors mouseover or hover on our ad?
Negative Feedback from Users—Post (Facebook)	5. Engagement/Interaction	How many unique users expressed a negative action regarding our Post?
Negative Feedback from Users—Page (Facebook)	5. Engagement/Interaction	How many unique people generated a negative action on our Page?
New App Users*	2. Audience/Traffic	How many new app users used our app?
New Likes—Page (Facebook)	2. Audience/Traffic	How many new likes did our page generate?
New Visitor	2. Audience/Traffic	How many unique visitors came to our site for the first time during a reporting period?
New Visitor (Percent)*	2. Audience/Traffic	What percentage of our visitors are new visitors?
Organic Impressions—Posts (Facebook)	1. Advertising	How many times were our posts seen organically in news feeds, tickers or on the page itself?
Organic Reach—Page (Facebook)	2. Audience/Traffic	How many people saw any of our content organically on Facebook?
Organic Reach—Post (Facebook)	2. Audience/Traffic	What is the organic reach of our page post?
Page	1. Advertising	What is a Page?
Page (Facebook, LinkedIn)	1. Advertising	What is a Facebook Page or LinkedIn Company Page?

Metrics Listed Alphabetically

Metric	Category	Answers Question
Page Exit Rate	3. Site Navigation/Site Performance	Which pages did Visitors exit from?
Page Load Times*	3. Site Navigation/Site Performance	How long does it take a specific page to load?
Page Post (Facebook)	1. Advertising	What is a Facebook Page Post?
Page View (Facebook)	4. Media Consumption	How many times did our page display on a particular day?
Page View, Logged-in (Facebook)	4. Media Consumption	How many people who viewed our page were logged-in to Facebook at the time?
Page View*	4. Media Consumption	Which Pages on our site are viewed most often?
Page Views per Visit*	4. Media Consumption	What is the average number of pages viewed each visit, over a specific time frame?
Paid Impression—Page (Facebook)	1. Advertising	How many Paid Impressions did our Sponsored Stories and Ads generate on Facebook?
Paid Impressions—Post (Facebook)	1. Advertising	How many impressions did our paid advertising generate?
Paid Reach - Page (Facebook)	2. Audience/Traffic	What is the number of people reached by our Facebook page's ad or sponsored story?
Paid Reach - Post (Facebook)	2. Audience/Traffic	What is the number of people reached by our Facebook post?
Pay Per Click (PPC)	1. Advertising	What is the amount we are paying per click?
People Engaged—Post (Facebook)	5. Engagement/Interaction	How many unique people liked, commented or shared our post?
People Talking About This—Page (Facebook)	6. Amplification/Endorsement	How engaged are people with our page?
People Talking About This—Post (Facebook)	6. Amplification/Endorsement	How many unique people created stories from our page post?

Metrics Listed Alphabetically

Metric	Category	Answers Question
Phone Brand	2. Audience/Traffic	Which phone brands accessed our mobile Web site?
Phone Type	2. Audience/Traffic	Which phone types accessed our mobile Web site?
Pinners	2. Audience/Traffic	How many unique people pinned something from our Website?
Pins	6. Amplification/Endorsement	How many things were pinned from our website, over a reporting period?
Playlist Average Playing Time	4. Media Consumption	How long was our playlist listened to, on average?
Playlist Completions	5. Engagement/Interaction	How many times was our playlist listened or viewed through to the end?
Playlist Starts	5. Engagement/Interaction	"How many times was our playlist listened to or watched?"
Program Completion Rate	5. Engagement/Interaction	Of all the times a program was started, what is the percentage of programs that played all the way through?
Program Completions	5. Engagement/Interaction	How many times was our program listened or viewed through to the end?
Program Repeated Completions	5. Engagement/Interaction	How many times was our program repeated and listened or viewed through to the end?
Program Repeated Starts	5. Engagement/Interaction	How many times was our program repeatedly watched or listened to?
Program Starts	5. Engagement/Interaction	How many times was our program watched or listened to?
Program Stops	5. Engagement/Interaction	How many times was our program stopped?
Reach*	2. Audience/Traffic	What percentage of the target audience had the opportunity to see a specific ad at least once, over a reporting period?
Recipe Downloads	7. Conversion	How many recipes were downloaded?

Metrics Listed Alphabetically

Metric	Category	Answers Question
Referral Traffic*	2. Audience/Traffic	Where is our site traffic coming from?
Repeat Visitors	2. Audience/Traffic	Are people coming back to our Website, app or brand page within a certain time period, and how many?
Repinners	2. Audience/Traffic	How many unique people repinned our pins, over a reporting period?
Repins	6. Amplification/Endorsement	How many times were pins on our website repinned, over a reporting period?
Return Visitor*	2. Audience/Traffic	How many Visitors come back to our site in this reporting period who visited in an earlier reporting period?
Retweets	6. Amplification/Endorsement	How many times was a specific tweet re-tweeted?
Revenue Over Email Delivered*	8. E-Commerce	What is the average amount of revenue earned for each delivered email?
Reviews (product)*	6. Amplification/Endorsement	How many reviews did a product receive over a specific time period?
Rich Media Interactive Impressions	1. Advertising	How many impressions did our rich media ad generate?
Screen View	4. Media Consumption	How many screen views were recorded over a certain period of time?
Screen Views per Visit	4. Media Consumption	How many screen views did our mobile site receive over a reporting period?
Search Traffic	2. Audience/Traffic	Which search engines are sending traffic to our site?
Sentiment*	6. Amplification/Endorsement	What is the opinion expressed towards my brand?
Share of Active Days	2. Audience/Traffic	When people go on the Web, what percent of visits go to our site?
Share of Streams	4. Media Consumption	What is the relative popularity of our streaming video or audio files?

Metrics Listed Alphabetically

Metric	Category	Answers Question
Sharing*	6. Amplification/Endorsement	How often is our content, ad or app being shared with friends, contacts or connections?
Social Click Rate	5. Engagement/Interaction	How many clicks did our ads get that had social context?
Social Clicks	5. Engagement/Interaction	How many clicks did our Facebook ad receive from friends?
Social Impressions (Facebook)	1. Advertising	How many impressions of our ad included social context?
Social Percentage (Facebook)	6. Amplification/Endorsement	What percentage of our ads have a social element?
Song Downloads	7. Conversion	How many songs were downloaded?
Source	2. Audience/Traffic	Which sources within online media channels are Visitors using to arrive at our site?
Sponsored Story (Facebook)	1. Advertising	What is a Sponsored Story?
Story (Facebook)	5. Engagement/Interaction	How many Facebook Stories were created by people who interacted with our Page, app or event?
Streams per Unique Viewer*	4. Media Consumption	How many streams did Unique Viewers initiate over a reporting period?
Tab Views, Total (Facebook)	2. Audience/Traffic	Which Facebook Tabs were viewed on our Page?
Target Audience*	1. Advertising	Who are we targeting with our online advertising?
Target Impressions	1. Advertising	How many impressions were served to our target audience for a particular media buy?
Time Spent Viewing, Average*	4. Media Consumption	What is the average length of time a specific video stream is played per viewer, for a reporting period?
Time Spent Viewing, Total	4. Media Consumption	How much time were our videos viewed?

Metrics Listed Alphabetically

Metric	Category	Answers Question
Time to Purchase*	8. E-Commerce	How many days and visits does it take for a visitor to purchase an item from our website?
Top Viewed Pages*	4. Media Consumption	Which are the top viewed pages on our Site?
Total Impressions—Page (Facebook)	1. Advertising	How many impressions did our page generate?
Total Impressions—Post (Facebook)	1. Advertising	How many impressions did our post generate?
Total Reach—Page (Facebook)	2. Audience/Traffic	How many unique people saw any content associate with our page?
Total Reach—Post (Facebook)	2. Audience/Traffic	How many unique people saw our Page Post?
Unduplicated Video Reach	2. Audience/Traffic	How many unique people did our video reach?
Unfollow/Unsubscribe*	2. Audience/Traffic	How many people have unsubscribed from our content?
Unique App Users*	2. Audience/Traffic	How many unique users does our app have?
Unique Clicks	5. Engagement/Interaction	How many unique people clicked on our ad?
Unique Program Viewers or Listeners	2. Audience/Traffic	How many unique people watched or listened to some amount of our program?
Unique Viewers*	2. Audience/Traffic	How many unique people viewed some portion of our video?
Unique Visitors (Unique Browsers)*	2. Audience/Traffic	How many unique visitors came to our site over a reporting period?
Unlike / Dislike*	6. Amplification/Endorsement	How many Unlikes is our content getting?
Unlikes—Page (Facebook)	6. Amplification/Endorsement	How many Unlikes is our page getting?

Metrics Listed Alphabetically

Metric	Category	Answers Question
Video—Audience Retention	5. Engagement/Interaction	How long are people watching our video?
Viewable Impression*	1. Advertising	How many of the impressions our campaign delivered had an opportunity to be seen?
Views	1. Advertising	What is a view?
Views, Videos*	4. Media Consumption	How many times was our video viewed?
Viral Impressions—Page (Facebook)	6. Amplification/Endorsement	How many impressions did our page generated virally?
Viral Impressions—Post (Facebook)	6. Amplification/Endorsement	How many viral impressions did our page post generate?
Viral Reach—Post (Facebook)	2. Audience/Traffic	How many people did our post reach through stories created by friends?
Viral Reach—Page (Facebook)	2. Audience/Traffic	How many unique people saw any of our Facebook brand page content through a friend's Story?
Virality/Engagement Rate—Post (Facebook)	6. Amplification/Endorsement	What percentage of people who saw our post engaged with it by liking, sharing, commenting, or clicking?
Visit (Session)*	2. Audience/Traffic	How many times did someone come to do something on our website?
Visits—Buy Now Section	8. E-Commerce	How many visits to our site's Buy Now section are we attracting?
Visits—Customer Service / Support Section	5. Engagement/Interaction	How many visits is the support section of our site getting?
Visits—Store Locator Section	8. E-Commerce	How often was the store locater feature visited?

Metrics Listed by Category

Category	Metric	Answers Question
1. Advertising	Ad Impression*	What is an ad impression and how are they counted?
1. Advertising	Bounce—Email*	How many emails bounced because they could not be delivered?
1. Advertising	Bounce Rate—Email	What percentage of our emails bounced?
1. Advertising	Cost per Action (CPA)*	What cost per action are we paying?
1. Advertising	Cost per Click (CPC)*	How much are we paying for each click on our ad?
1. Advertising	Cost per Lead (CPL)*	What cost per lead we are paying?
1. Advertising	Cost per Targeted Thousand Impressions (CPTM)	How much are we paying for one thousand targeted ad impressions?
1. Advertising	Cost per Thousand (CPM) Impressions*	How much are we paying for each thousand impressions?
1. Advertising	Cost per Transaction	What did it cost to generate one sales transaction?
1. Advertising	Cost per Unique Visitor	What is the average cost of our ad placement or app, per Unique Visitor?
1. Advertising	Earned Impression*	How many earned impressions did our ad generate?
1. Advertising	Email Delivered*	How many of our emails were actually received?
1. Advertising	Email Delivery Rate*	What percentage of our emails were completely received?
1. Advertising	Email Inbox Delivered*	How many emails were delivered to inboxes?
1. Advertising	Email Inbox Delivered Rate	How many emails were delivered to inboxes as a percentage of emails delivered?
1. Advertising	Email Open Rate*	What is the percentage of unique subscribers that opened an email message?

Metrics Listed by Category

Category	Metric	Answers Question
1. Advertising	Email Opens*	How many times did a person look at our email?
1. Advertising	Email Sent to Open Ratio*	How many of the unique emails we sent were opened?
1. Advertising	Frequency*	How many times did a person see a specific ad or other piece of content?
1. Advertising	Gross Ratings Points (GRP)*	How much advertising weight did we purchase?
1. Advertising	Organic Impressions—Posts (Facebook)	How many times were our posts seen organically in news feeds, tickers or on the page itself?
1. Advertising	Page	What is a Page?
1. Advertising	Page (Facebook, LinkedIn)	What is a Facebook Page or LinkedIn Company Page?
1. Advertising	Page Post (Facebook)	What is a Facebook Page post?
1. Advertising	Paid Impression—Page (Facebook)	How many Paid Impressions did our sponsored stories and ads generate on Facebook?
1. Advertising	Paid Impressions—Post (Facebook)	How many impressions did our paid advertising generate?
1. Advertising	Pay Per Click (PPC)	What is the amount we are paying per click?
1. Advertising	Rich Media Interactive Impressions	How many impressions did our rich media ad generate?
1. Advertising	Social Impressions (Facebook)	How many impressions of our ad included social context?
1. Advertising	Sponsored Story (Facebook)	What is a sponsored story?
1. Advertising	Target Audience*	Who are we targeting with our online advertising?
1. Advertising	Target Impressions	How many impressions were served to our target audience for a particular media buy?

Metrics Listed by Category

Category	Metric	Answers Question
1. Advertising	Total Impressions—Page (Facebook)	How many impressions did our page generate?
1. Advertising	Total Impressions—Post (Facebook)	How many impressions did our post generate?
1. Advertising	Viewable Impression*	How many of the impressions our campaign delivered had an opportunity to be seen?
1. Advertising	Views	What is a view?
2. Audience/Traffic	Active User Rate (Mobile Apps)*	What percentage of people who downloaded our app are using it?
2. Audience/Traffic	Bounce (Website or Social Network)*	How many people came to our site and saw only one page?
2. Audience/Traffic	Browser	What is a web browser?
2. Audience/Traffic	Channel	Which online media channels are visitors using to arrive at our site?
2. Audience/Traffic	Consumers—Page (Facebook)	How many unique people clicked on any of our page content?
2. Audience/Traffic	Consumers—Post (Facebook)	How many unique people clicked on anything in our post?
2. Audience/Traffic	Cookie	What is a cookie?
2. Audience/Traffic	Direct Traffic Visitors	How many visitors came to our site or page directly?
2. Audience/Traffic	Email Unsubscribe Rate*	What percentage of unique people unsubscribed from our email?
2. Audience/Traffic	Entry Type*	How did visitors arrive at our site?
2. Audience/Traffic	Fan (Facebook)	What is a Facebook fan?
2. Audience/Traffic	Followers/Subscribers*	How many people subscribe to our content?
2. Audience/Traffic	Friends of Fans (Facebook)	What is the maximum number of people we could reach through people who Like our page?

Metrics Listed by Category

Category	Metric	Answers Question
2. Audience/Traffic	Hit	How many hits did our site receive over a reporting period?
2. Audience/Traffic	Incoming Links (Backlinks)	Which sites are linking to our website and specific web pages?
2. Audience/Traffic	IP Address	What is the IP address of a visitor's device?
2. Audience/Traffic	Mobile Browser Version	Which mobile browsers were used to visit our mobile website?
2. Audience/Traffic	Mobile Operating System	Which mobile operating systems accessed our mobile website?
2. Audience/Traffic	New App Users*	How many new app users used our mobile app?
2. Audience/Traffic	New Likes—Page (Facebook)	How many new likes did our page generate?
2. Audience/Traffic	New Visitor	How many Unique Visitors came to our site for the first time during a reporting period?
2. Audience/Traffic	New Visitor (Percent)*	What percentage of our visitors are new visitors?
2. Audience/Traffic	Organic Reach—Page (Facebook)	How many people saw any of our content organically on Facebook?
2. Audience/Traffic	Organic Reach—Post (Facebook)	What is the organic reach of our page post?
2. Audience/Traffic	Paid Reach—Page (Facebook)	What is the number of people reached by our Facebook page's ad or sponsored story?
2. Audience/Traffic	Paid Reach—Post (Facebook)	What is the number of people reached by our Facebook post?
2. Audience/Traffic	Phone Brand	Which phone brands accessed our mobile website?
2. Audience/Traffic	Phone Type	Which phone types accessed our mobile website?

Metrics Listed by Category

Category	Metric	Answers Question
2. Audience/Traffic	Pinners	How many unique people pinned something from our website?
2. Audience/Traffic	Reach*	What percentage of the target audience had the opportunity to see a specific ad at least once, over a reporting period?
2. Audience/Traffic	Referral Traffic*	Where is our site traffic coming from?
2. Audience/Traffic	Repeat Visitors	Are people coming back to our website, app or brand page within a certain time period, and how many?
2. Audience/Traffic	Repinners	How many unique people repinned our pins, over a reporting period?
2. Audience/Traffic	Return Visitor*	How many visitors come back to our site in this reporting period who visited in an earlier reporting period?
2. Audience/Traffic	Search Traffic	Which search engines are sending traffic to our site?
2. Audience/Traffic	Share of Active Days	When people go on the web, what percent of visits go to our site?
2. Audience/Traffic	Source	Which sources within online media channels are visitors using to arrive at our site?
2. Audience/Traffic	Tab Views, Total (Facebook)	Which Facebook Tabs were viewed on our page?
2. Audience/Traffic	Total Reach—Page (Facebook)	How many unique people saw any content associated with our page?
2. Audience/Traffic	Total Reach—Post (Facebook)	How many unique people saw our page post?
2. Audience/Traffic	Unduplicated Video Reach	How many unique people did our video reach?
2. Audience/Traffic	Unfollow/Unsubscribe*	How many people have unsubscribed from our content?

Metrics Listed by Category

Category	Metric	Answers Question
2. Audience/Traffic	Unique App Users*	How many unique users does our app have?
2. Audience/Traffic	Unique Program Viewers or Listeners	How many unique people watched or listened to some amount of our program?
2. Audience/Traffic	Unique Viewers*	How many unique people viewed some portion of our video?
2. Audience/Traffic	Unique Visitors (Unique Browsers)*	How many Unique Visitors came to our site over a reporting period?
2. Audience/Traffic	Viral Reach—Post (Facebook)	How many people did our post reach through stories created by friends?
2. Audience/Traffic	Viral Reach—Page (Facebook)	How many unique people saw any of our Facebook brand page content through a friend's story?
2. Audience/Traffic	Visit (Session)*	How many times did someone come to do something on our website?
3. Site Navigation/Site Performance	Bounce Rate (Site or Network)*	What is the percentage of times a page bounces?
3. Site Navigation/Site Performance	Click Stream	What path did visitors take through our site?
3. Site Navigation/Site Performance	Entry Page (Top Entry Pages)*	Which pages did visitors access to enter our site?
3. Site Navigation/Site Performance	Exit Page*	At which page did visitors leave our site or process?
3. Site Navigation/Site Performance	Page Exit Rate	Which pages did visitors exit from?
3. Site Navigation/Site Performance	Page Load Times*	How long does it take a specific page to load?
4. Media Consumption	Average Time Spent on Page*	How long is a specific page being viewed on average?
4. Media Consumption	Estimated Minutes Watched*	How many minutes was our video watched?

Metrics Listed by Category

Category	Metric	Answers Question
4. Media Consumption	Page View (Facebook)	How many times did our page display on a particular day?
4. Media Consumption	Page View, Logged-in (Facebook)	How many people who viewed our page were logged-in to Facebook at the time?
4. Media Consumption	Page View*	Which pages on our site are viewed most often?
4. Media Consumption	Page Views per Visit*	What is the average number of pages viewed each visit, over a specific time frame?
4. Media Consumption	Playlist Average Playing Time	How long was our playlist listened to, on average?
4. Media Consumption	Screen View	How many screen views were recorded over a certain period of time?
4. Media Consumption	Screen Views per Visit	How many screen views did our mobile site receive over a reporting period?
4. Media Consumption	Share of Streams	What is the relative popularity of our streaming video or audio files?
4. Media Consumption	Streams per Unique Viewer*	How many streams did Unique Viewers initiate over a reporting period?
4. Media Consumption	Time Spent Viewing, Average*	What is the average length of time a specific video stream was played per viewer, for a reporting period?
4. Media Consumption	Time Spent Viewing, Total	How much time were our videos viewed?
4. Media Consumption	Top Viewed Pages*	Which are the top viewed pages on our site?
4. Media Consumption	Views, Videos*	How many times was our video viewed?

Metrics Listed by Category

Category	Metric	Answers Question
5. Engagement/Interaction	Actions Rate (Facebook)	What is the number of actions generated by our paid ad impressions?
5. Engagement/Interaction	Actions (Facebook)	How many actions were taken on our ad, Page, app or event after our ad was served?
5. Engagement/Interaction	Average Time Spent on Site (Session Length)*	How much time did visitor spend on our site, on average, for a reporting period?
5. Engagement/Interaction	Click	What is a click?
5. Engagement/Interaction	Click-Through	How many times was our ad, or content, clicked on?
5. Engagement/Interaction	Click-Through Rate (CTR)*	How often do people click on our ad or content after they have seen it?
5. Engagement/Interaction	Click-Through Rate After Video Exposure	How many click-throughs did our video generate?
5. Engagement/Interaction	Comments*	How many comments did an ad, post, or item of content receive?
5. Engagement/Interaction	Consumptions—Post (Facebook)	How many clicks did our post receive?
5. Engagement/Interaction	Conversation Relevant Sites	How many sites are there with conversation relevant to our brand?
5. Engagement/Interaction	Conversation*	How many conversations are people having about our brand?
5. Engagement/Interaction	Email Click to Open Rate*	How many clicks did our emails generate from messages that were opened?
5. Engagement/Interaction	Engaged Users—Post (Facebook)	How many unique people took any sort of action on our post?
5. Engagement/Interaction	Engagement—Tweet (Twitter)	What percentage of our Tweet impressions generated an action?
5. Engagement/Interaction	Engagement—Video	What percentage of our videos generated some type of engagement?

Metrics Listed by Category

Category	Metric	Answers Question
5. Engagement/Interaction	Engagement*	How are people interacting with our ad, content, or app?
5. Engagement/Interaction	Episode Completions	How many times was our episode viewed through to the end?"
5. Engagement/Interaction	Episode Starts	How many times was a specific episode in our program started?
5. Engagement/Interaction	Event	What is an Event?
5. Engagement/Interaction	Event Tracking*	What are the types of interactions people are having with our site?
5. Engagement/Interaction	In-Unit Click	How many clicks did our ad receive that took a visitor to another page within our site?
5. Engagement/Interaction	Interactions—In Ad	How did visitors interact with our ad or app over a reporting period?
5. Engagement/Interaction	Likes—Page (Facebook)	How many people Like our brand page?
5. Engagement/Interaction	Mouseover	How long did visitors mouseover or hover on our ad?
5. Engagement/Interaction	Negative Feedback from Users —Post (Facebook)	How many unique users expressed a negative action regarding our post?
5. Engagement/Interaction	Negative Feedback from Users —Page (Facebook)	How many unique people generated a negative action on our page?
5. Engagement/Interaction	People Engaged—Post (Facebook)	How many unique people liked, commented on, or shared our post?
5. Engagement/Interaction	Playlist Completions	How many times was our playlist listened or viewed through to the end?
5. Engagement/Interaction	Playlist Starts	How many times was our playlist listened to or watched?
5. Engagement/Interaction	Program Completion Rate	Of all the times a program was started, what is the percentage of programs that played all the way through?

Metrics Listed by Category

Category	Metric	Answers Question
5. Engagement/Interaction	Program Completions	How many times was our program listened or viewed through to the end?
5. Engagement/Interaction	Program Repeated Completions	How many times was our program repeated and listened or viewed through to the end?
5. Engagement/Interaction	Program Repeated Starts	How many times was our program repeatedly watched or listened to?
5. Engagement/Interaction	Program Starts	How many times was our program watched or listened to?
5. Engagement/Interaction	Program Stops	How many times was our program stopped?
5. Engagement/Interaction	Social Click Rate	How many clicks did our ads get that had social context?
5. Engagement/Interaction	Social Clicks	How many clicks did our Facebook ad receive from friends?
5. Engagement/Interaction	Story (Facebook)	How many Facebook stories were created by people who interacted with our page, app, or event?
5. Engagement/Interaction	Unique Clicks	How many unique people clicked on our ad?
5. Engagement/Interaction	Video—Audience Retention	How long are people watching our video?
5. Engagement/Interaction	Visits—Customer Service/Support Section	How many visits is the support section of our site getting?
6. Amplification/Endorsement	Brand Advocate*	What are brand advocates and what impact do they have?
6. Amplification/Endorsement	Check-Ins—Page (Facebook)	How many people checked-in to our place?
6. Amplification/Endorsement	Email Complaint Rate	What percentage of people complained about our email?
6. Amplification/Endorsement	Email Complaints	How many people marked our email as spam or junk?

Metrics Listed by Category

Category	Metric	Answers Question
6. Amplification/Endorsement	Email Forwards*	How many times was our email forwarded?
6. Amplification/Endorsement	Influencer*	What are Influencers and how do they work for brands?
6. Amplification/Endorsement	Like*	How many Likes did our ad or content receive?
6. Amplification/Endorsement	Mentions*	How many mentions did our brand receive in social media?
6. Amplification/Endorsement	People Talking About This—Page (Facebook)	How engaged are people with our page?
6. Amplification/Endorsement	People Talking About This—Post (Facebook)	How many unique people created stories from our page post?
6. Amplification/Endorsement	Pins	How many things were pinned from our website, over a reporting period?
6. Amplification/Endorsement	Repins	How many times were pins on our website repinned, over a reporting period?
6. Amplification/Endorsement	Retweets	How many times was a specific Tweet retweeted?
6. Amplification/Endorsement	Reviews (product)*	How many reviews did a product receive over a specific time period?
6. Amplification/Endorsement	Sentiment*	What is the opinion expressed towards my brand?
6. Amplification/Endorsement	Sharing*	How often is our content, ad, or app being shared with friends, contacts, or connections?
6. Amplification/Endorsement	Social Percentage (Facebook)	What percentage of our ads have a social element?
6. Amplification/Endorsement	Unlike/Dislike*	How many Unlikes is our content getting?
6. Amplification/Endorsement	Unlikes—Page (Facebook)	How many Unlikes is our page getting?

Metrics Listed by Category

Category	Metric	Answers Question
6. Amplification/Endorsement	Viral Impressions—Page (Facebook)	How many impressions did our page generate virally?
6. Amplification/Endorsement	Viral Impressions—Post (Facebook)	How many viral impressions did our page post generate?
6. Amplification/Endorsement	Virality/Engagement Rate—Post (Facebook)	What percentage of people who saw our post engaged with it by liking, sharing, commenting, or clicking?
7. Conversion	Abandonment Rate (Page)*	On which pages are visitors abandoning the conversion path?
7. Conversion	Abandonment Rate (Shopping Cart)*	What percent of visitors abandoned the shopping cart on our site?
7. Conversion	Brochure Downloads	How many of our brochures were downloaded over a period of time?
7. Conversion	Browse to Buy Ratio	What percentage of browsers to our site converted to place an order?
7. Conversion	Conversion Funnel*	What are the steps we expect visitors to take to complete an action we want?
7. Conversion	Conversion Goal*	What is a conversion goal?
7. Conversion	Conversion Rate*	What is the conversion rate for any conversion action on our site or through our email?
7. Conversion	Conversion*	Which conversion actions were performed on the site or in our email over a reporting period?
7. Conversion	Coupon Downloads	How many coupons were downloaded over a specific time period?
7. Conversion	Email Capture Rate	How many email addresses are we capturing on our website?
7. Conversion	Form Submissions*	How many forms were submitted on our site?
7. Conversion	Key Content Downloads (Coupons, Recipes, Apps, etc.)*	Which of our content files were downloaded, and how many times?

Metrics Listed by Category

Category	Metric	Answers Question
7. Conversion	Mobile App Downloads	How many times was our app downoaded?
7. Conversion	Recipe Downloads	How many recipes were downloaded?
7. Conversion	Song Downloads	How many songs were downloaded?
8. E-Commerce	Average Order Value*	What is the average order value on our site?
8. E-Commerce	Cost per Order	How much did it cost to generate one sale?
8. E-Commerce	Cost per Sale (CPS)	How much did it cost us to close one sale over a reporting period?
8. E-Commerce	Customers*	How many unique browsers placed an order on our site?
8. E-Commerce	First Orders	What is the number of first purchase orders our site received?
8. E-Commerce	Revenue Over Email Delivered*	What is the average amount of revenue earned for each delivered email?
8. E-Commerce	Time to Purchase*	How many days and visits does it take for a visitor to purchase an item from our website?
8. E-Commerce	Visits—Buy Now Section	How many visits to our site's Buy Now section are we attracting?
8. E-Commerce	Visits—Store Locator Section	How often was the store locater feature visited?
9. Ad Effectiveness	Ad Awareness*	What percentage of our target customers are aware of our brand's advertising?
9. Ad Effectiveness	Brand Awareness*	What percentage of our target market is aware of our brand?
9. Ad Effectiveness	Brand Lift*	Did exposure to our advertising campaign have an impact on our brand lift measures?
9. Ad Effectiveness	Key Performance Indicator (KPI)*	What is a Key Performance Indicator?

Metrics Listed by Marketing Stage

Marketing Stage	Metric	Answers Question
1. Capture	Ad Awareness*	What percentage of our target customers are aware of our brand's advertising?
1. Capture	Ad Impression*	What is an ad impression and how are they counted?
1. Capture	Bounce—Email*	How many emails bounced because they could not be delivered?
1. Capture	Bounce (Website or Social Net-work)*	How many people came to our site and saw only one page?
1. Capture	Bounce Rate—Email	What percentage of our emails bounced?
1. Capture	Bounce Rate (Site or Network)*	What is the percentage of times a page bounces?
1. Capture	Brand Awareness*	What percentage of our target market is aware of our brand?
1. Capture2. Connect3. Close	Brand Lift*	Did exposure to our advertising campaign have an impact on our brand lift measures?
1. Capture	Browser	What is a web browser?
1. Capture	Channel	Which online media channels are visitors using to arrive at our site?
1. Capture	Cookie	What is a cookie?
1. Capture	Cost per Action (CPA)*	What cost per action are we paying?
1. Capture	Cost per Click (CPC)*	How much are we paying for each click on our ad?
1. Capture	Cost per Lead (CPL)*	What is the cost per lead we are paying?
1. Capture	Cost per Targeted Thousand Impressions (CPTM)	How much are we paying for one thousand targeted ad impressions?
1. Capture	Cost per Thousand (CPM) Impressions*	How much are we paying for each thousand impressions?

Metrics Listed by Marketing Stage

Marketing Stage	Metric	Answers Question
1. Capture	Cost per Unique Visitor	What is the average cost of our ad placement or app, per Unique Visitor?
1. Capture	Email Delivered*	How many of our emails were actually received?
1. Capture	Email Delivery Rate*	What percentage of our emails was completely received?
1. Capture	Email Forwards*	How many times was our email forwarded?
1. Capture	Email Inbox Delivered*	How many emails were delivered to inboxes?
1. Capture	Email Inbox Delivered Rate	How many emails were delivered to inboxes as a percent-age of emails delivered?
1. Capture	Email Open Rate*	What is the percentage of unique subscribers that opened an email message?
1. Capture	Email Opens*	How many times did a person look at our email?
1. Capture	Email Unsubscribe Rate*	What percentage of unique people unsubscribed from our email?
1. Capture	Entry Page (Top Entry Pages)*	Which pages did visitors access to enter our site?
1. Capture	Entry Type*	How did visitors arrive at our site?
1. Capture2. Connect3. Close4. Keep	Exit Page*	At which page did visitor leave our site or process?
1. Capture	Frequency*	How many times did a person see a specific ad or other piece of content?
1. Capture	Friends of Fans (Facebook)	What is the maximum number of people we could reach through people who Like our page?
1. Capture	Gross Ratings Points (GRP)*	How much advertising weight did we purchase?

Metrics Listed by Marketing Stage

Marketing Stage	Metric	Answers Question
1. Capture	Hit	How many hits did our site receive over a reporting period?
1. Capture	Incoming Links (Backlinks)	Which sites are linking to our website and specific web pages?
1. Capture	IP Address	What is the IP address of a visitor's device?
1. Capture2. Connect3. Close4. Keep	Key Performance Indicator (KPI)*	What is a Key Performance Indicator?
1. Capture	Mobile Browser Version	Which mobile browsers were used to visit our mobile web-site?
1. Capture	Mobile Operating System	Which mobile operating systems accessed our mobile web-site?
1. Capture	New Visitor	How many Unique Visitors came to our site for the first time during a reporting period?
1. Capture	New Visitor (Percent)*	What percentage of our visitors are new visitors?
1. Capture	Organic Impressions—Posts (Facebook)	How many times were our posts seen organically in news feeds, tickers, or on the page itself?
1. Capture	Organic Reach—Page (Facebook)	How many people saw any of our content organically on Facebook?
1. Capture	Organic Reach—Post (Facebook)	What is the organic reach of our page post?
1. Capture	Page	What is a Page?
1. Capture	Page (Facebook, LinkedIn)	What is a Facebook Page or LinkedIn Company Page?
1. Capture	Page Load Times*	How long does it take a specific page to load?
1. Capture	Page Post (Facebook)	What is a Facebook Page post?
1. Capture	Paid Impression—Page (Facebook)	How many Paid Impressions did our sponsored stories and ads generate on Facebook?

Metrics Listed by Marketing Stage

Marketing Stage	Metric	Answers Question
1. Capture	Paid Impressions—Post (Facebook)	How many impressions did our paid advertising generate?
1. Capture	Paid Reach—Page (Facebook)	What is the number of people reached by our Facebook page's ad or sponsored story?
1. Capture	Paid Reach—Post (Facebook)	What is the number of people reached by our Facebook post?
1. Capture	Pay Per Click (PPC)	What is the amount we are paying per click?
1. Capture	Phone Brand	Which phone brands accessed our mobile website?
1. Capture	Phone Type	Which phone types accessed our mobile website?
1. Capture	Pinners	How many unique people pinned something from our web-site?
1. Capture	Reach*	What percentage of the target audience had the opportunity to see a specific ad at least once, over a reporting period?
1. Capture	Referral Traffic*	Where is our site traffic coming from?
1. Capture	Repinners	How many unique people repinned our pins, over a reporting period?
1. Capture	Rich Media Interactive Impressions	How many impressions did our rich media ad generate?
1. Capture	Search Traffic	Which search engines are sending traffic to our site?
1. Capture	Social Impressions (Facebook)	How many impressions of our ad included social context?
1. Capture	Social Percentage (Facebook)	What percentage of our ads has a social element?
1. Capture	Source	Which sources within online media channels are visitors using to arrive at our site?

Metrics Listed by Marketing Stage

Marketing Stage	Metric	Answers Question
1. Capture	Sponsored Story (Facebook)	What is a sponsored story?
1. Capture	Target Audience*	Who are we targeting with our online advertising?
1. Capture	Target Impressions	How many impressions were served to our target audience for a particular media buy?
1. Capture	Total Impressions—Page (Facebook)	How many impressions did our page generate?
1. Capture	Total Impressions—Post (Facebook)	How many impressions did our post generate?
1. Capture	Total Reach—Page (Facebook)	How many unique people saw any content associated with our page?
1. Capture	Total Reach—Post (Facebook)	How many unique people saw our page post?
1. Capture	Unduplicated Video Reach	How many unique people did our video reach?
1. Capture	Unique App Users*	How many unique users does our app have?
1. Capture	Unique Program Viewers or Listeners	How many unique people watched or listened to some amount of our program?
1. Capture	Unique Visitors (Unique Browsers)*	How many Unique Visitors came to our site over a reporting period?
1. Capture	Viewable Impression*	How many of the impressions our campaign delivered had an opportunity to be seen?
1. Capture	Views	What is a view?
1. Capture	Viral Impressions—Page (Facebook)	How many impressions did our page generate virally?
1. Capture	Viral Impressions—Post (Facebook)	How many viral impressions did our page post generate?

Metrics Listed by Marketing Stage

Marketing Stage	Metric	Answers Question
1. Capture	Viral Reach—Post (Facebook)	How many people did our post reach through stories created by friends?
1. Capture	Viral Reach—Page (Facebook)	How many unique people saw any of our Facebook brand page content through a friend's story?
1. Capture	Visit (Session)*	How many times did someone come to do something on our website?
1. Connect	Fan (Facebook)	What is a Facebook fan?
2. Connect	Actions Rate (Facebook)	What is the number of actions generated by our paid ad impressions?
2. Connect	Actions (Facebook)	How many actions were taken on our ad, Page, app or event after our ad was served?
2. Connect	Active User Rate (Mobile Apps)*	What percentage of people who downloaded our app is using it?
2. Connect	Average Time Spent on Page*	How long is a specific page being viewed on average?
2. Connect	Average Time Spent on Site (Session Length)*	How much time did visitors spend on our site, on average, for a reporting period?
2. Connect	Brand Advocate*	What are brand advocates and what impact do they have?
2. Connect	Brochure Downloads	How many of our brochures were downloaded over a period of time?
2. Connect	Check-Ins—Page (Facebook)	How many people checked-in to our place?
2. Connect	Click	What is a click?
2. Connect	Click Stream	What path did visitors take through our site?
2. Connect	Click-Through	How many times was our ad, or content, clicked on?

Metrics Listed by Marketing Stage

Marketing Stage	Metric	Answers Question
2. Conn	Click-Through Rate (CTR)*	How often do people click on our ad or content after they have seen it?
2. Connect	Click-Through Rate After Video Exposure	How many click-throughs did our video generate?
2. Connect	Comments*	How many comments did an ad, post, or item of content receive?
2. Connect	Consumers—Page (Facebook)	How many unique people clicked on any of our page con-tent?
2. Connect	Consumers—Post (Facebook)	How many unique people clicked on anything in our post?
2. Connect	Consumptions—Post (Facebook)	How many clicks did our post receive?
2. Connect	Conversation Relevant Sites	How many sites are there with conversation relevant to our brand?
2. Connect	Conversation*	How many conversations are people having about our brand?
2. Connect	Direct Traffic Visitors	How many visitors came to our site or page directly?
2. Connect	Earned Impression*	How many earned impressions did our ad generate?
2. Connect	Email Capture Rate	How many email addresses are we capturing on our web-site?
2. Connect	Email Click to Open Rate*	How many clicks did our emails generate from messages that were opened?
2. Connect	Email Complaint Rate	What percentage of people complained about our email?
2. Connect	Email Complaints	How many people marked our email as spam or junk?
2. Connect	Email Sent to Open Ratio*	How many of the unique emails we sent were opened?
2. Connect	Engaged Users—Post (Facebook)	How many unique people took any sort of action on our post?

Metrics Listed by Marketing Stage

Marketing Stage	Metric	Answers Question
2. Connect	Engagement—Tweet (Twitter)	What percentage of our Tweet impressions generated an action?
2. Connect	Engagement—Video	What percentage of our videos generated some type of engagement?
2. Connect	Engagement*	How are people interacting with our ad, content, or app?
2. Connect	Episode Completions	How many times was our episode viewed through to the end?"
2. Connect	Episode Starts	How many times was a specific episode in our program started?
2. Connect	Estimated Minutes Watched*	How many minutes was our video watched?
2. Connect	Event	What is an Event?
2. Connect3. Close4. Keep	Event Tracking*	What are the types of interactions people are having with our site?
2. Connect	Followers/Subscribers*	How many people subscribe to our content?
2. Connect	Form Submissions*	How many forms were submitted on our site?
2. Connect	In-Unit Click	How many clicks did our ad receive that took a visitor to another page within our site?
2. Connect	Influencer*	What are Influencers and how do they work for brands?
2. Connect	Interactions—In Ad	How did visitors interact with our ad or app over a reporting period?
2. Connect	Key Content Downloads (Coupons, Recipes, Apps, etc.)*	Which of our content files were downloaded, and how many times?
2. Connect	Like*	How many Likes did our ad or content receive?
2. Connect	Likes—Page (Facebook)	How many people Like our brand page?

Metrics Listed by Marketing Stage

Marketing Stage	Metric	Answers Question
2. Connect	Mentions*	How many mentions did our brand receive in social media?
2. Connect	Mobile App Downloads	How many times was our app downloaded?
2. Connect	Mouseover	How long did visitors mouseover or hover on our ad?
2. Connect	Negative Feedback from Users—Post (Facebook)	How many unique users expressed a negative action regarding our post?
2. Connect	Negative Feedback from Users—Page (Facebook)	How many unique people generated a negative action on our page?
2. Connect	New App Users*	How many new app users used our mobile app?
2. Connect	New Likes—Page (Facebook)	How many new likes did our page generate?
2. Connect	Page Exit Rate	Which pages did visitors exit from?
2. Connect	Page View (Facebook)	How many times did our page display on a particular day?
2. Connect	Page View, Logged-in (Facebook)	How many people who viewed our page were logged-in to Facebook at the time?
2. Connect	Page View*	Which pages on our site are viewed most often?
2. Connect	Page Views per Visit*	What is the average number of pages viewed each visit, over a specific time frame?
2. Connect	People Engaged—Post (Facebook)	How many unique people liked, commented on, or shared our post?
2. Connect	People Talking About This—Page (Facebook)	How engaged are people with our page?
2. Connect	People Talking About This—Post (Facebook)	How many unique people created stories from our page post?

Metrics Listed by Marketing Stage

Marketing Stage	Metric	Answers Question
2. Connect	Pins	How many things were pinned from our website, over a reporting period?
2. Connect	Playlist Average Playing Time	How long was our playlist listened to, on average?
2. Connect	Playlist Completions	How many times was our playlist listened or viewed through to the end?
2. Connect	Playlist Starts	How many times was our playlist listened to or watched?"
2. Connect	Program Completion Rate	Of all the times a program was started, what is the percent-age of programs that played all the way through?
2. Connect	Program Completions	How many times was our program listened or viewed through to the end?
2. Connect	Program Repeated Completions	How many times was our program repeated and listened or viewed through to the end?
2. Connect	Program Repeated Starts	How many times was our program repeatedly watched or listened to?
2. Connect	Program Starts	How many times was our program watched or listened to?
2. Connect	Program Stops	How many times was our program stopped?
2. Connect	Recipe Downloads	How many recipes were downloaded?
2. Connect	Repeat Visitors	Are people coming back to our website, app, or brand page within a certain time period, and how many?
2. Connect	Repins	How many times were pins on our website repinned, over a reporting period?
2. Connect3. Close4. Keep	Return Visitor*	How many visitors come back to our site in this reporting period who visited in an earlier reporting period?

Metrics Listed by Marketing Stage

Marketing Stage	Metric	Answers Question
2. Connect	Retweets	How many times was a specific Tweet retweeted?
2. Connect	Reviews (product)*	How many reviews did a product receive over a specific time period?
2. Connect	Screen View	How many screen views were recorded over a certain period of time?
2. Connect	Screen Views per Visit	How many screen views did our mobile site receive over a reporting period?
2. Connect	Sentiment*	What is the opinion expressed towards my brand?
2. Connect	Share of Active Days	When people go on the web, what percent of visits go to our site?
2. Connect	Share of Streams	What is the relative popularity of our streaming video or audio files?
2. Connect	Sharing*	How often is our content, ad, or app being shared with friends, contacts, or connections?
2. Connect	Social Click Rate	How many clicks did our ads get that had social context?
2. Connect	Social Clicks	How many clicks did our Facebook ad receive from friends?
2. Connect	Song Downloads	How many songs were downloaded?
2. Connect	Story (Facebook)	How many Facebook stories were created by people who interacted with our page, app, or event?
2. Connect	Streams per Unique Viewer*	How many streams did Unique Viewers initiate over a reporting period?
2. Connect	Tab Views, Total (Facebook)	Which Facebook Tabs were viewed on our page?
2. Connect	Time Spent Viewing, Average*	What is the average length of time a specific video stream is played per viewer, for a reporting period?

Metrics Listed by Marketing Stage

Marketing Stage	Metric	Answers Question
2. Connect	Time Spent Viewing, Total	How much time were our videos viewed?
2. Connect	Top Viewed Pages*	Which are the top viewed pages on our site?
2. Connect	Unique Clicks	How many unique people clicked on our ad?
2. Connect	Unique Viewers*	How many unique people viewed some portion of our video?
2. Connect	Video—Audience Retention	How long are people watching our video?
2. Connect	Views, Videos*	How many times was our video viewed?
2. Connect	Virality/Engagement Rate— Post (Facebook)	What percentage of people who saw our post engaged with it by liking, sharing, commenting, or clicking?
2. Connect	Visits—Customer Service/Support Section	How many visits is the support section of our site getting?
3. Close	Abandonment Rate (Page)*	On which pages are visitors abandoning the conversion path?
3. Close	Abandonment Rate (Shopping Cart)*	What percent of visitors abandoned the shopping cart on our site?
3. Close	Average Order Value*	What is the average order value on our site?
3. Close	Browse to Buy Ratio	What percentage of browsers to our site converted to place an order?
3. Close	Conversion Funnel*	What are the steps we expect visitors to take to complete an action we want?
3. Close	Conversion Goal*	What is a conversion goal?
3. Close	Conversion Rate*	What is the conversion rate for any conversion action on our site or through our email?

Metrics Listed by Marketing Stage

Marketing Stage	Metric	Answers Question
3. Close	Conversion*	Which conversion actions were performed on the site or in our email over a reporting period?
3. Close	Cost per Order	How much did it cost to generate one sale?
3. Close	Cost per Sale (CPS)	How much did it cost us to close one sale over a reporting period?
3. Close	Cost per Transaction	What did it cost to generate one sales transaction?
3. Close	Coupon Downloads	How many coupons were downloaded over a specific time period?
3. Close	Customers*	How many unique browsers placed an order on our site?
3. Close	First Orders	What is the number of first purchase orders our site received?
3. Close	Revenue Over Email Delivered*	What is the average amount of revenue earned for each delivered email?
3. Close	Time to Purchase*	How many days and visits does it take for a visitor to purchase an item from our website?
3. Close	Visits—Buy Now Section	How many visits to our site's Buy Now section are we attracting?
3. Close	Visits—Store Locator Section	How often was the store locater feature visited?
4. Keep	Unfollow/Unsubscribe*	How many people have unsubscribed from our content?
4. Keep	Unlike/Dislike*	How many Unlikes is our content getting?
4. Keep	Unlikes—Page (Facebook)	How many Unlikes is our page getting?

Guide to the Metrics Entries

Every entry presents identical fields of information in the same format. Each entry provides definitions, calculations, calculation examples, and categorization into buckets relevant to practitioners. Many metrics also include commentary, referenced research or articles, and cross-references to related terms. When information is not available or not relevant for a particular item, the field is left blank. This approach creates a standardized structure, which makes locating the knowledge you need quick and easy. A field listing follows. Take a moment to familiarize yourself with this list of 12 fields and their values. Doing so will help you get the most from the *Field Guide*.

The 12 Fields in the Metrics Entries

The *Field Guide*'s 12 entries are found on the entry page. Each metric is formatted as shown in Figure 1, below.

1 **Actions (Facebook)**

2 **AUTHORITY:**
Facebook

3 **MEDIA:**
Paid
Owned

4 **STAGE:**
2. Connect

5 **CATEGORY:**
5. Engagement/
Interaction

6 **APPLIES TO:**
Social

7 **ANSWERS QUESTION:**
Which actions were taken after viewing or clicking on our ad, widget, app or content?

8 **DEFINITION:**
Actions are behaviors people take after viewing or clicking on an ad, widget , app or content.

Some common actions are recorded when a person:
- Shares, likes or comments on your Page or post
- Joins your event
- Installs, shares, uses an app
- Claims or shares your offer
- Creates user-generated content
- Views a video

Note: Actions create Stories on Facebook.

9 **TECH NOTES:**
On Facebook: Count of actions taken: a) within 24-hours after viewing a paid ad or Sponsored Story, or b) clicks on your ad or Sponsored Story and then takes an action within 28 days, over a reporting period

10 **ARF COMMENTS:**
The number of clicks and the number of actions may be different because not all clicks generate actions. Tracking actions may be helpful to brands to understand the appeal of different content and use that to optimize its mix and user experience.

Regarding Facebook, the company allows third-party developers to create apps that are compatible with the Facebook platform. In their apps developers can define and add any types of action they want. There are no limitations. For example, Payvment, an enabler of commerce on Facebook, adds "I want this" and "I own this" to catalog displays. Clicking a button generates a Story. In their documentation, Facebook suggests other examples of actions like "cook," "read," "listen," "plan," and "review." Any verb can become an action.

Facebook sees actions as a way to create a greater variety of Stories and easily share them with Friends. The music streaming service Spotify is one example. The app enables Facebook users to generate Stories about the songs they listen to and have them appear in their friends' news feeds. Advertisers can turn Stories into Sponsored Stories to increase their reach.

Some Facebook observers see Actions as the next generation of sharing, as more of one's life can be shared. Facebook CEO Zuckerberg has even stated that "like buttons were limited" adding that Actions are a "new language for how people connect."

11 **CITED RESEARCH:**
Facebook Developers (2012). Define Actions. http://goo.gl/LOnwh
AllThingsD (2012). Facebook Actions Could be Unveiled as soon as Tomorrow. http://goo.gl/s68od
Venture Beat (2012). Facebook's biggest change yet: Actions are here. http://goo.gl/kpEyv

12 **SEE ALSO:**
Story (Facebook)

Figure 1: A Metrics Entry Example

1. Metric: This field contains the metric's name. An asterisk (*) following a metric's name indicates that it is a core metric. In most cases, the names are generic. In some instances, especially regarding Facebook, the name (Facebook) is added in parentheses to signify the metric's uniqueness to that social network. Additionally, Facebook reports many of its metrics at two levels: the Page and the Post. When that applies, the level is also included in the metric name.

2. Authority: The source(s) consulted for the definitions. Sources include publicly available definitions from standards bodies, measurement and analytics companies; services providers; and experts. Variations in a name for a particular metric or differences in calculation are noted in other metrics fields where appropriate, usually the Definition, Calculation, Technical Note, or ARF Comments. A list of authorities and the authoritative documents is provided (see the section Authorities for Metrics Definitions).

3. Media (Paid, Owned, and Earned): Digital advertising and marketing strategies increasingly utilize a mix of Paid, Owned, and Earned Media. Knowing which metrics apply to which medium helps brands accurately measure performance. The *Field Guide* classifies metrics as relating to those media types. Paid Media is advertising that brands pay for to run on commercial properties. Digitally, paid media often takes the form of display ads, paid search, promoted information and sponsorships. Owned Media refers to outlets that a brand controls, such as their own websites, mobile presences, Twitter accounts, Facebook brand pages, or YouTube channel. Earned Media results when people promote a brand by acting with a brand's content in some way, commonly occurring through mentions, blog posts, comments, or sharing. When metrics apply to two or more media types—Page View supplies one such example, the *Field Guide* lists them all.

4. Stage: Digital communications changed the way many think about the marketing funnel—that linear progression consumers move through from awareness to purchase. Alternatives proposed by ARF, McKinsey, Google, and others replace the funnel metaphor with an erratic, elliptical path in which people bounce around, stop, continue, restart, or finish, and use combinations of media. These newer models see consumers as "always on," Owing to these developments, marketers and advertisers started re-framing their digital activities in ways befitting the interactive, social, mobile, engaged world in which brands operate. The *Field Guide* adopts a scheme reflecting the tasks marketers and advertisers need to perform that are independent of media or type of advertising: Capture, Connect, Close, and Keep. Capture refers to attracting consumers to a brand. Connect means engaging them. Close relates to closing the sale, although it does not necessarily require that the transaction occur online. Keep concerns retention and loyalty. The *Field Guide* notes which metrics fall into which marketing stage. When metrics slot into two or more categories, all are mentioned.

5. Category: The *Field Guide* categorizes the metrics into nine areas of analytic interest. Here are the categories and brief descriptions. Advertising—impressions ad pricing approaches. Audience/Traffic—visitors and traffic sources. Site Navigation/Site Performance—entry, path through site, exit and technical factors such as page load times that affect user experience. Media Consumption—time spent reading, listening, or watching. Engagement/Interaction—actions people take with content. Amplification/Endorsement—liking, sharing, influencing, advocating. Conversion—actions brands want people to take. E-commerce—activities related to purchase. Ad Effectiveness—ad awareness and brand lift.

6. Applies to (Email, Mobile, Social, Website): Digital metrics come from four areas: email, mobile, social, and web. As with Media above, metrics may apply to one or more of these sources. When they do, illustrating again with Page View, the *Field Guide* reports the overlaps.

7. Answers Question: Metrics do more than measure something; they answer questions regarding those "somethings," such as site usage, media consumption, actions people take, and so forth. The *Field Guide* presents frequently asked questions about digital metric, providing another way to grasp the meaning or utility of a metric, and another avenue to promote conversation among your colleagues.

8. Definition: A statement of the meaning of the metric. If two or more sources vary in their definitions, differences are identified.

9. Tech Notes: When necessary, the *Field Guide* highlights any technical considerations concerning the metric's measurement. For example, the use of HTML IMG tags is explained for calculating email opens.

10. ARF Comments: Review of publicly available research and trade articles generally concerning advertising or marketing issues related to a metric. These mini-essays are valuable for the context they provide and issues they raise.

11. Cited Research: Research and articles mentioned in ARF Comments or Tech Notes are referenced, with URLs provided where appropriate. (URLs were shortened using Google URL Shortener.)

12. See Also: Cross-referenced terms that provide access to related measures.

Sources for Metrics Data

Confidence in metrics, confidence in their analysis, and confidence in using them for decision-making ultimately comes down to confidence in the underlying data. Practitioners and analysts both need to be certain that their reportable numbers are properly sourced, that they know the data's boundaries, strengths, and limitations, and that they understand the issues affecting the data's quality—factors which instill confidence in metrics and their interpretation.

Here is a rundown of data sources, their data collection methods, and data issues for the metrics covered in the *Field Guide*: email, social media, website, and mobile.

Email. Brands often use third-party email service providers (ESPs) for their email needs. ESPs furnish email services through a variety of business models, with software as a service (SaaS) platforms or agency-type email providers the two most common. (Agencies offer some combination of consulting, strategy, creative, execution, data, training, and reporting services.) ESPs deploy emails based on lists of targeted users or by retargeting cookied users who have visited a website. The links contained in these emails are tracked by both the ESP and the brand via tracking parameters appended to the URLs contained in links from the email to the website. If conversion is being monitored, a pixel is often placed on a web page, which equates to conversion. This could be a "Thank You" page following submission of a form or a purchase. The ESP's tracking will yield a "first touch" perspective of users who clicked a link and eventually took an action on the site, while the brand's web tracking will see only instances where the click on the email was the "last touch."

Social Media. Social media is a catch-all term for online sites that enable people to create, share, and exchange ideas or content in virtual communities or networks. Types of social media include blogs, comments, discussion sites, ratings and reviews, social bookmarking, wikis, media sharing sites, and social networks (Wikipedia 2013). Social media data are captured through a variety of methods including screen scraping, RSS and XML feeds, API of Page and Post level data from the social media site, campaign tracking parameters embedded in social media links, panel-based data, and referral data being captured by commercially or freely available web-tracking tools. Social media may be protected by privacy settings that users configure. For this reason, social media datasets contain information that is publicly available and may not reflect the complete range of people's thoughts, opinions, preferences, intentions, or desires. Social media data are frequently integrated with a brand's data sources by the brand itself or through its partners or suppliers.

Website. Websites collect data in several ways. Most commonly, they "drop" a third-party tracking cookie onto a user who visits their website. This cookie is a unique number that stays on their computer until the user deletes it. Every time a user visits the website, their activity is recorded in a web log file which tracks the pages they visit, the images they see, the buttons they click on, etc. These files are fed into a data warehouse, which becomes available through a user interface such as Google Analytics. Campaign tracking codes are embedded in links feeding to the website, to include measurement of advertising activity and social media initiatives. Referring websites are naturally captured by the refer-ring URL, allowing the web tool to see where users are coming in from. Additionally, marketing research companies often assemble statistically representative samples of specific populations by placing a tracking device on the computers of users who have agreed to be part of a panel. Sophisticated methods allow these companies to project entire populations based on their panel data and see all user activity across multiple websites. Finally, surveys are utilized to supplement other data sources and provide insight into user experience, behavior, profile, and demographics.

Several factors affect website measurement accuracy. For counts relying on cookies, cookie deletion, people using multiple browsers on one device, people using multiple devices, people accessing sites from different locations (e.g. home or work), or users sharing browsers can generate errors in the number or type of users. Additionally, spider and robot activity artificially inflates visitor counts if not filtered and removed. Unfortunately, server- and tracking-based measures offer sparse demographic information on users.

Mobile: Of all the metric areas, mobile is arguably the most complex and challenging today. The complexity arises from mobile not being one channel, but three: mobile websites, mobile applications, and text messaging (Gluck 2011). Mobile websites are measured similarly to PC-based websites. App measurement concerns downloads, installs, usage and time spent. SMS metrics share commonalities with email. Although the metrics ring familiar, brands face the challenge of bringing together myriad data sources from the three channels. The Mobile Marketing Association (2012) forcefully argues for the silos to be broken down, data standards established, and open APIs to enable seamless data sharing and integration. The aim is to promote industry cooperation and bring about meaningful metrics.

Mobile data collection methods include survey panels, meters, carrier-reported information, tagging, mobile web-server logs, mobile app providers, and surveys. Additionally, websites, social media sites, and email suppliers may capture and then report mobile activity through their analytics offerings or through third parties. Additionally complicating measurement is that some sites operate a separate mobile site and some have responsively designed sites that adjust to mobile.

Digital Metrics Field Guide Entries

Abandonment Rate (Page)*

AUTHORITY:	MEDIA:	STAGE:	CATEGORY:	APPLIES TO:
IAB, Farris et al.	Owned	3. Close	7. Conversion	Website Social Mobile

ANSWERS QUESTION:

On which pages are visitors abandoning the conversion path?

DEFINITION:

Abandonment rates are the percentage of web page visitors who, upon landing on a particular page along a conversion path, exit without linking to other pages on the site over a reporting period.

TECH NOTES:

None

ARF COMMENTS:

Abandonment Rate (Page) is typically used when referring to a page along a Conversion Funnel path. The aim is to track the effectiveness of pages along the way. Pages with high abandonment rates prior to purchase may be candidates for optimizing content, calls to action, or page load time, for example. Abandonment rates need to be interpreted in the context of brand goals. For example, purchase confirmation pages often have high abandonment rates, but that would be expected and not a concern because the abandonment occurs at the conclusion of a transaction. If a product description page early in the Conversion Funnel had a high abandonment rate, that would demand attention.

For pages that are not part of a conversion funnel, the Page Exit Rate metric is analyzed.

CITED RESEARCH:

None

SEE ALSO:

Page

Page Exit Rate

Abandonment Rate (Shopping Cart)*

AUTHORITY:	**MEDIA:**	**STAGE:**	**CATEGORY:**	**APPLIES TO:**
IAB, Farris et al.	Owned	3. Close	7. Conversion	Website Social Mobile

ANSWERS QUESTION:

What percent of visitors abandoned the shopping cart on our site?

DEFINITION:

The percentage that visitors leave a shopping cart with something in it prior to completing the transaction, over a reporting period.

TECH NOTES:

None

ARF COMMENTS:

Abandonment Rate (Shopping Cart) is typically used to understand the productivity of the Conversion Funnel path. Carts are often abandoned because visitors may be looking to determine the full price of an item or basket of items, such as to learn shipping costs, for comparison with other shopping sites. Carts with high abandonment rates may be candidates for optimizing content, calls to action, or page load time, for example.

UPS research (2013) reports that cart abandonment rates have increased to 88% in 2013 from 81% in 2012. The key reasons were: shipping costs pushed the price up more than expected (54%); person was doing price research but not ready to buy (50%) or was not ready to buy but wanted to save the cart (49%).

Several ways recommended to optimize include: reducing and simplifying the number of checkout steps; price guarantees; showing competitive prices; click-to-call; putting shipping costs upfront, and showing stock availability, among others. A very good practice is to present an exit survey to learn reasons why the cart was abandoned (Eisenberg 2003, Moth 2013).

CITED RESEARCH:

Eisenberg, Brian (2003). 20 Tips to Minimize Shopping Cart Abandonment, Part 1 (http://goo.gl/WToZ3).

Eisenberg, Brian (2003). 20 Tips to Minimize Shopping Cart Abandonment, Part 2 (http://goo.gl/bmGoW).

Moth, David (2013). Seven User Shortcuts that Will Help Reduce Checkout Abandonment. (http://goo.gl/bE2sw).

UPS (2013). UPS Pulse of the Online Shopper (http://goo.gl/CkW6X, registration required for download).

SEE ALSO:

Abandonment Rate (Page)
Conversion Funnel

Actions Rate (Facebook)

AUTHORITY:	MEDIA:	STAGE:	CATEGORY:	APPLIES TO:
Facebook	Paid	2. Connect	5. Engagement/ Interaction	Social

ANSWERS QUESTION:

What is the number of actions generated by our paid ad impressions?

DEFINITION:

For Facebook advertising, it is the number of actions a paid ad received divided by the number of impressions for a reporting period, expressed as a percentage.

TECH NOTES:

Actions Rate was included in older Facebook Advertising Performance reports, and was retired.

ARF COMMENTS:

▌ See Actions (Facebook) for comments on Actions.

CITED RESEARCH:

None

SEE ALSO:

Actions (Facebook)
Conversion Rate

Actions (Facebook)

AUTHORITY:	MEDIA:	STAGE:	CATEGORY:	APPLIES TO:
Facebook	Paid Owned	2. Connect	5. Engagement/ Interaction	Social

ANSWERS QUESTION:

How many actions were taken on our ad, Page, app or event after our ad was served?

DEFINITION:

The number of actions taken on your ad, Page, app or event after your ad was served to someone, even if they didn't click on it.

Some common actions are recorded when a person:
- Shares, likes, or comments on your page or post
- Joins your event
- Installs, shares, uses an app
- Claims or shares your offer
- Creates user-generated content
- Views a video

Note: Actions create stories on Facebook. If you are interested in the number of stories created for each action type, Facebook offers the Post Stories by Action Type metric. If the number of unique people creating stories about your post is of interest, Facebook offers Post Storytellers by Action Type.

TECH NOTES:

None

ARF COMMENTS:

The number of clicks and the number of actions may be different because not all clicks generate actions. Tracking actions may be helpful to brands to understand the appeal of different content and use that to optimize its mix and user experience.

Regarding Facebook, the company allows third-party developers to create apps that are compatible with the Facebook platform. In their apps developers can define and add any types of action they want. There are no limitations. For example, Payvment, an enabler of commerce on Facebook, adds "I want this" and "I own this" to catalog displays. Clicking a button generates a story. In their documentation, Facebook suggests other examples of actions like "cook," "read," "listen," "plan," and "review." Any verb can become an action.

Facebook sees actions as a way to create a greater variety of stories and easily share them with Friends. The music streaming service Spotify is one example. The app enables Facebook users to generate stories about the songs they listen to and have them appear in their friends' news feeds.

Some Facebook observers see Actions as the next generation of sharing, as more of one's life can be shared. Facebook CEO Zuckerberg has even stated that "like buttons were limited" adding that Actions are a "new language for how people connect."

CITED RESEARCH:

Facebook Developers (2012). Define Actions. (http://goo.gl/LOnwh).

AllThingsD (2012). Facebook Actions Could Be Unveiled as Soon as Tomorrow. (http://goo.gl/s68od).

Venture Beat (2012). Facebook's Biggest Change Yet: Actions Are Here. (http://goo.gl/kpEyv).

SEE ALSO:

Story (Facebook)

Active User Rate (Mobile Apps)*

AUTHORITY:	**MEDIA:**	**STAGE:**	**CATEGORY:**	**APPLIES TO:**
Millward Brown Digital, Webtrends	Owned	2. Connect	2. Audience/Traffic	Mobile

ANSWERS QUESTION:

What percentage of people who downloaded our app are using it?

DEFINITION:

The number of mobile app users as a percentage of the total number of mobile app downloads.

TECH NOTES:

None

ARF COMMENTS:

Active User Rate is an indication of engagement and also audience size. According to Webtrends, "trends in Active User Rate help sites gauge whether they are gaining or losing audience."

CITED RESEARCH:

Rickson, E. (2010). "Top Metrics for Mobile Apps: Measure What Matters," Webtrends, http://goo.gl/n6NfV

SEE ALSO:

Mobile App Downloads

Ad Awareness*

AUTHORITY:	MEDIA:	STAGE:	CATEGORY:	APPLIES TO:
ARF, Millward Brown Digital	Paid	1. Capture	9. Ad Effectiveness	Website Social Email Mobile

ANSWERS QUESTION:

What percentage of our target customers are aware of our brand's advertising?

DEFINITION:

The campaign's contribution to ad awareness (aided/unaided), usually expressed as a difference (delta) or relative difference (lift). Ad Awareness can be specific to a campaign, individual media, or all advertising.

Unaided Ad Awareness is unprompted (top of mind); Aided Ad Awareness is prompted.

TECH NOTES:

None

ARF COMMENTS:

According to Romaniuk et al. (2004) "Awareness assesses both the reach and the cut-through of the advertising, in that it records the proportion of the market with long term memories of having noticed the brand advertising."

Aided and Unaided Ad Awareness are standard measures of advertising effectiveness. These have long been relied upon because the dominant models regarding advertising effectiveness assume a "hierarchy of effects." These models, often called AIDA models (Awareness, Interest, Desire, Action), start with the idea that consumers must progress through a series of stages: first become aware of products, then learn about them, then develop supporting attitudes to want them, and finally to act on them. Ad awareness has been very well studied across every media type. Research companies have established norms for various brand measures that enable advertisers to compare their results with those norms. Such comparisons are often used to make decisions about improving or running ads.

It is worth noting that the industry is reevaluating AIDA models because they rely on the conscious processing of advertising messages and the ability of people to accurately state their awareness of the ads. Although in wide use, AIDA models are being challenged today because ad awareness may exist below the level of conscious thought, as the industry is learning through research on low attention processing (Heath 2009) and on the subconscious processing of ideas and emotions through neuroscience approaches (ARF 2011). Consequently, the industry is seeking alternatives to AIDA that are based in contemporary research and understanding. Several essays in Viewpoints II point towards non-AIDA models that are desired or being proposed . A more detailed discussion of AIDA models is available in the entry on Brand Awareness.

CITED RESEARCH:

ARF (2011). Neurostandards Collaboration Project. Available from ARF, fee for non-members).

Heath, Robert (2009). Emotional Engagement: How Television Builds Big Brands at Low Attention, Journal of Advertising Research, Vol. 49, No. 1, Mar 2009, pp. 62-73.

Romaniuk, Jenni et al. (2004). Brand and Advertising Awareness: A Replication and Extension of a Known Empirical Generalisation, Australasian Marketing Journal 12 (3), 2004 (http://goo.gl/67FcD).

SEE ALSO:

Brand Awareness
Brand Lift

Ad Impression*

AUTHORITY:	MEDIA:	STAGE:	CATEGORY:	APPLIES TO:
IAB, Nielsen, Yahoo!, Microsoft, MMA, MRC, Pinterest	Paid	1. Capture	1. Advertising	Website Social Email Mobile

ANSWERS QUESTION:

What is an ad impression and how are they counted?

DEFINITION:

An impression is an ad which is served to a user's browser. Ads can be requested by the user's browser (referred to as pulled ads) or they can be pushed, such as e-mailed ads.

Impressions are also called "opportunities to see," often abbreviated OTS, or "exposures."

Note: Mobile ad impressions may be prepended or appended to an SMS message, seen on a mobile web or web page, within a video clip, or in related media.

TECH NOTES:

Two methods are used to deliver ad content to users: a) server-initiated, and b) client-initiated. Server-side counting counts an ad impression as soon as it is requested. Client-side counting counts an ad impression only when it is successfully delivered to a device. Discrepancies in the numbers of ad impressions often arise between the two counting methods because not all ads that are requested are delivered: server-initiated counts are often higher.

Since 2004, Guidelines issued by the Interactive Advertising Bureau (IAB 2013a) with industry partner organizations Mobile Marketing Association (MMA) and Media Ratings Council (MRC) mandate client-initiated measurement over server-side based on the principle that client-initiated impressions are closest to the user actually seeing the ad. For that reason, client-initiated counts are believed to give media buyers and sellers "confidence that the measurements are accurate and can be relied upon as a currency" (McDermott 2013). Not all organizations use client-initiated methods. "For organizations that use a server-initiated ad counting method," the IAB (2012) offers that, "counting should occur subsequent to the ad response at either the publisher's ad server or the web content server." In other words, ad impressions should be counted after they are served, not before.

Regarding impressions in dynamic mobile applications, jointly issued IAB, MMA, and MRC Guidelines (2013b) propose that an ad impression is a measurement of exposure to an in-application ad that meets established minimum thresholds for quality and the terms and conditions established between ad seller and buyer. Further, because apps may be used offline, the notion of the "deferred ad impression" is incorporated into Guidelines. Those impressions are collected when the user returns online, meaning that there is a time gap to consider and that a robust means of counting and reporting back on the impressions delivered is needed. In-app ads point towards a future of evolving measurement complexity for what is, and has been, one of the bedrock measures for media exposure, and media planning and buying.

One example of the unfolding complexity is counting impressions across mobile apps and the different interfaces to a platform a platform offers to its services. For example, ads in Facebook's mobile apps are counted as served when they are viewed for the first time. On all other Facebook interfaces, an ad is served the first time it is placed in a person's News Feed or each time it is placed in the right hand column.

ARF COMMENTS:

Advertisements take many forms online including, but not limited to, display ads, search ads, in-app ads, rich media ads, and sponsored content. Ad Impressions are the primary basis for buying, selling, and accounting for paid advertising, with the cost often quoted in cost per thousand (CPM) impressions.

Impression counting is a matter of great debate, especially as digital media and mobile advance technologically and new types of advertising become adopted. Industry organizations and private companies are exploring new ways of counting. Foremost among these are methods to account for discrepancies between server-initiated and client-initiated impression counts, recommendations to move away from "served" impressions to "viewable" impressions (which are those that have an opportunity to be seen, and are more comparable to TV ad impressions), and handling new media, such as mobile applications.

Brands and agencies that count advertising impressions need to understand the various approaches available by measurement companies, ad servers, and publishers, weigh their strengths and weaknesses, and select the method(s) that best fit their business needs. Moreover, brands must be knowledgeable regarding the newer forms of ad impressions brought about by social and mobile media, such as ads with social elements, the earned impression, and in-app advertising impression.

CITED RESEARCH:

Abraham, Linda et al. (2012). Changing How the World Views Digital Advertising. comScore (http://goo.gl/vId9h, free to download, registration required).

Hemann, Chuck and Ken Burbary (2013). Digital Marketing Analytics: Making Sense of Consumer Data in a Digital World. Indianapolis: QUE.

IAB (2012). IAB Wiki entry for "Ad Impression" (http://goo.gl/YbW2Rz).

IAB, MMA and MRC (2013a). Mobile Web Advertising Measurement Guidelines: Adapted from IAB (US) Ad Impression Measurement Guidelines.(http://goo.gl/qKJAU3).

IAB, MMA, and MRC (2013b). Mobile Application Advertising Measurement Guidelines, Version 1.0 Final Release July 2013 (http://goo.gl/2w9zOZ).

Pinterest Help (2014). Your Pinterest Profile Analytics (http://goo.gl/eGYzlo).

SEE ALSO:

Cost per Thousand (CPM) Impressions

Earned Impression

Frequency

Gross Ratings Points (GRP)

Reach

Viewable Impression

Average Order Value*

AUTHORITY:	MEDIA:	STAGE:	CATEGORY:	APPLIES TO:
comScore, Experian Marketing Services, Google, Millward Brown Digital	Owned	3. Close	8. E-Commerce	Website Social Email Mobile

ANSWERS QUESTION:

What is the average order value on our site?

DEFINITION:

Average Order Value may be computed on a Total or Unique Basis.

Total: Sum of order values received through a website or email divided by the number of orders for a defined time period.

Unique: Average order value by browser is the total order value divided by the number of unique browsers.

TECH NOTES:

Email service providers, such as Experian's CheetahMail, may offer a "track to purchase" functionality that reports the contribution of emails to transactions. Check with your email service provider to determine its availability.

ARF COMMENTS:

Total average order value and Unique browser average order value answer two different questions. Total is helpful when we want to know: "What is the average order on my site?" When we want to know what individual people (unique browser) are spending, the Unique average order value gets at that: "For the people who buy from my site, what is the size of their average order?" Terry Cohen, Digitas SVP Strategy and Analysis, makes the point that "associating Average Order Value with a source of acquisition—either the whole channel, or even a website used in a banner campaign—enables us to optimize ROI or allows us to spend a higher CPM in those placements or channels that give us higher value customers."

For pure-play e-commerce providers, revenue numbers are often captured by a tracking capability or program that can report sales over their site(s). Omnichannel retailers need to make sure that relevant revenues from all their outlets are rolled-up. For many retailers this is a challenge. eConsultancy (2013) reports that only about 20% of companies spending $5 million or more annually currently have capabilities for "real-time data," "integrated data across marketing channels," and a "single customer view from all data sources." Only 15% "gain insights from big data" or "unstructured data." Most firms are working on or planning for these capabilities.

CITED RESEARCH:

Cohen, Terry (2014). Personal communication.

Tornquist, Stefan (2013). What Aren't We Seeing? The Data Iceberg: New Report (http://goo.gl/Y2HuS).

SEE ALSO:

Conversion

Average Time Spent on Page*

AUTHORITY:	MEDIA:	STAGE:	CATEGORY:	APPLIES TO:
Yahoo!, IAB, Google, Nielsen, comScore, Kaushik	Owned	2. Connect	4. Media Consumption	Website Social Mobile

ANSWERS QUESTION:

How long is a specific page being viewed on average?

DEFINITION:

Average time visitors spent on a web page during a visit (session). In mobile applications, Page Views are often called Screen Views.

Note: Nielsen NetRatings calls this metric Duration of Web Page Viewed. comScore calls it Average Page View Duration.

TECH NOTES:

According to web analysts Kaushik and Batra, the counting of Average Time Spent on Page (as well as On Site) this metric has some issues. Batra lists five:

1. Last page viewed in a visit is not counted in this metric.
2. Single Page Visits are not counted in this metrics.
3. Visitors are multitasking, causing inaccuracies in actual time spent on the site.
4. Tabbed Browsing, causing inaccuracies in actual time spent on the site.
5. Download time of the page—time spent on page calculation includes time taken to download the page.

According to the IAB time spent ". . . should represent the activity of a single cookied browser or user for a single access session to the website or property."

ARF COMMENTS:

Average Time on Page should be evaluated in the context of your site's or site's section goals. Pages that are information-rich or provide product details, for example, might target long durations, whereas contact pages or directories would most likely aim for short durations. Pages whose durations are different from what's expected are candidates for optimization. Because pages may contain advertisements or be a step along a Conversion Funnel, relating Average Page View Duration to specific outcomes or conversions can be another way to evaluate the effectiveness of individual pages

Even with the measurement inaccuracies mentioned above, Batra states that Time on Page and Time on Site metrics can be helpful for diagnosing issues with site navigation, search engine optimization, or users' behavior (Batra, 2007).

CITED RESEARCH:

Batra, Anil (2007). "Understanding the 'Time Spent on the Site' Metrics—Web Analytics, Behavioral Targeting and Optimization," (http://goo.gl/EHjf8).

Kaushik, Avinash (2008). "Standard Metrics Revisited: #4 : Time on Page & Time on Site," (http://goo.gl/bbVLp).

SEE ALSO:

Average Time Spent on Site (Session Length)
Page View

Average Time Spent on Site (Session Length)*

AUTHORITY:	MEDIA:	STAGE:	CATEGORY:	APPLIES TO:
Google, Millward Brown Digital, Nielsen, IAB, Yahoo!	Owned	2. Connect	5. Engagement/ Interaction	Website Social Mobile

ANSWERS QUESTION:

How much time did visitors spend on our site, on average, for a reporting period?

DEFINITION:

Average time visitors spent on your site, section, or community for a defined reporting period.

Also called Session Length.

TECH NOTES:

According to web analysts Kaushik and Batra, the counting of Average Time Spent on Site (and On Page) metric has some issues. Batra lists five:

1. Last page viewed in a visit is not counted in this metric.
2. Single Page Visits are not counted in this metric.
3. Visitors are multitasking, causing inaccuracies in actual time spent on the site.
4. Tabbed Browsing, causing inaccuracies in actual time spent on the site.
5. Download time of the page—time spent on page calculation includes time taken to download the page.

According to the IAB time spent "… should represent the activity of a single cookied browser or user for a single access session to the website or property."

ARF COMMENTS:

Even with the inaccuracies, Batra states that Time on Page and Time on Site metrics can be helpful. (Batra, 2007)

"Sudden changes in time spent could indicate a problem with site navigation, search engine optimization or users behavior. It can show that one of the factors on your site has changed.

a. Single Page Visits: Change in single page visits will affect this metric. If you search engine rankings have changed that can affect single page visits and hence time spent on site.

b. Navigation on your site: It either is obstructing finding the correct information (time spent goes up) or has improved so users are getting right to they content they are looking for (time spent goes down).

c. Problems with a page: This can cause users to exit the site prematurely, causing time spent on the site to go down unless the problem is on one of the pages with very high exit ratio. Since the last page is never counted in calculating time spent, a user who exits after seeing this page or exits after getting an error on this page won't make much difference in time spent on the site calculations.

d. User Behavior: If nothing else changed, then users might be either multitasking more than before or are using tabbed browsing. This will result in changes in the time spent on the site."

CITED RESEARCH:

Batra, Anil. "Understanding the 'Time Spent on the Site' Metrics—Web Analytics, Behavioral Targeting and Optimization," (http://goo.gl/EHjf8).
Kaushik, Avinash (2008). "Standard Metrics Revisited: #4 : Time on Page & Time on Site," (http://goo.gl/bbVLp), also Kaushik, A. (2010). "Web Analytics 2.0," Sybex.

SEE ALSO:

Average Time Spent on Page

Bounce—Email*

AUTHORITY:	MEDIA:	STAGE:	CATEGORY:	APPLIES TO:
IAB, Experian Marketing Services	Owned	1. Capture	1. Advertising	Email

ANSWERS QUESTION:

How many emails bounced because they could not be delivered?

DEFINITION:

Count of emails that could not be delivered and are sent back to the email service provider that sent it.

The IAB categorizes email bounces as "hard" or "soft." They define "hard" bounces as the failed delivery of email due to a permanent reason, such as a nonexistent address. "Soft" bounces are the failed delivery of email due to a temporary issue, such as a full inbox or an unavailable ISP server.

Note: Email bounces are different from bounces on website or social networks. Email bounces are concerned with deliverability, site bounces are visits that have a single page view.

TECH NOTES:

None

ARF COMMENTS:

A high number of bounces indicates a list with inaccurate email addresses or issues with the sender, such as being on blacklists. The reasons for high bounce numbers should be discovered and corrected to increase the opportunities for an advertiser's or marketer's message to reach the intended recipients.

According to MailChimp (2012), an email service provider, too many hard bounces is a sign of an old, stale list. Soft bounces usually mean the recipient is "temporarily unavailable," such as on vacation. Across industries, hard bound rates range from 0.1% to 2%; soft bounces from 0.3% to 2.2%.

According to Vertical Response, a leading email service provider, "the frequency with which you mail can also have an impact on the number of bounces you receive (2012). To keep bounces low, Vertical Response offers these tips: a) Mail at least once per month—this helps to solidify your relationship with your subscriber base, especially the ones who've just recently signed up; b) Provide offers or newsletters that your recipients will miss if they change email accounts; c) Offer your recipients a way to update their email address and other account details somewhere on your website; d) If you do get a bounced email, call or mail your customer a postcard to let them know their email bounced and you'd like to get an updated email address.

CITED RESEARCH:

MailChimp (2012). Email Marketing Benchmarks. (http://goo.gl/0E4ZP).
Vertical Response (2012). Acceptable Bounce and Unsubscribe Rates. (http://goo.gl/5GOsS).

SEE ALSO:

Bounce (Website or Social Network)
Bounce Rate—Email

Bounce (Website or Social Network)*

AUTHORITY:	MEDIA:	STAGE:	CATEGORY:	APPLIES TO:
Digital Analytics Association	Owned	1. Capture	2. Audience/Traffic	Website Social Mobile

ANSWERS QUESTION:

How many people came to our site and saw only one page?

DEFINITION:

Count of visits that consist of one Page View over a reporting period.

Note: Email bounces are different from bounces on website or social networks. Email bounces are concerned with deliverability.

TECH NOTES:

It is important to filter out automated visits to a website from crawlers, robots, or spiders in order to calculate an accurate count.

ARF COMMENTS:

Except for sites that are optimized for one-page viewing, bounces may provide indications of the appeal and value of specific pages. In general, pages with a high number of bounces may indicate that the traffic directed to a site is not relevant or that the site's content or structure is not encouraging visitors to travel more deeply into the website. Conversely, pages with a low number of bounces may indicate that the content is of interest. Pages with a high number of bounces need to be assessed in the context of site and brand goals, and may be candidates for optimization that increases their relevance.

CITED RESEARCH:

Kaushik, A. (2010). "Web Analytics 2.0," Sybex.

SEE ALSO:

Bounce—Email

Bounce Rate (Website or Social Network)

Bounce Rate - Email

AUTHORITY:	MEDIA:	STAGE:	CATEGORY:	APPLIES TO:
IAB, Experian Marketing Services	Owned	1. Capture	1. Advertising	Email

ANSWERS QUESTION:

What percentage of our emails bounced?

DEFINITION:

The Bounce Rate is the percentage of subscribers that did not receive a mailing because the subscribers' email addresses bounced.

TECH NOTES:

Email service providers may count total bounces or only hard bounces.

ARF COMMENTS:

A high number of bounces indicates a list with inaccurate email addresses or issues with the sender, such as being on blacklists. The reasons for high bounce numbers should be discovered and corrected to increase the opportunities for an advertiser's or marketer's message to reach the intended recipients.

Too many hard bounces is a sign of an old, stale list. Soft bounces usually mean the recipient is "temporarily unavailable," such as on vacation (MailChimp 2012). Across industries, hard bound rates range from 0.1% to 2%; soft bounces from 0.3% to 2.2%.

"The frequency with which you mail can also have an impact on the number of bounces you receive" (Vertical Response 2012). To keep bounces low, Vertical Response offers these tips: a) Mail at least once per month—this helps to solidify your relationship with your subscriber base, especially the ones who've just recently signed up; b) Provide offers or newsletters that your recipients will miss if they change email accounts; c) Offer your recipients a way to update their email address and other account details somewhere on your website; d) If you do get a bounced email, call or mail your customer a postcard to let them know their email bounced and you'd like to get their updated email address.

CITED RESEARCH:

MailChimp (2012). Email Marketing Benchmarks. (http://goo.gl/0E4ZP).

Vertical Response (2012). Acceptable Bounce and Unsubscribe Rates. (http://goo.gl/5GOsS).

SEE ALSO:

Bounce—Email

Bounce Rate (Website or Social Network)

Bounce Rate (Site or Network)*

AUTHORITY:	MEDIA:	STAGE:	CATEGORY:	APPLIES TO:
Yahoo!, Google, Patel & Flores, ARF	Owned	1. Capture	3. Site Navigation/Site Performance	Website Social Mobile

ANSWERS QUESTION:

What is the percentage of times a page bounces?

DEFINITION:

The Bounce Rate is the number of Bounces as a percentage of the Number of Visits to a site page, over a reporting period.

TECH NOTES:

None

ARF COMMENTS:

A high bounce rate indicates a landing page that may not be working well and engaging the visitor. Pages with high bounce rates are candidates for redesign or tailoring to engage the viewer and promote the desired interactions, especially those that are most often used for entry into the site. According to Google Analytics, bounce rates can be minimized in search engine marketing campaigns by tailoring landing pages to each keyword and ad that is run. Landing pages should provide the information and services that were promised in the ad copy. Additionally, make sure that Referral Traffic sent by links on other sites are relevant to your site's content.

Bounce rate is not necessarily a relevant measure for many blogs because they are designed for reading a post and leaving. However, it can be relevant for blogs that intend to draw the reader in for engagement with content or offers.

CITED RESEARCH:

Google Analytics (2013). Bounce Rate (http://goo.gl/CI5Y1).

SEE ALSO:

Average Page Views Per Visit
Bounce
Page View
Referral Traffic
Visit (Session)

Brand Advocate*

AUTHORITY:	MEDIA:	STAGE:	CATEGORY:	APPLIES TO:
WOMMA, IPR	Earned	2. Connect	6. Amplification/ Endorsement	Social

ANSWERS QUESTION:

What are brand advocates and what impact do they have?

DEFINITION:

An individual who shows support for, pleads the case of or defends a brand, cause, product, or service while remaining formally unaffiliated with the brand and unremunerated.

Advocates have these characteristics:
- intermittent or one-time advocacy either about a brand or experience
- have positive sentiment towards the brand
- open and willing to share specific experiences with others
- independent from the brand

TECH NOTES:

None

ARF COMMENTS:

Followers and Subscribers may reflect an affinity for your brand, but need not be that involved. Brand advocates generate content and brand engagement. Dachis Group, a social business platform provider, tracks 30,000 brands and nearly 250,000 brand advocates. A recent analysis of their data revealed that brand advocates make up only 0.001% of a brand's social subscribers, but they are responsible for 5% of a brand's total social signal, and start 8% of all company-related conversations (Mastronardi 2012). BzzAgent, a social marketing company that uses word-of-mouth to drive sales, has a panel of brand advocates that it studied to learn about their habits, behaviors, and motivations. Findings showed that brand advocates are 2.5 times more likely to use social media to expand their social circles (half visit to meet new people and potentially expand their reach); they write and share more than twice as many online communications about brands and are 50% more likely to influence a purchase; and enjoy sharing information—they are three times more likely to share product information to relax (BzzAgent 2011). Zuberance, a firm that helps brands identify advocates and manage advocacy programs, studied advocates finding that 38% made a recommendation about once a month, and 12% said they did so several times a week. Recommendations are not one-time events: 70% recommended at least five products or services a year, and 16% recommended at least 15 products or services over that time (eMarketer 2012).

Brand advocates are allies that brands attract, nurture, and activate; they are a tribe. Advocates "target you, they like you, they want you and you need to respect and return that love" (Rabjohns 2013). Brands that seek to leverage their advocates institute a formal advocacy program. BzzAgent lists 10 tips to tap the power of your brand advocates. These include: engaging them in sites where they advocate; treat them specially; keep a laser-focus on your product; make content engaging, easy to find and share; recognize them and help make their voices heard; gauge their influence on others; and measure the sales impact of the program. Keep in mind that individual brand advocates may differ, with different interests, motivations and behaviors, so it is important to understand those differences and adjust your brand advocate program to accommodate their variety.

The Norton Advocates program is a classic example. This initiative identified customers as Norton Advocates. These advocates created and published thousands of reviews and testimonials, enabling Norton to double user ratings for its products on leading shopping and review sites. The Norton Advocates program enabled parent company Symantec to generate a significant quantity of highly valuable user-generated content that Norton leveraged to drive positive awareness, leads, and sales, which increased by Norton Advocates sharing thousands of promotional offers with friends and colleagues, boosting Norton sales. Those actions "generated five to ten times higher conversion rates than offers through other marketing programs" (Zuberance 2009).

In addition to the Norton example, other studies demonstrated relationships between brand advocacy and sales or market share, arguably the most important measure of effectiveness. As early as 2008, TNS research demonstrated a correlation between online advocacy and market share for HDTV brands, and clearly showed that brand advocacy can be stimulated by marketing communications spend (Nail & Chapman 2008). David Rabjohn's essay in this book explains that it is the number of advocates, not the number of conversations or level of buzz that drive sales; it is the changes in advocate levels that can predict the direction of next-month sales.

CITED RESEARCH:

BzzAgent (2011). A Field Guide to Brand Advocates: Insights for Marketers (http://goo.gl/yQN5U).

eMarketer (2012). Brand Advocates Are Here to Help (http://goo.gl/QtlaZ).

Mastronardi, David (2012). Six Brand Advocate Archetypes (http://goo.gl/2ccYL).

Nail, J. and J. Chapman (2008). Social Media Analysis for Consumer Insight: Validating and Enhancing Traditional Market Research Findings (ARF WebEx presentation).

Rabjohns, D. (2013). Personal communication.

Zuberance (2009). Zuberance, the Leading Word of Mouth Company, Wins Prestigious Social Media Award (http://goo.gl/6LbfU, reported in SmartBrief).

SEE ALSO:

Followers/Subscribers

Influencer

Brand Awareness*

AUTHORITY:	MEDIA:	STAGE:	CATEGORY:	APPLIES TO:
ARF, IAB, Millward Brown Digital	Paid	1. Capture	9. Ad Effectiveness	Website Social Email Mobile

ANSWERS QUESTION:

What percentage of our target market is aware of our brand?

DEFINITION:

Represents the campaign's contribution to brand awareness (aided/unaided), usually expressed as an absolute difference (delta) or relative difference (lift).

Unaided Brand Awareness is unprompted or "top of mind;" Aided Brand Awareness is prompted.

Can be calculated by campaign, medium, or all advertising.

TECH NOTES:

Awareness research may use one of two methods:

Control/Exposed—simultaneously surveying people who were not exposed to ads and people who were exposed to ads and comparing the differences.

Pre/Post—respondents surveyed before the campaign and then during/after the campaign.

ARF COMMENTS:

Aided and Unaided Brand Awareness have long been standard measures in brand research because the dominant models regarding advertising effectiveness assume a "hierarchy of effects." These models are often called AIDA (Awareness, Interest, Desire, Action) models. They start with the idea that consumers must progress through a series of stages: first become aware of brands, then learn about them, then develop supporting attitudes to want them, and finally to act on them. In these models, brand awareness arises from the conscious processing of advertising messages and the ability of people to state accurately that they are aware of the brands. Advertising's impact on brand awareness, and other common branding measures such as recall, message association, affinity, favorability, and purchase intention is, and has been, very well studied across every media type. Several research companies have established norms for various brand measures that enable advertisers to compare their results with those benchmarks. Norms are often used to make decisions about improving or running ads. From a different viewpoint, brand awareness is seen as the foundation for brand equity (Aaker 1991)

AIDA models rely on the conscious processing of advertising messages and the ability of people to state that they are aware of the brands advertised. However, AIDA models are being challenged today because contemporary research on low involvement processing (Heath 1999) and on the subconscious processing of advertising through neuroscience methods (ARF 2011) reveal that brand awareness often exists below the level of conscious thought and may not be consciously recalled. Although AIDA models remain widely used, many in the industry are searching for alternatives that take the new science into account. Essays in Viewpoints II describe several.

Moreover, those new models need to account for the many ways people have today for learning about and becoming aware of brands through search, the Internet, email, mobile media, and social media, not just advertising. The information and experiences accessed and shared through these tools are reshaping shopping and buying. Research from Group M (2011), the ARF (2012), and Google (2013) found that social media conversations, mobile media, search, websites, and email impact brand awareness and the entire purchase journey.

CITED RESEARCH:

Aaker, David (1991). *Managing Brand Equity: Capitalizing on the Value of a Brand Name. The Free Press: New York.*

ARF (2011). *Neurostandards Collaboration Project. Available from ARF (fee for non-members).*

ARF (2012). *Digital/Social Media in the Purchase Decision Process. White Paper available from ARF (fee for non-members).*

Google (2013). *The Customer Journey to Online Purchase (http://goo.gl/rxlCA).*

Group M and comScore (2011). *The Virtuous Circle: The role of search and social media in the purchase pathway, (http://goo.gl/EUGyg).*

Heath, Robert (1999). *The Low-involvement Processing Theory (Admap, March Issue).*

SEE ALSO:

Ad Awareness

Brand Lift

Brand Lift*

AUTHORITY:	MEDIA:	STAGE:	CATEGORY:	APPLIES TO:
ARF, Millward Brown Digital	Paid	1. Capture 2. Connect 3. Close	9. Ad Effectiveness	Website Social Email Mobile

ANSWERS QUESTION:

Did exposure to our advertising campaign have an impact on our brand lift measures?

DEFINITION:

The percentage increase in brand measures resulting from exposure to an advertising campaign, relative to a control group that was not exposed. Brand lift measures include, but are not limited to: brand awareness (aided and unaided), recall (aided and unaided), message association, attitudes, favorability, purchase intent, preference, and likelihood to recommend.

TECH NOTES:

Brand lift is researched using survey methods, typically using a test/control methodology.

ARF COMMENTS:

Brand lift measures are metrics of long standing. They are used to evaluate the effectiveness of brand advertising. Lifts may be calculated for the online campaign or for the total, multi-platform campaign. Lifts may also be segmented, such as by media placement, creative, target audience, or exposure frequency. Brand lift analysis is often used to optimize a brand's advertising campaign so that it can best achieve its objectives across the Capture, Connect, and Close stages.

Brand lift measures are poised, some say, to become even more important to evaluating brand advertising on digital platforms. Marketers are committing more advertising dollars to digital branding efforts and moving dollars from direct response. Further, marketers, agencies, and media sellers agree that brand lift is a suitable measure to determine the effectiveness of their digital branding campaigns. While marketers would first prefer sales lift, it is often difficult and/or costly to compute for every campaign, and their partners often do not have the sales data. Brand lift is considered a precursor to sales lift and can serve as a leading indicator. Advances in digital technologies allow for brand lift to be measured and optimized in near real-time, potentially increasing its value to marketers, agencies, and media sellers (Vizu 2013).

However, brand lift measures are derived from the Awareness-Interest-Desire-Action (AIDA) progressions that dominate our industry's mental models of how advertising works. With the rise of the Internet and social media, new research on consumer information processing, insights from neuroscience and recent economic findings regarding decision-making, the notion that consumers are persuaded by advertising, and then travel linear paths to purchase utilizing conscious and rational thought processes is being seriously questioned (see Brand Awareness for a more detailed discussion). The Part II Essays in Viewpoints point towards more contemporary approaches to understanding advertising effects. A more detailed discussion of AIDA models is available in the Brand Awareness entry.

CITED RESEARCH:

Vizu-A Nielsen Company (2013). Online Advertising Performance Outlook 2013 (available from Nielsen site, registration may be required. http://goo.gl/VoT0D).

SEE ALSO:

Ad Awareness
Brand Awareness

Brochure Downloads

AUTHORITY:	MEDIA:	STAGE:	CATEGORY:	APPLIES TO:
Patel & Flores	Owned	2. Connect	7. Conversion	Website Social Mobile

ANSWERS QUESTION:

How many of our brochures were downloaded over a period of time?

DEFINITION:

The number of times a brochure was downloaded over a reporting period.

TECH NOTES:

It is also important to count the number of download failures to learn if there is a problem with the file, a file transfer issue, or browser problem.

ARF COMMENTS:

Counts of brochure downloads indicate interest in content about a company, product or service, and the effectiveness of communications about the brochure. Most brochures are in PDF format, making them easy to share and print. When making brochures available to share, companies should have tracking capability. Sharing rates are another indicator of interest and also provide opportunities to communicate with or advertise to the person receiving the brochure. Often evaluating the impact of brochure downloads requires additional data from other corporate systems or resources.

CITED RESEARCH:

None

SEE ALSO:

Key Content Downloads (Coupons, Recipes, Apps, etc.)
Key Performance Indicator (KPI)

Browse to Buy Ratio

AUTHORITY:	MEDIA:	STAGE:	CATEGORY:	APPLIES TO:
comScore, Millward Brown Digital	Owned	3. Close	7. Conversion	Website Mobile

ANSWERS QUESTION:

What percentage of browsers to our site converted to place an order?

DEFINITION:

The number of unique browsers that placed an order as a percentage of all unique browsers in a reporting period.

TECH NOTES:

None

ARF COMMENTS:

For e-commerce sites, the Browse to Buy Ratio indicates the site's conversion productivity and ability to achieve the conversion goal of sales. Trends in this metric coupled with analyses of the product sales mix can suggest ways to help the site perform better.

CITED RESEARCH:

None

SEE ALSO:

Conversion
Conversion Funnel
Conversion Goal
Conversion Rate

Browser

AUTHORITY:	MEDIA:	STAGE:	CATEGORY:	APPLIES TO:
comScore, Millward Brown Digital, Wikipedia	Owned	1. Capture	2. Audience/Traffic	Site

ANSWERS QUESTION:

What is a web browser?

DEFINITION:

A web browser is an application software or program designed to enable users to access, retrieve, and view documents and other resources on a PC, mobile phone, or Internet-enabled device.

Many browsers are available. Several of the most popular are Internet Explorer, Google Chrome, Firefox, and Safari. These are released as major versions that are updated from time to time with minor version numbers. Examples: Chrome 23.0.1271, Internet Explorer 8.1.

TECH NOTES:

Browsers are usually identified by cookies that are placed on a computer by a web server or by a web browser. If a browser does not accept cookies an alternative unique identifier may be used, such as IP address (comScore).

ARF COMMENTS:

Browsers from different publishers provide many of the same features, but the implementation of those features, as well as unique capabilities, affect the user experience. Testing sites with multiple browsers and multiple versions is a best practice designed to maximize cross-browser compatibility for online and mobile sites.

CITED RESEARCH:

None

SEE ALSO:

Unique Browsers
Visit (Session)
Unique Visitors (Unique Browsers)

Channel

AUTHORITY:	MEDIA:	STAGE:	CATEGORY:	APPLIES TO:
comScore, Google	Paid Owned Earned	1. Capture	2. Audience/Traffic	Website Social Email Mobile

ANSWERS QUESTION:

Which online media channels are visitors using to arrive at our site?

DEFINITION:

An online media type through which you attract browsers to your website. Examples include: Cost-per-Click (also called PPC, pay-per-click, i.e., paid search), organic search, direct visits, RSS (Really Simple Syndication), email, and social media. Often reported as a total count and as a percent distribution.

Channels are comprised of one or more sources, such as Google, Yahoo, Twitter, and Facebook.

Note: Google uses the term "Medium" for Channel.

TECH NOTES:

None

ARF COMMENTS:

Understanding the channels used to reach your site provides guidance for gauging the strategy (e.g., "Is social media working as we would like?"), and the relative abilities of different channels to drive traffic. Channel and Source analysis is helpful for optimizing traffic—and the right traffic—to a site.

CITED RESEARCH:

None

SEE ALSO:

Source
Referral Traffic

Check-Ins—Page (Facebook)

AUTHORITY:	**MEDIA:**	**STAGE:**	**CATEGORY:**	**APPLIES TO:**
Facebook	Earned	2. Connect	6. Amplification/ Endorsement	Social

ANSWERS QUESTION:

How many people checked-in to our place?

DEFINITION:

Count of the total number of unique people who check-in to a Facebook place through their mobile device or by tagging your place in their posts. Facebook provides a total count and also a count of unique users who checked-in using their mobile.

Note: If you are interested in the numbers of times people checked-into a place instead of the number of people, Facebook offers two metrics - one for the total number of times, and the second for the mobile number of times.

TECH NOTES:

None

ARF COMMENTS:

Check-ins use a Facebook page type called place page. A place page is different from a brand page. Place pages show location and relevant information if it is provided. People who view place pages can see lists of friends who are there, or have visited.

Check-ins create stories which show up in the News Feeds of friends. In so doing, check-ins to place pages may enable Page owners to increase Impressions of their place and expand reach. However, not all friends will see check-ins in their News Feeds because of Facebook's optimization algorithm called EdgeRank, which determines what appears.

CITED RESEARCH:

None

SEE ALSO:

Story (Facebook)

Click

AUTHORITY:	MEDIA:	STAGE:	CATEGORY:	APPLIES TO:
IAB, comScore, Experian Marketing Services, Pinterest, Yahoo!	Paid Owned Earned	2. Connect	5. Engagement/ Interaction	Website Social Email Mobile

ANSWERS QUESTION:

What is a click?

DEFINITION:

The IAB provides four definitions for a "click."

1) metric that measures the reaction of a user to an Internet ad. There are three types of clicks: click-throughs, in-unit clicks, and mouseovers;

2) the opportunity for a user to download another file by clicking on an advertisement, as recorded by the server;

3) the result of a measurable interaction with an advertisement or key word that links to the advertiser's intended website or another page or frame within the website;

4) metric that measures the reaction of a user to linked editorial content.

Clicks are also counted for email.

TECH NOTES:

comScore counts clicks called "clickin," "clickout," and "PDF." A "clickin" is a click on third-party banners and hyperlinks referring to your website, or for measuring internal links on your website. A "clickout" is a click on banners or hyperlinks on your website to third-party sites. PDF clicks are those that link to PDF files. (Note: PDF is the portable document format developed by Adobe used to share documents.)

Pinterest click reporting counts "clickouts"—the number of clicks and unique visits back to your website.

ARF COMMENTS:

The click is generally counted for ad campaigns to determine how often a particular campaign ad brought a visitor to an advertiser-specified online or mobile destination, such as a sign-up page, product page, or shopping cart, for example.

See the entries for Click-Through, Click-Through Rate, and Click-Through Rate—Email (Total and Unique) for detailed discussion of the issues around click counting.

CITED RESEARCH:

None

SEE ALSO:

Click-Through
Click-Through Rate (CTR)

Click Stream

AUTHORITY:	MEDIA:	STAGE:	CATEGORY:	APPLIES TO:
IAB, Millward Brown Digital, Yahoo	Owned	2. Connect	3. Site Navigation/Site Performance	Site

ANSWERS QUESTION:

What path did visitors take through our site?

DEFINITION:

A Click Stream is:

1) the electronic path a user takes while navigating from site to site, and from page to page within a site;

2) a comprehensive body of data describing the sequence of activity between a user's browser and any other Internet resource, such as a website or third party ad server.

Note: Yahoo! calls this "Visit Path."

TECH NOTES:

Web analytics software is a critical source for obtaining detailed Click Stream and path analyses for your owned sites. Panels are helpful for obtaining click stream across multiple sites.

ARF COMMENTS:

Click Streams record user behavior; they provide the foundations for measuring Visits, Visitors, Time on Site, Page Views, Bounce Rate, Sources, and many more metrics. Click Stream data describe what people did on a site, not why they did it. Click Stream analysis can be used for site optimization; overlaying Click Streams can show where people are clicking and where they are not (Parr 2009). Segmenting Click Stream by type of visitor or Referral Sources, for example, may reveal finer patterns that can be used to enhance the visitor experience and help the brand achieve site goals.

CITED RESEARCH:

Parr, Ben (2009). Clickstreams: What They Are and Why You Should Track Them. Mashable (http://goo.gl/IW2Tb).

SEE ALSO:

Click
Click-Through
Click-Through Rate (CTR)

Click-Through

AUTHORITY:	MEDIA:	STAGE:	CATEGORY:	APPLIES TO:
IAB, Digital Analytics Association, Facebook, Microsoft	Paid Owned	2. Connect	5. Engagement/ Interaction	Website Social Email Mobile

ANSWERS QUESTION:

How many times was our ad, or content, clicked on?

DEFINITION:

The action of following a link within an advertisement or editorial content to another website or another page or frame within the web or mobile site.

TECH NOTES:

On websites, ad click-throughs should be tracked and reported as a 302 redirect at the ad server and should filter out robotic activity (IAB).

According to the Digital Analytics Association, "click-throughs measured on the sending side (as reported by your ad server, for example) and on the receiving side (as reported by your web analytics tool) often do not match. Minor discrepancies are normal, but large discrepancies may require investigation (see their Web Analytics Definitions Version 4: http://goo.gl/6H3C3).

ARF COMMENTS:

Click-through is a long-used measure for gauging an advertisement's effectiveness for direct response and display advertising. Click-through is generally relied upon as a metric for direct response advertising. Quantcast (2013) notes that for search, clicks are a "natural currency" that are useful because people click to "go somewhere else," and clicks are fine for measurement and optimization. But clicks are controversial for measuring display advertising because click-throughs do not fully measure important contributions to brand building, such as image, sales, and the cumulative impact of ads. comScore research indicates that clicks "may not be a relevant measure of the impact of display advertising." Their research found that "the manner in which online display ads work in affecting consumer behavior, revealed that there are indeed latency effects and branding effects even when click rates are minimal." Subsequent research found that interaction capability and viewability are more highly correlated with conversion than click-throughs (Lipsman 2012).

Facebook's Brad Smallwood, head of Measurement and Insights, has even gone so far as to say that "clicks aren't the right metric for the broader set of marketing objectives beyond direct response." Facebook's research correlating ad exposure within the social network and offline purchasing revealed that 99% of purchases did not involve clicking (2012). This "view-through" behavior is also recognized by the Making Measurement Make Sense Initiative (3MS 2012) which states that "click-through will still be relevant and operative for transactions, but view-through is more relevant as a surrogate engagement measurement for brand marketers less interested in immediate transactions. Quantcast's study supports Facebook and 3MS, adding an important observation that the people who click on ads are not the same ones who buy (Feldman 2013).

For editorial content, click-throughs are often considered a measure of interest or engagement. Click-throughs are no longer confined to websites. Most social networking sites, such as Twitter, LinkedIn, Pinterest, and Facebook, furnish the ability to embed links to external sites in content; these have become important drivers of traffic (they are external referrers). Link shortening programs, from Bitly and Google to name two, add analytics about the clicks. Bitly's stats include the number of clicks, the number of clicks via the shortened URL, and the number of people who saved the link destination. Bitly supplies segmentation on the source of traffic to the shortened link and the countries that clicked. Analyzing tweets may provide guidance as to which types of content drive interest sufficiently that the reader will click-through. When coupled with analysis on the destination end, the value of that traffic can be assessed.

Concerning mobile advertising, click-through rates on mobile banners appear to be somewhat higher for certain categories than they are for standard banner ads (eMarketer 2011). In addition to category, smartphone capabilities influence clicking. These include factors such as the device type, use of mobile site links (which increase exposure on smartphone search engine results pages), and personalization, such as the dynamic insertion of location (Performics 2013).

CITED RESEARCH:

3MS (2012). Making Measurement Make Sense: Time to Get Up to Speed (http://goo.gl/fvuhK).

eMarketer (2011). "Mobile Ads Outperform Standard Banners" (http://goo.gl/aRXJ7).

Feldman, Konrad (2013). Display Ad Clickers Are Not Your Customers (http://goo.gl/vE02y).

Fulgoni, Gian M and Marie Pauline Mörn (2009). Whither the Click? Journal of Advertising Research, Vol. 49, No. 2, pp. 134–142.

Lipsman, Andrew (2012). For Display Ads, Being Seen Matters More than Being Clicked (http://goo.gl/OHXgY).

Performics (2013). Retailer has 62% Increased CTR for On-the-Go Boosts Smartphone Orders (http://goo.gl/iCR6Y).

Quantcast (2013). Beyond Last Touch: Understanding Campaign Effectiveness (available from http://goo.gl/0JPBb).

Smallwood, Brad (2012). Making Digital Brand Campaigns Better (http://goo.gl/yuy12).

SEE ALSO:

Click-Through Rate (CTR)
Cost per Click (CPC)
Mouseover
Referral Traffic

Click-Through Rate (CTR)*

AUTHORITY:	MEDIA:	STAGE:	CATEGORY:	APPLIES TO:
Digital Analytics Association,Experian Marketing Services, Facebook, Microsoft, Millward Brown Digital, Yahoo!	Paid Owned Earned	2. Connect	5. Engagement/ Interaction	Website Social Email Mobile

ANSWERS QUESTION:

How often do people click on our ad or content after they have seen it?

Definition: The Click-Through Rate (CTR) of online (web, social or mobile) advertisements or links within editorial content is the number of click-throughs for a specific link divided by the number of times that link was viewed, expressed as a percentage over a reporting period.

For emails, it is the number of clicks on one or more links within an email as a percentage of the number of emails delivered.

TECH NOTES:

None

ARF COMMENTS:

Click-Through Rate is a long-used measure for judging an advertisement's effectiveness for direct response and display advertising. Click-through is often used to evaluate direct response advertising—trends in clicks may indicate the utility of search key words for driving traffic and moving through a conversion funnel, but is controversial for measuring display advertising because click-through rates do not fully measure important contributions to brand building, such as image, sales, and the cumulative impact of ads. comScore research by Fulgoni and Morn (2009) indicates that clicks "may not be a relevant measure of the impact of display advertising." Their research found that "the manner in which online display ads work in affecting consumer behavior, revealing that there are indeed latency effects and branding effects even when click rates are minimal. Subsequent research found that interaction capability and viewability are more highly correlated with conversion than click-throughs (comScore 2012). For editorial content, click-throughs are often considered a measure of interest or engagement.

Click-through rates appear to be somewhat higher in mobile advertising for certain categories than they are for standard banner ads. This may be related to the current state of the mobile experience, which is less robust in general and more dependent on clicks. However, this bears watching because technology advances and their adoption may change the user experience and need to click (eMarketer 2011).

CITED RESEARCH:

For research on latency and branding effects, see: Gian M. Fulgoni and Marie Pauline Mörn. Journal of Advertising Research, Vol. 49, No. 2, June 2009, pp. 134-142.

comScore (2012). "For Display Ads, Being Seen Matters More than Being Clicked" (http://goo.gl/OHXgY).

eMarketer (2011). "Mobile Ads Outperform Standard Banners" (http://goo.gl/5JF7G).

SEE ALSO:

Click
Click-Through
Cost per Click (CPC)

Click-Through Rate After Video Exposure

AUTHORITY:	MEDIA:	STAGE:	CATEGORY:	APPLIES TO:
Yahoo!	Paid Owned	2. Connect	5. Engagement/ Interaction	Website Social Stream Mobile

ANSWERS QUESTION:

How many click-throughs did our video generate?

DEFINITION:

Number of click-throughs generated by the views of a brand's online video to the number of views, expressed as a percentage over a reporting period.

TECH NOTES:

None

ARF COMMENTS:

This metric reports the ability of a branded video or video ad to generate click-throughs and drive traffic to an advertiser-specified destination. Correlating clicks with actions taken on the destination, such as completing conversion actions like requesting information, signing up for newsletters or making purchases, may reveal the specific ways in which the ad is—or is not—effective in contributing to a desired outcome. For branding purposes, conducting surveys before and after exposure may reveal to what extent the video raised Brand Lift measures such as awareness, recall, likeabilty, or purchase intent, for example.

CITED RESEARCH:

A recent infographic-like review of stats on video advertising effectiveness is provided by Video Brewery (2012).
18 Big Video Marketing Statistics and What They Mean for Your Business. (http://goo.gl/xDLJE, accessed December 14, 2012.)

SEE ALSO:

Brand Lift
Click-Through Rate (CTR)
Conversion

Comments*

AUTHORITY:	MEDIA:	STAGE:	CATEGORY:	APPLIES TO:
ARF	Earned	2. Connect	5. Engagement/ Interaction	Social

ANSWERS QUESTION:

How many comments did an ad, post, or item of content receive?

DEFINITION:

A comment is an annotation that users write about an ad, post, or item of content, usually on a blog or social network. It is the count of user-generated comments a post or item of content receives over a reporting period.

TECH NOTES:

Comments are often tracked by site or social network analytics packages, such as Facebook Insights and Google Analytics, and third-party measurement services.

ARF COMMENTS:

Comment count is often used as a measure of engagement. The idea is that comments represent efforts by people to talk about or interact with a brand.

According to Socius, an online community software concern, computing a Post to Comment ratio can be a valuable metric to determine if the post, forum entries, idea submissions, or file uploads added to a site is driving interest and engagement.

If using comment count, it's important to consider the type of site and use of the comment feature. Trade and academic publisher Wiley, for example, recently devalued the number of comments metric as an indicator of impact or quality because the commenting feature is seldom used in scholarly publishing.

However, there's a big caution about using comment count: comment spam. There's a small industry in comment spam, much of which uses automated programs—spambots —to sites of all types and descriptions. If you use comment count, it is essential that you filter out the spam and off-topic counts to derive meaningful measures.

CITED RESEARCH:

Ryan, Tim (2011). "Article Metrics and Discoverability" on blogs.wiley.com (http://goo.gl/E9313).

Socius (2012). 6-Key-Customer-Engagement-Metrics-for-Improving-Online-Community-ROI (http://goo.gl/0sBiP).

SEE ALSO:

Mentions

Reviews

Consumers—Page (Facebook)

AUTHORITY:	MEDIA:	STAGE:	CATEGORY:	APPLIES TO:
Facebook	Paid Owned	2. Connect	2. Audience/Traffic	Social

ANSWERS QUESTION:

How many unique people clicked on any of our page content?

DEFINITION:

The number of people who clicked on any of your content, over a reporting period.

TECH NOTES:

Facebook reports metrics at the Page and Post levels. It is very important to make sure that you use the right ones for your analytic task. Post-level metrics are typically reported on a lifetime basis, whereas page-level metrics are typically reported for daily, weekly, and 28-day periods.

ARF COMMENTS:

Total Consumers counts the number of interactions people have with a page, and is considered a measure of user engagement. Analyzing trends may provide guidance on the types of content that users are presumably interested in.

CITED RESEARCH:

None

SEE ALSO:

Click-Through

Consumers—Post (Facebook)

AUTHORITY:	MEDIA:	STAGE:	CATEGORY:	APPLIES TO:
Facebook	Paid Owned	2. Connect	2. Audience/Traffic	Social

ANSWERS QUESTION:

How many unique people clicked on anything in our post?

DEFINITION:

The number of unique people who clicked anywhere in your post.

TECH NOTES:

Facebook reports metrics at the page and post levels. It is very important to make sure that you use the right ones for your analytic task. Post-level metrics are typically reported on a lifetime basis, whereas page-level metrics are typically reported for daily, weekly, and 28-day periods.

ARF COMMENTS:

Post Consumers counts the number of people who interact with a post, and is considered a measure of user engagement.

Analyzing trends in Post Consumers may provide guidance on the types of content that users are presumably interested in.

CITED RESEARCH:

None

SEE ALSO:

Click-Through

Consumptions—Post (Facebook)

AUTHORITY:	MEDIA:	STAGE:	CATEGORY:	APPLIES TO:
Facebook	Paid Owned	2. Connect	5. Engagement/ Interaction	Site Advertising Content

ANSWERS QUESTION:

How many clicks did our post receive?

DEFINITION:

The number of times people clicked anywhere in your posts without generating a story.

Note: Facebook also reports the number of people who clicked on the post without generating a story, in a metric called Post Consumptions (Unique).

TECH NOTES:

Clicks that generate stories are reported as "Other Clicks." Facebook also reports clicks segmented by consumption type.

ARF COMMENTS:

Post Consumption counts the number of interactions people have with a post, and is considered a measure of user engagement. Analyzing the clicks provides guidance on the types of post content that users are presumably interested in.

CITED RESEARCH:

None

SEE ALSO:

Consumers—Post (Facebook)

Conversation Relevant Sites

AUTHORITY:	MEDIA:	STAGE:	CATEGORY:	APPLIES TO:
IAB	Earned	2. Connect	5. Engagement/ Interaction	Social

ANSWERS QUESTION:

How many sites are there with conversation relevant to our brand?

DEFINITION:

The count of sites in the conversation whose content contains relevant conversations.

Often sites are identified by "conversation phrases" which are combinations of keywords and keyword phrases used to associate an author/site, its content, and audiences to a conversation

TECH NOTES:

The original IAB definition is from the perspective of targeting media plans to blog conversations; it stipulates that the count be from the client's Request for Proposal (RFP) or Insertion Order (IO).

ARF COMMENTS:

Brands targeting conversation phrases usually look beyond the mere number of relevant sites, to evaluating and selecting them on dimensions, such as audience size, number of conversations, breadth of topics, and the quality, depth, threading, and frequency of the postings. Advertisers should study conversation sites for seasonality and shifts in conversation topics to assure that their advertising and any engagement actions are tuned to the conversations, timely and appropriate.

CITED RESEARCH:

Rappaport, Stephen D. (2011). Listen First! Turning Social Media Conversations into Business Advantage. Hoboken: John Wiley & Sons.

SEE ALSO:

Conversation
Sentiment

Conversation*

AUTHORITY:	MEDIA:	STAGE:	CATEGORY:	APPLIES TO:
IAB, Coalition for Public Relations Research Standards, IPR	Earned	2. Connect	5. Engagement/ Interaction	Social

ANSWERS QUESTION:

How many conversations are people having about our brand?

DEFINITION:

A conversation is a collection of authors/sites and their audience linked by relevant content, usually blog posts, status updates, replies, reviews comments, or face-to-face interactions. Conversations may be online or offline, and may be between consumers, consumers and brands, or among other third parties.

TECH NOTES:

None

ARF COMMENTS:

Counting online conversations may be helpful to estimate the volume of buzz around a brand, but understanding its substance, sentiment, and importance for the brand requires the application of listening approaches, which are primarily social media monitoring and social research. The use of these approaches depends on business objectives. The most popular applications for monitoring are customer service and reputation management. For social research it is developing consumer insights for understanding mindsets, discovering new markets and unmet needs, competitive analysis, product innovation, and messaging. Conversation analysis is being used to target video and advertising on Twitter through Twitter Amplify, to augment traditional numbers like TV ratings by adding social context (social TV ratings), and to create new predictive analytics, such as forecasting near-term sales. See Rappaport (2011) for a detailed review of listening.

It is important to note that most brand conversations—about 90%—occur face-to-face or on the telephone, with roughly 10% of conversations online (Keller & Fay 2012). Brands studying conversations should make certain that they are capturing the conversations and conversation locations that are most relevant to them.

CITED RESEARCH:

Keller, Ed and Brad Fay (2012). The Face-to-Face Book: Why Real Relationships Rule in a Digital Marketplace. New York: Free Press.
Rappaport, Stephen D. (2011). Listen First! Turning Social Media Conversations into Business Advantage. Hoboken: John Wiley & Sons.

SEE ALSO:

Conversation Relevant Sites
Sentiment

Conversion Funnel*

AUTHORITY:	MEDIA:	STAGE:	CATEGORY:	APPLIES TO:
Google, comScore	Owned	3. Close	7. Conversion	Website Social Email Mobile

ANSWERS QUESTION:

What are the steps we expect visitors to take to complete an action we want?

DEFINITION:

A sequence of conversion goals that form a path to fulfilling a destination goal, such as a purchase or relationship objective between a site and visitors, or email campaigns and email recipients. Conversion funnels are usually custom-configured in analytics packages.

TECH NOTES:

comScore refers to steps as "checkpoints" that represent an online process. Page names, clickins, or clickouts can be checkpoints.

ARF COMMENTS:

Tracking where visitors get on or off the path can be helpful in optimizing the sequence. If visitors routinely exit at a page before the destination, that can suggest problems that might need remedy. Similarly, if visitors are skipping steps along the path on the way to the destination, that may reveal that the path the site owner described can be shortened or modified in some way to streamline the journey. Many analytic packages, such as Google Analytics, offer a "reverse goal path" that lists the URL paths used to reach the goal pages, and the number of conversions that each path generates. This is another way to learn how visitors are arriving at your goals, and to spot the pages that contribute to conversions.

On the email front, Google's Gmail Quick Actions may streamline the conversion path by providing two types of functionality without requiring that an email be opened: 1) Gmail actions such as replying to meeting requests or adding a product review, and 2) "go to" actions which add a "call to action" button that takes the email recipient to a page where an action can be performed, such as a check-in, travel itinerary change, purchase, and so forth. Google recommends Quick Actions for transactional emails that are expected to have high levels of interactivity; they are not recommended for bulk emails (Google Developers 2013).

comScore's Gian Fulgoni (2013) notes that "for conversion metrics that require tracking of a cookie over time, it's important to point out that one needs to take into account cookie deletion, which if ignored is going to lower the conversion rates substantially."

CITED RESEARCH:

Fulgoni, Gian (2013). Personal communication.
Google Developers (2013). Registering with Google (http://goo.gl/0Ak98).

SEE ALSO:

Conversion
Conversion Goal
Conversion Rate
Event Tracking

Conversion Goal*

AUTHORITY:	MEDIA:	STAGE:	CATEGORY:	APPLIES TO:
Google	Owned	3. Close	7. Conversion	Website Social Email Mobile

ANSWERS QUESTION:

What is a conversion goal?

DEFINITION:

A target action a site owner or email marketers wants visitors to take. There are two basic categories of goals:
1) so-called step, support, mini, or micro conversions because they precede an ultimate action, and
2) destination goal conversions, such as a purchase.

TECH NOTES:

Conversion goals are often assigned monetary goal values. In Google Analytics and similar programs, the types of goals typically fall into four types: URL destination, Visit Duration, Page per Visit (web) or Screen per Visit (mobile), and Events (which must be set up in Event Tracking).

ARF COMMENTS:

Goals are often linked into a sequence, generally called a "conversion funnel," which describes a pathway towards reaching a destination goal. Tracking where visitors get on or off the path can be helpful in optimizing the sequence. If visitors routinely exit at a page before the destination, that can suggest problems that might need remedy. Similarly, if visitors are skipping steps along the path on the way to the destination, that may reveal that the path the site owner described can be shortened or modified in some way to streamline the journey. Keep in mind that consumers may use different devices simultaneously, where an action on one device can trigger an action on another—such as going from a mobile device to a PC. Conversion goals and calls to action should not be limited to the device they were initially displayed on (Google 2012).

Goal conversions are logged when they are completed. The economic value of a conversion can be computed by assigning a monetary amount for each one. There are a variety of approaches to set conversion value, but one common one is to assign a dollar value based on the contribution the conversion makes to the final goal. Google provides one example: If 10% of people who convert to newsletter signup eventually go on to purchase a $500 product, the conversion value could be $50. If only 1% of the signups purchase, the goal could be $5.

comScore's Gian Fulgoni (2013) notes that "for conversion metrics that require tracking of a cookie over time, it's important to point out that one needs to take into account cookie deletion, which if ignored is going to lower the conversion rates substantially."

CITED RESEARCH:

Fulgoni, Gian (2013). Personal communication.
Google (2012). The New Multi-Screen World: Understanding Cross Platform Consumer Behavior (http://goo.gl/vbrEu).
Google Analytics (2012). Conversions: About Goals (http://goo.gl/koOSA).

SEE ALSO:

Conversion
Conversion Rate
Conversion Funnel
Event Tracking

Conversion Rate*

AUTHORITY:	MEDIA:	STAGE:	CATEGORY:	APPLIES TO:
Google, IAB, Yahoo!, Microsoft	Paid Owned	3. Close	7. Conversion	Website Social Email Mobile

ANSWERS QUESTION:

What is the conversion rate for any conversion action on our site or through our email?

DEFINITION:

Conversion rate is the number of conversions as a percentage of base number of interest, usually Unique Visitors or Visits on a Website or Email Opens or Unique Email Opens for a reporting period.

Conversions are any action of interest, such as registrations, newsletter signups, or transactions, for example.

TECH NOTES:

None

ARF COMMENTS:

When computing Conversion Rate, brands have the choice of Visits or Unique Visitors as the base. Selecting which base number (denominator) to use is a matter of "fit" with a company's business model. Analytics authority Avinash Kaushik explains that if Visits is used, the assumption is that every visit to the website is an opportunity for conversion. That may be perfectly suitable for businesses where a single visitor makes several purchases a week, such as ordering lunch from a local restaurant or a car dealership's service department ordering from parts suppliers. When Unique Visitors is employed, there's a different assumption, which is that it is perfectly fine for Unique Visitors to visit several times before converting. They may come first to learn, then make a series of visits before taking the action. Identify your business model and select the denominator that supports it. Whether it is web or email, know which denominator your web or email analytics tool uses or can make available; that way you'll calculate the conversion rate most closely matched to your business model. The business model you use has implications for strategy; it will influence the keywords, referring links, and other techniques used to drive traffic and expectations.

Conversion rate is influenced by the quality of the traffic coming into a site. For this reason it is a good idea to track conversion rates by sources of traffic to see how they are performing and to optimize one source, or the mix of sources, as necessary.

Many analytics packages offer the ability to create an expected pathway or funnel from entering the site to reaching the final goal. These can indicate when the paths are followed as expected, if there are shortcuts, if people are getting stuck, or if people are bouncing around. They also measure the drop off from one step to another. Recent ARF (2012) research on the purchase decision established that the sequence is not as linear as the funnel metaphor suggests, but is also a customer experience journey and should be considered as such.

However, many site owners seek to maximize the final conversion rate, such as a sale or transaction of some type. Focusing on the end-goal alone is understandable—it's where the business results come from—but also make sure to periodically review and optimize the pathways and preceding conversions because problems there may dissuade a person from buying or taking the ultimate action you want. Keep in mind that consumers may use different devices simultaneously, where an action on one device can trigger an action on another—such as going from a mobile device to a PC. Conversion goals and calls to action should not be limited to the device they were initially displayed on (Google 2012).

comScore's Gian Fulgoni (2013) notes that "for conversion metrics that require tracking of a cookie over time, it's important to point out that one needs to take into account cookie deletion, which if ignored is going to lower the conversion rates substantially."

CITED RESEARCH:

ARF (2012). Digital/Social Media in the Purchase Decision Process (Available from ARF).

Fulgoni, Gian (2013). Personal communication.

Google (2012). The New Multi-Screen World: Understanding Cross Platform Consumer Behavior (http://goo.gl/vbrEu).

Kaushik, Avinash (2010). Web Analytics 2.0. The Art of Online Accountability & Science of Customer Centricity. Sybex.

SEE ALSO:

Conversion

Referral Traffic

Source

Unique Visitors (Unique Browsers)

Visit (Session)

Conversion*

AUTHORITY:	MEDIA:	STAGE:	CATEGORY:	APPLIES TO:
Digital Analytics Association, Facebook, Google, IAB, Yahoo!	Paid Owned	3. Close	7. Conversion	Website Social Email Mobile

ANSWERS QUESTION:

Which conversion actions were performed on the site or in our email over a reporting period?

DEFINITION:

A visitor or email recipient completing a target action. Such actions come in every variety, such as 1) clicking on an ad, site registrations, visiting a section, Liking a page, downloading a white paper, or 2) signing up for a car test drive or completing a transaction. The first group of conversions are sometimes called step, support, mini, or micro conversions because they precede an ultimate action. The second group are considered destination goal conversions.

TECH NOTES:

Facebook reports conversions in two ways: Conversions by Impression Time, and Conversions by Conversion Time.

Conversions by Impression Time reports the number of conversions categorized by the length of time between a user's view or click on the ad and the conversion (i.e., 0–24 hours, 1–7 days, 8–28 days).

The Conversions by Conversion Time report will show you the number of conversions organized by the time of the conversion event (e.g., purchase time), categorized by the length of time between a user's view or click on a Facebook Ad and the conversion (i.e., 0–24 hours, 1–7 days, 8–28 days).

Google and other analytic packages typically report a Time to Purchase metric that includes the number of days and the number of visits required for purchase on a site.

ARF COMMENTS:

According to the Digital Analytics Association: "Conversions provide a general framework for segmenting visits or visitors and attributing various marketing activity and visitor actions to these segments. They provide the marketer an additional tool for segmenting visitors other than demographics. In practice the two approaches work together to understand the visitor and their on- and offline behavior with respect to various marketing activities. The best conversions indicate that a visitor has successfully completed an objective of the site or business."

Conversions are reported in many analytics packages. Almost always they require configuring the goals and actions that are relevant and that indicate the goal has been achieved. Conversions are logged when they are completed. The economic value of a conversion can be computed by assigning a monetary amount for each one. There are a variety of approaches to set conversion value, but one common one is to assign a dollar value based on the contribution the conversion makes to the final goal. Google provides one example: If 10% of people who convert to newsletter signup eventually go on to purchase a $500 product, the conversion value could be $50. If only 1% of the signups purchase, the goal could be $5.

Goals are often linked into a sequence, generally called a "funnel," which describes a pathway towards reaching a destination goal. Tracking where visitors get on or off the path can be helpful in optimizing the sequence. If visitors routinely exit at a page before the destination, that can suggest problems that might need remedy. Similarly, if visitors are skipping steps along the path on the way to the destination, that may reveal that the path the site owner laid down can be shortened or modified in some way to streamline the journey. Streamlining the path is important for the user experience on all devices, and especially on smartphones. Keep in mind that consumers may use different devices simultaneously, where an action on one device can trigger an action on another— such as going from a mobile device to a PC. Conversion goals and calls to action should not be limited to the device they were initially displayed on (Google 2012).

An important issue with conversion is called attribution, the ability to identify which clicks or actions contribute to the successful conversion. Additionally, ad campaigns seldom run on one website or one social network; they often combine several digital channels and properties as well as traditional media. Attribution is especially important for advertisers that pay-per-click or pay for some other performance action. Should they pay or not? Attribution is critical for spending precious budgets optimally.

The attribution problem is generally well-understood; solutions are imperfect but improving. The most common attribution models available from analytics programs and vendors are: "first click," "last click," "even click," and "split credit." Some companies have custom attribution models that map to their specific array of individual channels or properties (Kaushik 2010). However, progress is being made in the direction of working towards an holistic, multi-channel approach. Google, for example, offers "multi-channel conversion funnels," which enables search advertisers to integrate their digital sources and understand conversion. At press time, Facebook announced new capabilities through its Atlas ad platform. Facebook will be able to follow people across browsers and devices, and to link their ad interactions on Facebook, apps, and websites to their Facebook accounts (Ha 2014). At the enterprise level, Adobe and other large analytics vendors offer solutions that integrate many sources to give a more complete picture.

comScore's Gian Fulgoni (2013) notes that "for conversion metrics that require tracking of a cookie over time, it's important to point out that one needs to take into account cookie deletion, which if ignored is going to lower the conversion rates substantially."

CITED RESEARCH:

Fulgoni, Gian (2013). Personal communication.

Google Analytics (2012). About Goals (http://goo.gl/mDwo6).

Google (2012). The New Multi-Screen World: Understanding Cross Platform Consumer Behavior (http://goo.gl/vbrEu).

Ha, Anthony (2014). Facebook Relaunches Atlas Ad Platform With Cross-Device Targeting And Offline Sales Tracking (http://goo.gl/3JrozQ).

Kaushik, Avinash (2010). Web Analytics 2.0: The Art of Online Accountability & Science of Customer Centricity. Sybex.

SEE ALSO:

Conversion Funnel
Conversion Rate
Time to Purchase

Cookie

AUTHORITY:	MEDIA:	STAGE:	CATEGORY:	APPLIES TO:
comScore	Owned	1. Capture	2. Audience/Traffic	Website Social Email Mobile

ANSWERS QUESTION:

What is a cookie?

DEFINITION:

A text file that a web server sets on a device so as to store information about a session or the browser. Session cookies are typically used to store e-commerce shopping cart information or to remember information pertaining to the browser's current visit to the website.

Persistent cookies are typically used to store information pertaining to the browser so that it may be retrieved in subsequent visits to the website. These are often used to identify new and returning browsers (visitors) to your sites and to thread together information regarding a site visit.

TECH NOTES:

There are two classes of cookies: first-party and third-party. Cookies placed by a site that is delivering web content directly are first-party cookies. Their aim is to improve the site experience for visitors. Third-party cookies are not served by the site, but are embedded in the page. They provide a means for tracking user activity across a broad network.

ARF COMMENTS:

Users can delete cookies. comScore's family of cookie deletion studies across countries indicates that third-party cookies are deleted by 20%–40% of computers, and first-party cookies are deleted by 20% or more of computers in a month (comScore 2011).

Reviewing comScore's study (Nguyen 2011) identifies the following issues with cookie deletion:

Cookie deletion affects site-centric and ad-server measurements, and leads to inaccuracies "for those choosing to rely solely on server-based unique user/browser data for weekly or monthly audience numbers.

For site-centric measures, cookie deletion leads to the following inaccuracies when unique user/browser numbers are used as a proxy for Unique Visitors to a website:
• Overstatement of Unique Visitor counts
• Understatement of Repeat Visitor counts
• Understatement of conversion rates

Cookie deletion leads to the following inaccuracies in ad server measurement when unique user/browser numbers are used as a proxy for the count of the number of unique recipients of ads:
• Overstatement of reach
• Understatement of frequency
It is recommended that advertisers and publishers account for cookie deletion in order to gain an accurate understanding of a site's traffic.

Regarding advertising effectiveness research, the IAB concludes that cookie deletion is a "somewhat intractable problem for effectiveness research. In test and control studies, the control group "should not be contaminated by people who deleted their exposure cookies." The IAB states that "cookies are rapidly becoming an obsolete method to designate a control group. While cookie deletion presents challenges to learning if ad exposures had effects, the industry is developing methodologies that address or overcome issues raised by cookie deletion (IAB 2011).

Additionally, comScore's Gian Fulgoni (2013), adds that "cookie deletion is a problematic issue for every cookie-based tracking metric that has a longitudinal time dimension to it because in a month about 30% of Internet users will delete their first- and third-party cookies an average of 4 to 6 times."

CITED RESEARCH:

comScore (2011). The Impact of Cookie Deletion on Site-Server and Ad-Server Metrics in Australia: An Empirical comScore Study (http://goo.gl/t1D6d).

Fulgoni, Gian (2013). Personal communication.

IAB (2011). Best Practices for Conducting Online Ad Effectiveness Research (http://goo.gl/2RTJP).

Nguyen, Joe (2011). Cookie Deletion: Why It Should Matter to Advertisers and Publishers (http://goo.gl/VhCkW).

SEE ALSO:

Frequency

Gross Ratings Points (GRP)

Reach

Unique Visitors (Unique Browsers)

Cost per Action (CPA)*

AUTHORITY:	MEDIA:	STAGE:	CATEGORY:	APPLIES TO:
IAB, Yahoo!, Microsoft	Paid	1. Capture	1. Advertising	Website Social Email Mobile

ANSWERS QUESTION:

What cost per action are we paying?

DEFINITION:

Cost of advertising based on a visitor taking some specifically defined action in response to an ad. "Actions" include such things as completely filling out a form, completing a sales transaction, or subscribing to a newsletter for example. The action is the choice of the advertiser. It is sometimes called Pay per Action (PPA).

TECH NOTES:

None

ARF COMMENTS:

Cost per Action is an advertising model that enables advertisers to pay for performance and control budget. Cost per Action is one of the several performance-based pricing models for online advertising. The advertising budget is usually capped at a certain value, depending on the brand's goals and budgeting approach. In CPA advertising, the value of the action is negotiated in advance between an advertiser and publisher. Actions are often specified in a conversion funnel. "Cost per" measures, such as action or lead, are typically employed for direct marketing efforts, or for the direct marketing aspects of a brand campaign.

CITED RESEARCH:

Laubenstein, Christine (2010). What Is Cost Per Action Advertising? WordStream Blog (http://goo.gl/Ohhtv).

SEE ALSO:

Conversion Funnel

Cost per Click (CPC)*

AUTHORITY:	MEDIA:	STAGE:	CATEGORY:	APPLIES TO:
Yahoo!, IAB, Farris et al., Facebook, Microsoft	Paid	1. Capture	1. Advertising	Website Social Email Mobile

ANSWERS QUESTION:

How much are we paying for each click on our ad?

DEFINITION:

The amount of money an advertiser pays an online publisher each time the advertiser's ad is clicked from the publisher's site or Facebook page for a reporting period. It is also called pay-per-click advertising. The amount paid is either negotiated in advance or through a bidding process.

Cost per Click is also called Pay per Click.

TECH NOTES:

None

ARF COMMENTS:

CPC is a pay-for-performance advertising model that is used to measure or establish the cost-effectiveness of advertising. The aim of CPC advertising is to drive targeted traffic to an advertiser's website and control advertising costs. Keyword selection is critical, and branded and non-branded terms are important, as is using terms consumers use. When searching, people tend to use non-branded terms at the beginning and then use more branded terms as they narrow down their search or make head-to-head comparisons (Plummer et al. 2007).

An important issue with cost-per-click is called attribution, the ability to identify which clicks contribute to a successful conversion. Attribution is especially important for advertisers that pay-per-click or pay for some other performance action. Should they pay or not? Attribution is critical for spending precious budgets optimally.

The attribution problem is generally well-understood, but solutions are not. Despite their issues, "first click" and "last click" attribution models are widely used; some companies have attribution models for individual channels or properties. However progress has been made and continues to advance, with the newest direction working towards an holistic, multi-channel approach. Google, for example, recently offered "multi-channel conversion funnels," which enables search advertisers to integrate their digital sources and understand conversion. At the enterprise level, Adobe and other large analytics vendors offer solutions that integrate many sources.

Advertisers are increasingly interested in pay-for-performance models where they pay for a specific outcome. These advertising models are designed to minimize the problem of click fraud and also control the advertising budget. Cost per Action and Cost per Lead are two popular pay-for-performance options.

CITED RESEARCH:

Plummer, Joseph et al. (2007). The Online Advertising Playbook. Hoboken: John Wiley & Sons.

SEE ALSO:

Click
Click-Through
Click-Through Rate (CTR)

Cost per Lead (CPL)*

AUTHORITY:	MEDIA:	STAGE:	CATEGORY:	APPLIES TO:
IAB	Paid	1. Capture	1. Advertising	Website Social Email Mobile

ANSWERS QUESTION:

What is the cost per lead we are paying?

DEFINITION:

A performance-based pricing model for advertising. The cost per lead is the amount of money an advertiser agrees to pay an online publisher for each lead received.

TECH NOTES:

None

ARF COMMENTS:

Cost per Lead is one of the several performance-based pricing models for online advertising. The advertising budget may be capped at a certain value or not, depending on the brand's goals and budgeting approach. In CPL advertising, the value of the lead is negotiated in advance between an advertiser and publisher. "Cost per" measures, such as action or click, are typically employed for direct marketing efforts, or for the direct marketing aspects of a brand campaign.

CITED RESEARCH:

None

SEE ALSO:

Cost per Action (CPA)
Cost per Click (CPC)
Cost per Targeted Thousand Impressions (CPTM)
Cost per Thousand (CPM) Impressions

Cost per Order

AUTHORITY:
Farris et al., IAB,
Millward Brown Digital

MEDIA:
Paid

STAGE:
3. Close

CATEGORY:
8. E-Commerce

APPLIES TO:
Website
Social
Email
Mobile

ANSWERS QUESTION:
How much did it cost to generate one sale?

DEFINITION:
The advertiser's cost to generate one sales transaction.

Variations: Also called Cost per Sale and Cost per Transaction.

TECH NOTES:
None

ARF COMMENTS:
▌ See Cost per Sale (CPS) for details.

CITED RESEARCH:
None

SEE ALSO:
Cost per Sale (CPS)
Cost per Transaction

Cost per Sale (CPS)

AUTHORITY:	MEDIA:	STAGE:	CATEGORY:	APPLIES TO:
IAB, Farris et al.	Paid	3. Close	8. E-Commerce	Website Social Email Mobile

ANSWERS QUESTION:

How much did it cost us to close one sale over a reporting period?

DEFINITION:

The advertiser's cost to generate one sales transaction.

Variations: Also called Cost per Order and Cost per Transaction.

TECH NOTES:

If Cost of Sale is being used in conjunction with a media buy, a cookie can be offered on the content site and read on the advertiser's site after the successful completion of an online sale.

ARF COMMENTS:

Cost per Sale measures or establishes the cost-effectiveness of online advertising only. This model does not take into account the total costs of goods sold. Brands seeking to calculate the true cost per sale most often have to bring several data sources to bear. Brands can use Cost per Sale to compare sales costs across advertising media or specific media vehicles as a way to judge the relative performance of online advertising in the media mix.

CITED RESEARCH:

None

SEE ALSO:

Cost per Thousand (CPM) Impressions

Cost per Targeted Thousand Impressions (CPTM)

AUTHORITY:	MEDIA:	STAGE:	CATEGORY:	APPLIES TO:
IAB, Facebook	Paid	1. Capture	1. Advertising	Website Social Email Mobile

ANSWERS QUESTION:

How much are we paying for one thousand targeted ad impressions?

DEFINITION:

The cost of purchasing 1,000 impressions against a targeted audience that is defined by demographics or other specific characteristics, such as attitudes, interests, behaviors, or purchase. Often abbreviated as CPTM.

TECH NOTES:

None

ARF COMMENTS:

Cost per Targeted Thousand Impressions is used to measure the cost-effectiveness of online and mobile advertising, and has the advantage of being comparable to impression purchases in traditional media. CPTM differs from CPM in that CPM impressions are not targeted. A guide to commonly used online targeting approaches is found in Plummer et al. (2007).

CPM can be calculated on a cost per impression basis, but it is customary to denominate cost in thousands of impressions.

CITED RESEARCH:

Plummer, Joseph et al. (2007). The Online Advertising Playbook. Hoboken: John Wiley & Sons.

SEE ALSO:

Ad Impression

Cost per Thousand (CPM) Impressions

Cost per Thousand (CPM) Impressions*

AUTHORITY:	MEDIA:	STAGE:	CATEGORY:	APPLIES TO:
IAB, Facebook, Microsoft	Paid	1. Capture	1. Advertising	Website Social Email Mobile

ANSWERS QUESTION:

How much are we paying for each thousand impressions?

DEFINITION:

Media buying term describing the cost of purchasing 1,000 impressions against the total audience.

TECH NOTES:

None

ARF COMMENTS:

CPM is used to measure the cost-effectiveness of online, social, and mobile advertising, and has the advantage of being comparable to impression purchases in traditional media.

CPM can be calculated for specific target groups (see Cost per Thousand Targeted Impressions) or on a cost per impression basis.

CITED RESEARCH:

None

SEE ALSO:

Ad Impression
Cost per Impression
Cost per Targeted Thousand Impressions (CPTM)

Cost per Transaction

AUTHORITY:	MEDIA:	STAGE:	CATEGORY:	APPLIES TO:
IAB, Farris et al.	Paid	3. Close	1. Advertising	Website
				Social
				Email
				Mobile

ANSWERS QUESTION:

What did it cost to generate one sales transaction?

DEFINITION:

The advertiser's cost to generate one sales transaction.

Variations: Also called Cost per Sale and Cost per Order

TECH NOTES:

None

ARF COMMENTS:

▍ See Cost per Sale (CPS) for details.

CITED RESEARCH:

None

SEE ALSO:

Cost per Sale (CPS)

Cost per Unique Visitor

AUTHORITY:	MEDIA:	STAGE:	CATEGORY:	APPLIES TO:
IAB	Paid Owned	1. Capture	1. Advertising	Website Social Email Mobile

ANSWERS QUESTION:

What is the average cost of our ad placement or app, per Unique Visitor?

DEFINITION:

The total cost of a placement or app divided by the number of Unique Visitors.

TECH NOTES:

None

ARF COMMENTS:

▌ IAB reports this measure as one of its social media metrics. It is useful as a measure of cost-efficiency.

CITED RESEARCH:

None

SEE ALSO:

Unique Visitors (Unique Browsers)

Coupon Downloads

AUTHORITY:
Millward Brown Digital

MEDIA:
Owned

STAGE:
3. Close

CATEGORY:
7. Conversion

APPLIES TO:
Website
Social
Mobile

ANSWERS QUESTION:
How many coupons were downloaded over a specific time period?

DEFINITION:
The number of times a coupon was downloaded in a reporting period from a site.

TECH NOTES:
It is also important to count the number of download failures to learn if there is a problem with the file, a file transfer issue, or browser problem.

ARF COMMENTS:
Metric is used to gauge interest in a product or service, to promote product purchase, to stimulate trial for new or repositioned products, or to test price sensitivity. Manufacturers may offer coupons through their own sites, mobile sites or applications, or third-party sites such as Facebook, that can be downloaded and printed, or read directly from a mobile phone. This last option is expected to become more popular as mobile coupon readers are more widely installed. Some manufacturers offer coupons that can be loaded directly onto loyalty cards. P&G Everyday is one example of the latter (see their FAQ to learn how that type of program works: http://goo.gl/fsO8f).

Coupons may also be restricted by manufacturers in terms of how often they can be printed and/or by expiration date. They are also made available through dedicated coupon sites. Coupons may also be made available for a specific date or date range or targeted to a time period or daypart. Some years ago KFC, for example, encouraged trial of a new product by making a coupon for it available during the lunch hour across the four US time zones (see Plummer et al. 2007). When making coupons available to share, companies should have tracking capability. Sharing rates are another indicator of interest and also provide opportunities to communicate with or advertise to the person receiving the coupon.

Because of all the different ways coupons can be accessed, downloaded, or transferred, companies issuing coupons need to account for all the sources used to obtain an accurate count. An important companion measure is coupon redemption rate and the ratio of coupons downloaded to redeemed. Often evaluating the impact of coupon downloads requires additional data from other corporate systems or resources.

CITED RESEARCH:
eMarketer (2010), "Propelling the Pepsi Spirit with Mobile Apps" (http://goo.gl/D0IW6).
Plummer, Joseph et al. (2007). The Online Advertising Playbook. Hoboken: John Wiley & Sons.

SEE ALSO:
Key Content Downloads (Coupons, Recipes, Apps, etc.)
Key Performance Indicator (KPI)

Customers*

AUTHORITY:	MEDIA:	STAGE:	CATEGORY:	APPLIES TO:
comScore, Millward Brown Digital	Owned	3. Close	8. E-Commerce	Website Social Mobile

ANSWERS QUESTION:

How many unique browsers placed an order on our site?

DEFINITION:

The total number of unique browsers that placed an order, over a reporting period.

TECH NOTES:

None

ARF COMMENTS:

This metric can indicate the effectiveness of a campaign and/or website or mobile app in converting visits to sales and capturing customers during the reporting period. When analyzed in the context of total customers, first-time customers, and repeat customers, customer trends may suggest the vitality of the business and actions that can be taken to maximize its growth. Keep in mind that a "unique browser" (Unique Visitor) is identified for a specific period of time.

CITED RESEARCH:

None

SEE ALSO:

Average Order Value, Total and Unique
Conversion
Conversion Funnel
Conversion Goal
Conversion Rate
Unique Visitors (Unique Browsers)

Direct Traffic Visitors

AUTHORITY:

Facebook, Google, Kaushik, Millward Brown Digital, Webtrends

MEDIA:

Owned

STAGE:

2. Connect

CATEGORY:

2. Audience/Traffic

APPLIES TO:

Website
Social
Mobile

ANSWERS QUESTION:

How many visitors came to our site or page directly?

DEFINITION:

Direct Traffic Visitors are those visitors who clicked on a bookmark or who typed the URL directly into the browser to arrive at the site over a relevant time period. Also called "Direct Navigation" Visitors, "Unknown Referrer" Visitors, or "No Referrer" Visitors.

Direct Traffic differs from traffic sent to a site by Referring Sites and Search Keywords.

TECH NOTES:

Direct traffic bucket includes bookmark traffic and typed URLs, but often can and does include other sources that are not reported, such as links in some emails and links included in documents. Webtrends (2014) presents a list of 19 reasons why referrers may be unknown. Importantly, Webtrends notes, the amount of Direct Traffic without referrers is on the rise because of moves by search engines Yahoo! and Bing to anonymize their traffic. For this reason it is very important to separate out the visits from typed-in URLs and bookmarks from the others.

ARF COMMENTS:

Direct traffic, when properly accounted for (see Tech Notes above), can be an indicator of a high value consumer connection with a brand's content. This is because it identifies the page(s) the consumer made the effort to either bookmark or remember well enough to type accurately into the browser. For this reason, Direct Traffic metrics can be used to optimize the site. Direct Traffic should be evaluated in light of the other types of Referral Traffic a site receives, the type of website you have, its objectives, and marketing strategy. For those sites that aim to engage with consumers and retain them, for example, higher numbers are generally considered better than lower numbers. Analyst Avinash Kaushik (2012) points out that analyzing Direct Traffic trends over time is a good practice, for it can identify seasonality and patterns of interest that reflect when people may be more highly engaged and interested.

CITED RESEARCH:

Google Analytics (2013). Direct Traffic (http://goo.gl/NS7gL).

Kaushik, Avinash, (2007), "Web Analytics Demystified" (http://goo.gl/eVjqJ).

Webtrends 2014. "What is Direct Traffic?" (http://goo.gl/zClzC6.)

SEE ALSO:

Referral Traffic

Earned Impression*

AUTHORITY:	MEDIA:	STAGE:	CATEGORY:	APPLIES TO:
comScore	Earned	2. Connect	1. Advertising	Social

ANSWERS QUESTION:

How many earned impressions did our ad generate?

DEFINITION:

Earned impressions are advertising messages people pass on to their friends and associates via social networks, functioning as bonus advertising providing additional exposures at no added cost.

The Digital Analytics Association has a draft definition for impression in social media out for comment. They define an impression as: "the number of times an ITEM was displayed." In their definition: "An ITEM of content is a post, micro-post, article or other instance appearing for the first time in digital media." The word ITEM replaces such terms as "clip," "post" or other "unclear terms." ITEMs contain one or more MENTIONS, which can refer to a brand, organization, campaign, or entity that is being tracked.

TECH NOTES:

On Twitter, Hemann and Burbary (2013) note, impression counting is "controversial as some analytics tools calculate impressions by including replies." When replying on Twitter the only people seeing it are the sender, the recipient, and the followers in common. Consult with your social media analytics tool supplier regarding their method for calculating impressions on Twitter and if counting replies is appropriate for your brand's requirements.

ARF COMMENTS:

Social media content sharing, brands named in posts or comments, endorsements such as "Liking" on Facebook or retweeting on Twitter, generated interest in the unpaid pass-along value of brand mentions for advertising and marketing. Many consider these mentions akin to ad impressions and call them "earned impressions." These impressions are considered valuable: Nielsen global research revealed that 92% of consumers around the world say "they trust earned media, such as word-of-mouth and recommendations from friends and family, above all other forms of advertising—an increase of 18 percent since 2007. Online reviews are trusted by 70% (Nielsen 2012).

A great deal of industry discussion concerns earned impressions, so much so that they are considered along with traditional paid impressions and impressions in "owned" or brand-controlled media. Due to the size of its user base, seamless sharing philosophy and, arguably, its pioneering efforts in social advertising, Facebook dominates conversation and research about earned impressions. However, earned impressions are generated many ways, such as through Twitter, mentions, reviews, and social sharing.

The literature on earned impressions is growing. The key topics being researched are: reach and frequency; the impact of paid and owned impressions on sharing; branding effectiveness of earned impressions compared with other types; purchase lift; engagement level with a brand and its effects; and creative elements in the ad, such as ads that mention friends. A trend in the research is to begin moving away from simple counts and volume measures of social activity, but to focus on the recipients of the messages and to examine the effects of earned media through social networks of fans, friends, friends of fans, and followers.

Several recent studies examined earned impressions. comScore studies are available for free download but require registration or login. "The Power of Like 2: How Social Marketing Works" (2012) focuses on the impact of branded earned impressions on the behavior of Facebook Fans and Friends of Fans. "The Power of Like Europe: How Social Marketing Works for Retail Brands" (2012) "illustrates how popular consumer brands are utilizing Facebook to deliver media impressions at scale, achieve brand amplification and resonance, and ultimately drive desired behaviors among key customer segments." Nielsen's (2010) study "Nielsen/Facebook Report: The Value of Social Media Ad Impressions" showed that paid Facebook ads combined with social media impressions raise lift for three traditional effectiveness measures: Ad Recall, Awareness, and Purchase Intent.

The ability of earned Facebook impressions to generate new brand growth is the subject of research from Karen Nelson-Field and colleagues of Ehrenberg-Bass Institute. They take issue with the value of fans and friends of friends, the reach of brand messages, the importance of brand engagement, and the impact of the cluttered Facebook environment on effectiveness measures (such as ad recall), and, most importantly, on brand growth. Their findings raise concern over Facebook's ability to reach light users who, Ehrenberg-Bass research concludes, are necessary to drive brand growth. Brand fans are heavy users who are important for volume but less so for growth. Nelson-Field suggests several ways to make the most of Facebook earned brand impressions: a) focus less on getting "loved" and more on being seen by light buyers, b) embrace recency planning, c) use mass media branding rules to cut through the clutter, and d) nurture the heavy users (fans), but don't over-invest to change their patterns. However, fans may be valuable for insights, pre-testing, and emerging products.

CITED RESEARCH:

comScore (2012). *The Power of Like 2: How Social Marketing Works (http://goo.gl/eY4Os).*

comScore (2012). *The Power of Like Europe: How Social Marketing Works for Retail Brands (http://goo.gl/awndP).*

Digital Analytic Association (2013). Proposed Social Media Standard Definitions for Reach and Impressions, from the Digital Analytics Association (http://goo.gl/FQugv).

Hemann, Chuck and Ken Burbary (2013). Digital Marketing Analytics: Making Sense of Consumer Data in a Digital World. Indianapolis: QUE.

Nielsen (2010). Nielsen/Facebook Report: The Value of Social Media Ad Impressions (http://goo.gl/rzEV).

Nielsen (2012). Global Consumers' Trust in Earned Media Advertising Grows in Importance (http://goo.gl/Evucr).

Nelson-Field, Karen et al. (2012). What's Not to "Like?" Can a Facebook Fan Base Give a Brand the Advertising Reach it Needs? Journal of Advertising Research, Vol. 52, No. 2, pp. 262–269.

SEE ALSO:

Ad Impression

Email Capture Rate

AUTHORITY:	MEDIA:	STAGE:	CATEGORY:	APPLIES TO:
	Owned	2. Connect	7. Conversion	Email

ANSWERS QUESTION:

How many email addresses are we capturing on our website?

DEFINITION:

The number of email addresses captured on a website expressed as a percentage of visitors over a reporting period. Email addresses are usually captured through a registration, submission, or signup form.

TECH NOTES:

None

ARF COMMENTS:

Email capture is an opt-in method for building lists, and developing and nurturing relationships. Generally, email capture tactics stress collecting them on the landing page, and as early as possible in the signup, registration, or submission processes. Test the text, calls to action, design, colors, and buttons in email capture forms to optimize their effectiveness.

CITED RESEARCH:

None

SEE ALSO:

Conversion

Email Click to Open Rate*

AUTHORITY:
IAB, Experian
Marketing Services

MEDIA:
Owned

STAGE:
2. Connect

CATEGORY:
5. Engagement/
Interaction

APPLIES TO:
Email

ANSWERS QUESTION:

How many clicks did our emails generate from messages that were opened?

DEFINITION:

The number of clicks an email generates as a percentage of the number of opens.

This metric can be computed on a Total Open or Unique Open basis.

TECH NOTES:

None

ARF COMMENTS:

Estimates the effectiveness of email message content and the advertiser's "call to action" to induce recipients to click-through to an advertiser's landing page. These ratios should be computed for each specific campaign and list. The click can be a source of referral traffic and may also be counted as a conversion event.

People are opening more emails and responding to them faster, according to Experian Marketing Services research reported in Lucia Moses in Adweek (2013).

Consumers use mobile devices to open emails. YesMail (2013) reports that 49% of emails are opened on mobile devices. Studying 6 billion marketing emails in Q2 2013, YesMail discovered that Clicks to Open differ on desktops and mobile, with mobile clicks coming in at about half the rate (11%) of desktop clicks (23%). The links in mobile emails are being looked at but actions are not being taken, yet the same emails viewed on desktops are clicked on more frequently. This finding suggests that content and creative execution be optimized for the mobile platform.

Analyzing this metric on a Total or Unique basis depends on the analytic objective. Total answers the question: "How many times was my email opened and clicked on?" whereas the Unique basis answers the questions: "How many individual people opened my email and clicked on it one or more times?" and may be viewed as a type of engagement.

CITED RESEARCH:

Moses, Lucia (2013). What's the Best Time of Day to Send an Email? Adweek.com (http://goo.gl/UcwqT).
YesMail (2013). Study: Almost Half of All Brand Emails Opened on Mobile Devices (http://goo.gl/0EYC1v).

SEE ALSO:

Click-Through Rate (CTR)
Conversion
Email Opens
Email Sent to Open Ratio

Email Complaint Rate

AUTHORITY:	MEDIA:	STAGE:	CATEGORY:	APPLIES TO:
IAB	Owned	2. Connect	6. Amplification/ Endorsement	Email

ANSWERS QUESTION:

What percentage of people complained about our email?

DEFINITION:

The number of people who clicked a link in their email software to mark an email as "spam" or "junk" as a percentage of email delivered.

TECH NOTES:

None

ARF COMMENTS:

Tracking and trending Email Complaint Rate can be used to identify emails that lead people to report mail or junk back to their email service provider. Monitoring this rate can be helpful to email marketers and advertisers who change their message frequency, drop, modify or offer different types of content, or whose lists have many "lazy unsubscribers"— people who click the spam or junk button instead of properly unsubscribing. Email complaint rates are often less than 0.1% across a variety of industries (MailChimp 2012). However, given the increasing popularity of email over Mobile devices, brands should be vigilant about complaint rates.

CITED RESEARCH:

MailChimp (2012). Email Marketing Benchmarks (http://goo.gl/0E4ZP).

SEE ALSO:

Email Complaints

Email Complaints

AUTHORITY:	MEDIA:	STAGE:	CATEGORY:	APPLIES TO:
IAB	Owned	2. Connect	6. Amplification/ Endorsement	Email

ANSWERS QUESTION:

How many people marked our email as spam or junk?

DEFINITION:

Count of the number of people who clicked a link in their email software to mark an email as "spam" or "junk."

TECH NOTES:

None

ARF COMMENTS:

Email Complaints can affect email delivery and the impressions they represent. Often, email service providers will take the volume and severity of complaint actions to let mail through or not. Given the increasing popularity of email over mobile devices, brands should be vigilant about complaints.

TrustE, the reputation organization, and Epsilon, an email service provider, offers these guidelines for minimizing email complaints (2006):
a) Be clear about what the consumer is signing up for and deliver on their expectations
b) Provide permission and consent mechanisms
c) Be relevant and timely, provide value
d) Let people control Preferences
e) Make Unsubscribe feature visible
f) Brand email and remind consumers
g) Participate in industry self-regulation programs
h) Register for feedback loops
i) Analyze problematic messaging and implement improvements.

These recommendations pass the test of time; they were further supported in a post by Linhorst (2013).

CITED RESEARCH:

Linhorst, Michael (2013). Five Tips for Reducing Email Spam Complaints (http://goo.gl/QzkCf).

TrustE and Epsilon (2006). Best Practices that Minimize Email Complaints (http://goo.gl/8OY2T).

SEE ALSO:

Email Complaint Rate

Email Delivered*

AUTHORITY:	MEDIA:	STAGE:	CATEGORY:	APPLIES TO:
IAB	Owned	1. Capture	1. Advertising	Email

ANSWERS QUESTION:

How many of our emails were actually received?

DEFINITION:

The number of emails that were completely received by the intended recipient's mailbox provider without generating a bounce or delivery error. Calculation occurs before any rules are applied, such as those that route an email to a specific folder or apply an action, such as forwarding. However, messages that are accepted and placed in "junk" email folders are generally not counted as delivered.

TECH NOTES:

None

ARF COMMENTS:

According to IAB, Emails Delivered is currently the most common metric used to purchase email advertising by CPM or third-party list rental.

Because emails delivered are impressions for email marketers and advertisers, taking steps to help ensure that the maximum number end up in mailboxes contributes towards effectiveness. Experian Marketing Services (2012) details three pillars for successful email delivery: data integrity, relevance, and reputation. Additional guidance is available from the Email Experience Council (2012) and Exact Target (2012).

CITED RESEARCH:

Email Experience Council (2012). Five Ways to Improve Email Deliverability with Gmail (http://goo.gl/HVeEV).

ExactTarget (2012). Best Practices: Understand Your Deliverability (http://goo.gl/i6Pz7).

Experian Marketing Services (2012). Three Pillars of Successful Email Deliverability: Ensuring Safe Arrival and Optimum Placement in the Inbox (http://goo.gl/KuehF).

SEE ALSO:

Bounce— Email

Bounce Rate—Email

Cost per Thousand (CPM) Impressions

Email Delivery Rate*

AUTHORITY:	MEDIA:	STAGE:	CATEGORY:	APPLIES TO:
IAB	Owned	1. Capture	1. Advertising	Email

ANSWERS QUESTION:

What percentage of our emails were completely received?

DEFINITION:

The number of emails that were completely received by the intended recipient's mailbox as a percentage of emails sent, for a reporting period.

Note: Email Bounce Rate and Email Delivery Rate should add up to 100%.

TECH NOTES:

None

ARF COMMENTS:

Email Delivery Rate indicates whether or not delivery is smooth or is problematic. Low Email Delivery Rates suggest that email advertisers and marketers investigate the reasons why email messages are not getting through and take steps to overcome them. Delivery problems reduce the number of impressions generated by the email. Taking steps to help ensure that the maximum number end up in mailboxes contributes towards effectiveness. Experian Marketing Services (2012) details three pillars for successful email delivery: data integrity, relevance, and reputation. Additional guidance is available from the Email Experience Council (2012) and Exact Target (2012).

CITED RESEARCH:

Email Experience Council (2012). Five Ways to Improve Email Deliverability with Gmail (http://goo.gl/HVeEV).

ExactTarget (2012). Best Practices: Understand Your Deliverability (http://goo.gl/i6Pz7).

Experian Marketing Services (2012). Three Pillars of Successful Email Deliverability: Ensuring Safe Arrival and Optimum Placement in the Inbox (http://goo.gl/KuehF).

SEE ALSO:

Bounce—Email

Bounce Rate— Email

Email Delivered

Email Forwards*

AUTHORITY:	MEDIA:	STAGE:	CATEGORY:	APPLIES TO:
IAB	Owned	1. Capture	6. Amplification/ Endorsement	Email

ANSWERS QUESTION:

How many times was our email forwarded?

DEFINITION:

Count of the number of times an email was sent from the original recipient to a new recipient, over a reporting period.

TECH NOTES:

None

ARF COMMENTS:

Email forwards potentially expand reach because recipients are sharing with their community. Tracking and trending email forwards may suggest the types of emails, subject lines, content, and offers that promote forwarding and the implied endorsement that comes from one friend passing an email along to another. It can also be thought of as a measure of virality.

CITED RESEARCH:

None

SEE ALSO:

Email Opens
Reach

Email Inbox Delivered*

AUTHORITY:	MEDIA:	STAGE:	CATEGORY:	APPLIES TO:
IAB	Owned	1. Capture	1. Advertising	Email

ANSWERS QUESTION:

How many emails were delivered to inboxes?

DEFINITION:

The number of emails that were delivered to a recipient's inbox.

TECH NOTES:

According to IAB, this metric is often computed using a sample of email accounts.

ARF COMMENTS:

Metric indicates how successful the email campaign was at actually getting into the inbox, and potentially generating an ad impression. Helpful for understanding the impression delivery differences between those that were delivered to any folder in the mailbox and those that made it into the inbox. Size of the disparity should trigger looking into reasons preventing the emails from showing up and identify ways to overcome them, if necessary.

CITED RESEARCH:

None

SEE ALSO:

Bounce—Email
Email Delivered

Email Inbox Delivered Rate

AUTHORITY:	MEDIA:	STAGE:	CATEGORY:	APPLIES TO:
IAB	Owned	1. Capture	1. Advertising	Email

ANSWERS QUESTION:

How many emails were delivered to inboxes as a percentage of emails delivered?

DEFINITION:

The number of emails that were delivered to a recipient's inbox expressed as a percentage of emails delivered.

TECH NOTES:

According to IAB, this metric is often computed using a sample of email accounts.

ARF COMMENTS:

Metric indicates how successful the email campaign was at actually getting into the inbox and potentially generating an ad impression. Helpful for understanding the percentage of impression delivery differences between those that were delivered to any folder in the mailbox and those that made it into the inbox. A lower than average rate should trigger looking into reasons preventing the emails from showing up and identify ways to overcome them, if necessary.

CITED RESEARCH:

None

SEE ALSO:

Email Delivered

Email Open Rate*

AUTHORITY:	MEDIA:	STAGE:	CATEGORY:	APPLIES TO:
Experian Marketing Services	Owned	1. Capture	1. Advertising	Email

ANSWERS QUESTION:

What is the percentage of unique subscribers that opened an email message?

DEFINITION:

Count of the number of times an email was recorded as opened usually by loading of an invisible pixel or recipients taking an action, such as downloading images or clicking on a link, expressed as a percentage of emails received, over a reporting period.

May be computed on a Total or Unique basis. Unique Email Opens counts individuals who open an email only once, irrespective of the number of times they open it.

TECH NOTES:

See Email Opens for issues related to undercounting of Opens.

ARF COMMENTS:

Higher Open rates are generally considered a positive indicator for email marketing. In addition to the technical reasons that may affect the number of opens, Email Open rates are influenced by creative factors including the subject line (Experian Marketing Services 2012a, 2012b), landing page quality, email format and its appeal, relevancy, and the deliverability of the message (did it get through), and browser image settings, for example. Testing these factors and comparing open rates for emails in a campaign helps email marketers identify the elements most likely to generate the desired responses and optimize them. Open rates vary by industry. In conjunction with Click to Open rates, email senders can get a picture of the of productivity of the opened email in generating engagement.

Open rates may be viewed as a basic type of engagement and measure of ad effectiveness. Open rates (unique) vary across industries.

It is important to keep in mind that email opens on mobile devices are increasing. From March 2012 to February 2013, the percentage of Opens on mobile increased from 32% to 43% (Litmus 2013). Experian Marketing Services (2013) and YesMail (2013) confirm the growing share of mobile Opens, reporting that half occur on mobile devices. Moreover, Experian and YesMail reports that 53% of email subscribers and 61% of consumers, respectively, view email exclusively on a mobile device or use mobile and desktop devices interchangeably. Email advertisers need to make certain that their emails are mobile- and desktop-friendly. In addition, the type of devices, such as Android or Apple, influences Opens, clicks, and transactions. Experian advises that email marketers analyze and leverage device preferences and platforms to spot trends, monitor changes, and optimize their programs

New developments, such as Google's Gmail Quick Actions, may reduce the need to Open emails and lower the Open Rate. Quick Actions provide two types of functionality: 1) Gmail actions such as replying to meeting requests or adding a product review, and 2) "go to" actions which add a "call to action" button that takes the email recipient to a page where an action can be performed, such as a check-in, travel itinerary change, purchase, and so forth. Google recommends Quick Actions for transactional emails that are expected to have high levels of interactivity; they are not recommended for bulk emails (Google Developers 2013). Quick Actions and related innovations offered by email providers have the potential to reduce the number of steps required in a transaction or conversion path. Google Actions along with changes to email interfaces, such as Google Tabs and similar features from other email clients, that auto-categorize email into categories other than the main inbox, can also affect Open rates. Advertisers should analyze their campaign performances in the context of Actions, auto-categorization, and related to judge their impacts and adapt accordingly.

Analyzing this metric on a Total or Unique basis depends on the analytic objective. Total answers the question: "What is the percentage of emails opened among those we sent?" The Unique basis answers the question: "What percentage of unique people opened our emails?"

CITED RESEARCH:

Experian Marketing Services (2012a). It's All in the Wording; A Guide to Optimizing Your Email Subject Lines (http://goo.gl/UTzUi).

Experian Marketing Services (2012b). Three Pillars of Successful Email Deliverability: Ensuring Safe Arrival and Optimum Placement in the Inbox (http://goo.gl/KuehF).

YesMail (2013). Study: Almost Half of All Brand Emails Opened on Mobile Devices (http://goo.gl/0EYC1v).

SEE ALSO:

Email Click to Open Rate

Email Opens

Email Sent to Open Ratio

Email Opens*

AUTHORITY:	MEDIA:	STAGE:	CATEGORY:	APPLIES TO:
IAB, Experian Marketing Services	Owned	1. Capture	1. Advertising	Email

ANSWERS QUESTION:

How many times did a person look at our email?

DEFINITION:

Count of the number of times an email was recorded as opened, usually by loading of an invisible pixel or recipients taking an action, such as downloading images or clicking on a link.

Computed on a Total or Unique basis. Total includes multiple opens by the same subscriber. Unique email opens counts individuals only once who open an email, irrespective of the number of times they open it.

TECH NOTES:

Email opens may be undercounted for a variety of reasons: 1) Users may have their image settings disabled, 2) Some users have a "text only" email option selected that does not count the tag, 3) The email may be viewed on a mobile device, or 4) The email may be loaded into a preview pane but is not actually clicked-on to be viewed by the recipient.

ARF COMMENTS:

An opened email is an advertising impression.

Higher opens are generally considered a positive indicator for email marketing. In addition to the technical reasons that may affect the number of opens, email opens are influenced by creative factors including the subject line, landing page quality, email format, and its appeal, relevancy, and the deliverability of the message (did it get through), and browser image settings, for example (Experian Marketing Services 2012a, 2012b). Testing these factors and comparing open rates for emails in a campaign helps email marketers identify the elements most likely to generate the desired responses and optimize them. Open rates may be viewed as a basic type of engagement and measure of ad effectiveness. Open rates vary across industries, day of week, and time of day.

Analyzing this metric on a Total or Unique basis depends on the analytic objective. Total answers the question: "How many times was my email opened?" whereas the Unique basis answers the questions: "How many individual people opened my emails?"

It is important to keep in mind that email opens on mobile devices are increasing. From March 2012 to February 2013, the percentage of Opens on mobile increased from 32% to 43% (Litmus 2013). Experian Marketing Services (2013) and YesMail (2013) confirm the growing share of mobile Opens, reporting that half occur on mobile devices. Moreover, Experian and YesMail reports that 53% of email subscribers and 61% of consumers, respectively, view email exclusively on a mobile device or use mobile and desktop devices interchangeably. Email advertisers need to make certain that their emails are mobile- and desktop-friendly. In addition, the type of devices, such as Android or Apple influences Opens, clicks, and transactions. Experian advises that email marketers analyze and leverage device preferences and platforms to spot trends, monitor changes, and optimize their programs

New developments, such as Google's Gmail Quick Actions, may reduce the need to open emails by providing two types of functionality: 1) Gmail actions such as replying to meeting requests or adding a product review, and 2) "go to" actions which add a "call to action" button that takes the email recipient to a page where an action can be performed, such as a check-in, travel itinerary change, purchase, and so forth. Google recommends Quick Actions for transactional emails that are expected to have high levels of interactivity; they are not recommended for bulk emails (Google Developers 2013). Quick Actions and related innovations offered by email providers have the potential to reduce the number of steps required in a transaction or conversion path. Google Actions along with changes to email interfaces, such as Google Tabs and similar features from other email clients, that auto-categorize email into categories other than the main inbox, can also affect Opens. Advertisers should analyze their campaign performances in the context of Actions, auto-categorization, and other automated routines to judge their impacts and adapt accordingly.

CITED RESEARCH:

Experian Marketing Services (2012a). It's All in the Wording; A Guide to Optimizing Your Email Subject Lines (http://goo.gl/UTzUi).

Experian Marketing Services (2012b). Three Pillars of Successful Email Deliverability: Ensuring Safe Arrival and Optimum Placement in the Inbox (http://goo.gl/KuehF).

Google Developers (2013). Registering with Google (http://goo.gl/0Ak98).

Litmus (2013). Emails Opened on Mobile? Start Designing for Fingers and Thumbs (http://goo.gl/tFL02).

YesMail (2013). Study: Almost Half of All Brand Emails Opened on Mobile Devices (http://goo.gl/0EYC1v).

SEE ALSO:

Email Open Rate
Email Sent to Open Ratio

Email Sent to Open Ratio*

AUTHORITY:	MEDIA:	STAGE:	CATEGORY:	APPLIES TO:
IAB	Owned	2. Connect	1. Advertising	Email

ANSWERS QUESTION:

How many unique emails were opened that we sent?

DEFINITION:

Email Sent to Open Ratio is the percentage of unique email messages opened by people who received and opened an email in a reporting period.

TECH NOTES:

Email Open rates are tracked by having a client or browser display an HTML IMG tag. However, due to many browsers having this feature disabled by default, this rate often understates of actual amount of opens. Email opens may also be undercounted when users have "text only" email options selected, view the email on a mobile device, or when the email is loaded into a preview pane but not actually viewed by the recipient.

ARF COMMENTS:

Higher open rates are generally considered a positive indicator for email marketing—presumably the recipient was interested enough to be exposed to the messages. However, an "opened" email does not necessarily mean that it was read by the recipient. Open rates can be affected by a number of factors including sender recognition, the subject line, landing page quality, email format, and its appeal, relevancy, and the deliverability of the message (did it get through), and browser image settings for example (Experian Marketing Services 2012a, 2012b).

The quality of the email opened can be assessed by relating conversion actions email recipients later take on sites or social networks, such as Page Views, newsletter signups, commenting, requesting a test drive, or purchasing. Several analytics packages include the ability to create hybrid metrics like these that combine data from different sources, or they can be computed by in-house analysts (Kaushik 2011).

CITED RESEARCH:

Experian Marketing Services (2012a). It's All in the Wording: A Guide to Optimizing Your Email Subject Lines (http://goo.gl/UTzUi).

Experian Marketing Services (2012b). Three Pillars of Successful Email Deliverability: Ensuring Safe Arrival and Optimum Placement in the Inbox (http://goo.gl/KuehF).

Kaushik, Avinash (2011). Email Marketing: Campaign Analysis, Metrics, Best Practices (http://goo.gl/LLSlc, accessed December 14, 2012).

SEE ALSO:

Conversion
Email Open Rate
Email Opens
Impressions

Email Unsubscribe Rate*

AUTHORITY:	MEDIA:	STAGE:	CATEGORY:	APPLIES TO:
Experian Marketing Services	Owned	1. Capture	2. Audience/Traffic	Email

ANSWERS QUESTION:

What percentage of unique people unsubscribed from our email?

DEFINITION:

The number of unique people who unsubscribed from an email campaign as a percentage of the number of emails delivered.

TECH NOTES:

None

ARF COMMENTS:

Email Unsubscribe Rate can be considered a measure of relevancy and engagement, and affect the number of impressions delivered by the email. This metric can be helpful for gauging the email campaign's ability to retain and grow lists, list churn, and also for optimizing email. Tracking and trending Unsubscribe rates identify those emails that encourage people to stay on or leave from the list. Unsubscribe rates range from 0.2% to 0.4% across a range of industries. They provide a variety of email marketing benchmarks that are frequently updated (MailChimp 2012). Check with your email services provider to get stats for your brands and categories.

CITED RESEARCH:

MailChimp (2012). Email Marketing Benchmarks (http://goo.gl/0E4ZP).

SEE ALSO:

Email Unsubscribe
Unfollow/Unsubscribe

Engaged Users—Post (Facebook)

AUTHORITY:	MEDIA:	STAGE:	CATEGORY:	APPLIES TO:
Facebook	Paid Owned	2. Connect	5. Engagement/ Interaction	Social

ANSWERS QUESTION:

How many unique people took any sort of action on our post?

DEFINITION:

Engaged Users reports the number of people who clicked anywhere in your posts, who took any sort of action on your page. It includes any type of click.

Depending on the type of click, it may or may not create a story.

TECH NOTES:

None

ARF COMMENTS:

Engaged Users provides the number of unique people who interacted in any way with your post and provides a measure of the overall level of activity. Facebook has been moving towards measures that more precisely capture actions which are presumably more relevant to advertisers. People Engaged is a good example of this direction, focusing only on four types that imply meaningful engagement, instead of any type.

CITED RESEARCH:

None

SEE ALSO:

Actions (Facebook)
People Engaged—Post (Facebook)
Story (Facebook)

Engagement—Tweet (Twitter)

AUTHORITY:	MEDIA:	STAGE:	CATEGORY:	APPLIES TO:
Twitter	Paid	2. Connect	5. Engagement/ Interaction	Social

ANSWERS QUESTION:

What percentage of our Tweet impressions generated an action?

DEFINITION:

Percentage of Tweet impressions that generated a click, retweet, reply, or follow. Available for Twitter's Promoted Tweets, Trends, and Accounts.

TECH NOTES:

Segmentation available by action type: click, retweet, reply, follow.

The performance of all Tweets, promoted and regular, are also available in a Timeline format through Twitter Analytics. The timeline shows all activity including: clicks, retweets, replies, mentions, reaches, follows, and unfollows.

ARF COMMENTS:

Engagement on Twitter is similar to Engaged Users and People Engaged on Facebook: They both measure the actions people take with your content. Understanding the types of actions people take and their trends over time may help optimize campaigns.

CITED RESEARCH:

None

SEE ALSO:

Engaged Users—Post (Facebook)
Engagement
Engagement—Video

Engagement—Video

AUTHORITY:	Owned	**CATEGORY:**		**APPLIES TO:**	Mobile
YouTube	**STAGE:**	5. Engagement/	Website
MEDIA:	2. Connect	Interaction	Social

ANSWERS QUESTION:

What percentage of our videos generated some type of engagement?

DEFINITION:

Percentage of videos that generate some type of social engagement action, such as likes, dislikes, favoriting, subscribing, rating, retweeting, replying, commenting, or sharing.

TECH NOTES:

None

ARF COMMENTS:

Engagement indicates a video's appeal. When comparing one video to another, lists of videos ordered by engagement can provide guidance on popularity and ability to generate social interaction. While the total is very helpful, further analyzing by the type of engagement action can identify those whose social actions are in or out of line with the desired outcomes of a marketing or advertising strategy. For example, if a brand wants a video to be liked and shared so it has a chance to go viral, the brand can determine if liking and sharing trends may be creating a viral hit or not. Understanding that can suggest tactics to promote the desired behavior or overcome obstacles that are preventing the video from breaking out.

CITED RESEARCH:

None

SEE ALSO:

Engagement

Engagement*

AUTHORITY:	MEDIA:	STAGE:	CATEGORY:	APPLIES TO:
ARF	Paid Owned Earned	2. Connect	5. Engagement/ Interaction	Website Social Email Mobile

ANSWERS QUESTION:

How are people interacting with our ad, content, or app?

DEFINITION:

Engagement is a catchall term for measuring the types of actions that people take with a brand's advertising, content, or app.

TECH NOTES:

None

ARF COMMENTS:

Measuring engagement means identifying the actions that reflect involvement and interaction that you consider important to achieving your brand or advertising objectives and outcomes and which you can relate to Key Performance Indicators. There is no standard definition. Engagement is a term, not a metric.

As a very general rule of thumb, engagement measures for websites center on time spent and media consumption metrics, such as: time spent on page, page views, click-through rate, or estimated minutes watched of a video. These are measures of what people are doing on the site, not merely counting traffic measures such as Unique Visitor or Visits.

Social engagement focuses more on what people are doing with your content, ad, or app. This is a large and always expanding list. Some of the more common metrics are: comments, downloads, subscriptions, posting, rating, liking/unliking, following, and sharing.

CITED RESEARCH:

None

SEE ALSO:

Key Performance Indicator (KPI)
Sharing

Entry Page (Top Entry Pages)*

AUTHORITY:	MEDIA:	STAGE:	CATEGORY:	APPLIES TO:
Digital Analytics Association, Google, Millward Brown Digital	Owned	1. Capture	3. Site Navigation/Site Performance	Website Social Mobile

ANSWERS QUESTION:

Which pages did visitors access to enter our site?

DEFINITION:

An Entry Page is the first page of a Visit. It may be a home page, but is often a different page on the site. Top Entry Pages are a rank ordering of the most frequently accessed Entry Pages for a reporting period.

TECH NOTES:

None

ARF COMMENTS:

Entry Pages and Top Entry Pages provide understanding on the ways people enter a site. The most common way in may not be the home page but may be to a specific page (sent by a search engine result or email) or link embedded in a Tweet or status update on a social networking site. For example, if a person is shopping for the Nike Olympics sneaker, search results for them would include URLs to product pages as well as the Nike home page. Taking a different example, if a link embedded in a Tweet or LinkedIn or Facebook post, the person clicking would be taken directly to that page. Research from the Nieman Journalism Lab (2012) revealed that at many media company sites, such as *The New York Times* and *Wall Street Journal*, a majority of traffic is coming in through the "side door," bypassing the home page. For this reason they see the home page as becoming more a branding mechanism and downplaying its traditional role as a traffic driver.

Entry Page analysis is beneficial for analyzing the different ways people reach your site, and determining if they are in line with marketing and advertising strategy or not. Examining Entry Page trends over time may reveal shifts in traffic sources and patterns, product interest and, in conjunction with related metrics, such as Bounce Rate, analyses may be used to optimize site content and increase its relevancy, whether for content or commerce.

CITED RESEARCH:

La France, Adrian (2012). *Coming in the Side Door: The Value of Homepages Is Shifting from Traffic-Driver to Brand* (http://goo.gl/IEVsN).

SEE ALSO:

Bounce
Bounce Rate (Website or Social Network)
Exit Page

Entry Type*

AUTHORITY:	MEDIA:	STAGE:	CATEGORY:	APPLIES TO:
comScore, Millward Brown Digital	Owned	1. Capture	2. Audience/Traffic	Website Social Mobile

ANSWERS QUESTION:

How did visitors arrive at our site?

DEFINITION:

The method browsers use to enter a website. This can be via a search engine, an external referrer, or direct entry when they type the URL directly in their web browser or when they enter the website via a bookmark. If clickins are used to measure a link to a website, then the entry type is registered as a clickin.

TECH NOTES:

None

ARF COMMENTS:

When rank ordered, Entry Type can be helpful for broadly understanding the popularity of different methods people use to reach a site. When examined in the context of Channel and Source, the combination may reflect on the effectiveness of traffic-driving strategies and tactics. For example, if a campaign relied heavily on generating traffic through the Entry Type of search, the comparative popularity and ranking of search gives guidance on how well it is working.

CITED RESEARCH:

None

SEE ALSO:

Channel
Referral Traffic
Source

Episode Completions

AUTHORITY:	MEDIA:	STAGE:	CATEGORY:	APPLIES TO:
comScore	Owned	2. Connect	5. Engagement/ Interaction	Website Social Mobile

ANSWERS QUESTION:

How many times was our episode viewed through to the end?

DEFINITION:

The total number of times an episode was completely played over a period of time. Typically a threshold is set at which a playback is considered fully played, such as 90%.

An episode is the name of show within a program; it can be designated by season and number, such as Season 2 Episode 3 of *Modern Family,* or by its name, which in this case is "Earthquake."

TECH NOTES:

None

ARF COMMENTS:

A basic interaction measure. The depth of engagement may be analyzed through related metrics, such as episode completions and average playing time. This metric may be helpful to optimize program selection.

CITED RESEARCH:

None

SEE ALSO:

Episode Starts

Episode Starts

AUTHORITY:	MEDIA:	STAGE:	CATEGORY:	APPLIES TO:
comScore	Owned	2. Connect	5. Engagement/ Interaction	Website Social Mobile

ANSWERS QUESTION:

How many times was a specific episode in our program started?

DEFINITION:

The total number of times of first and repeated episode starts, over a reporting period.

An episode is the name of show within a program; it can be designated by season and number, such as Season 2 Episode 3 of *Modern Family,* or by its name, which in this case is "Earthquake."

TECH NOTES:

None

ARF COMMENTS:

A basic interaction measure. The depth of engagement may be analyzed through related metrics, such as episode completions and average playing time. Metric may be helpful to optimize program selection.

CITED RESEARCH:

None

SEE ALSO:

Episode Completions

Estimated Minutes Watched*

AUTHORITY:	MEDIA:	STAGE:	CATEGORY:	APPLIES TO:
YouTube, comScore	Owned	2. Connect	4. Media Consumption	Website Social Mobile

ANSWERS QUESTION:

How many minutes was our video watched?

DEFINITION:

Count of the number of minutes a YouTube video, or videos in a channel, were watched, over a period of time.

Note: comScore names this measure "Total Minutes."

TECH NOTES:

None

ARF COMMENTS:

Estimated minutes watched is a measure of engagement with the video, and must be evaluated against the length of the video and the marketing or advertising objective. Estimated minutes watched may be helpful for optimizing videos.

CITED RESEARCH:

None

SEE ALSO:

Video—Audience Retention
Video Plays

Event

AUTHORITY:	MEDIA:	STAGE:	CATEGORY:	APPLIES TO:
Google	Owned	2. Connect	5. Engagement/ Interaction	Website Social Mobile

ANSWERS QUESTION:

What is an Event?

DEFINITION:

An event is an action visitors take on a website that does not create a new Page View.

TECH NOTES:

Events may include, but not be limited to, interacting with a video player or audio player, setting the zoom in a map, or a widget of some kind. According to Google's Analytics Advocate Justin Cutroni, these types of events once were counted as Page Views in Google Analytics. For events to be reported, they must first be defined. Consult with your analytics vendor to learn how events are defined and reported.

ARF COMMENTS:

Event counting is very helpful for understanding the interactions visitors have with the content on a web page. Trends identify patterns in usage that can be used to optimize the page and site experience.

CITED RESEARCH:

Cutroni, J. (2007). "Event Tracking Pt. 1: Overview & Data Model" (http://goo.gl/oPZYi).

SEE ALSO:

Page View

Event Tracking*

AUTHORITY:	MEDIA:	STAGE:	CATEGORY:	APPLIES TO:
Google, Facebook	Owned	2. Connect 3. Close 4. Keep	5. Engagement/ Interaction	Website Social Mobile

ANSWERS QUESTION:

What are the types of interactions people are having with our site?

DEFINITION:

Event tracking is a method for recording the interactions visitors have with website elements. If it can be defined as an event, it can be tracked. Some common events tracked are, but not limited to, a video play button, link click, purchase, flash play, comment, PDF download, or cost calculator.

TECH NOTES:

Many analytics packages provide for Event Tracking. Google Analytics is pretty typical, requiring a Category (group of items you want to track), an Action (such as play, click, or download), and optionally a Label (for description, such as video title, PDF file name, etc.), a Value (assigning a number or dollar value to an action, such as the number of seconds it takes for a video player to load or trigger a dollar value when a certain location during video playback is reached), and Implicit Count (a counting of total events and unique events).

ARF COMMENTS:

Event tracking is an important step forward from the standard page metrics. Event Tracking reports reveal what people are doing on the site and with its content, making it very relevant for the Connect, Close, and Keep stages. Not limited to websites, event tracking is used in social networks to track such things as shares, comments, retweets, views, etc. (see Facebook Actions). In this regard, we are seeing a movement towards focusing on interactions people have with sites and content, and not merely counting what a site or network did, such as serve a page for a certain amount of time. Event Tracking is especially useful when you want to measure assets on your site that do not link to a page or generate a page view. It is often used for measuring videos. With Event Tracking every video action that can be defined is measurable and trackable, such as starts, stops, pauses, drop-off rates, and length of time the video was played.

Event tracking is helpful for optimizing a site. It can tell you which links are popular, which videos are started and stopped quickly and, in combination with other metrics, can point out problems. For example, using Event Tracking a University discovered that a box with a link to start the application process was not working as expected: the number of submitted applications was about 80% less than the number of clicks. After some internal deliberation the people realized that the drop-off was occurring because visitors didn't expect to be taken directly to the application on a click. The University added a couple of information pages beforehand in order to set expectations and motivate visitors. Pages per visit went up by two, time on site increased, and general click-throughs went up 50%. "Without event tracking, I would have never been able to identify the problem or measure the results of the change" (Fienen 2011).

CITED RESEARCH:

The case study on Event Tracking is from: Feinen, Michael (2011). The Idiot's Guide to Event Tracking (http://goo.gl/TDWLP).

SEE ALSO:

Actions (Facebook)

Conversion

Engagement

Event

Exit Page*

AUTHORITY:
comScore, Google, Yahoo!

MEDIA:
Owned

STAGE:
1. Capture
2. Connect
3. Close
4. Keep

CATEGORY:
3. Site Navigation/Site Performance

APPLIES TO:
Website
Social
Mobile

ANSWERS QUESTION:
At which page did a visitor leave our site or process?

DEFINITION:
Two definitions: 1) The last page in a session, 2) the page at which visitors exit from a conversion funnel.

TECH NOTES:
None

ARF COMMENTS:
Exit Pages identify where people are leaving the site (typically during the Connect stage), or at which page they abandon the conversion funnel (Close stage). Those pages may indicate whether or not visitors are exiting from locations that are on or off strategy, and suggest ways to optimize them. If visitors are bailing at a micro-conversion page, then that page becomes a candidate for improving its content or functionality.

CITED RESEARCH:
None

SEE ALSO:
Abandonment Rate (Page)
Conversion Funnel
Page Exit Rate

Fan (Facebook)

AUTHORITY:	MEDIA:	STAGE:	CATEGORY:	APPLIES TO:
Facebook	Earned	1. Connect	2. Audience/Traffic	Social

ANSWERS QUESTION:

What is a Facebook fan?

DEFINITION:

A Facebook fan is a person who Likes a page.

TECH NOTES:

None

ARF COMMENTS:

When a person Likes a page they are making, in Facebook terminology, a connection to the page. After that happens, a Story about that Like will appear on a person's Timeline and may also appear in their News Feed. The person may be displayed on the Page they connected to, in advertisements about that Page or in social plugins next to the content the Like.

The person may see updates to in their feeds and the feeds of their friends from Pages they like. They may also receive messages. Their connection to the page may also be shared with apps on the Facebook Platform.

However, "Liking" a page is not the same as "Liking" a post, update, video link, or similar content from a friend. Liking a friend's content lets your friend know that you Like it but are not commenting on it.

CITED RESEARCH:

Facebook (2013). Updating Page Insights (http://goo.gl/X5f29E).

SEE ALSO:

Like
Likes (Facebook)
Unlike a Page (Facebook)

First Orders

AUTHORITY:	MEDIA:	STAGE:	CATEGORY:	APPLIES TO:
comScore, Millward Brown Digital	Owned	3. Close	8. E-Commerce	Website Social Mobile

ANSWERS QUESTION:

What is the number of first purchase orders our site received?

DEFINITION:

The total number of first orders by unique browsers over a reporting period.

TECH NOTES:

None

ARF COMMENTS:

First Orders answer the question: "How many of the orders we are getting come from unique buyers?" This metric can indicate the effectiveness of a campaign and/or website or mobile app in converting visits to sales and capturing new customers during the reporting period. When analyzed in the context of total orders and repeat orders from unique people (browsers), First Order trends may suggest the vitality of the business and actions that can be taken to maximize its growth. Keep in mind that a "unique browser" (Unique Visitor) is identified for a specific period of time.

CITED RESEARCH:

None

SEE ALSO:

Average Order Value, Total and Unique
Conversion
Conversion Funnel
Conversion Goal
Conversion Rate
Unique Visitors (Unique Browsers)

Followers/Subscribers*

AUTHORITY:	MEDIA:	STAGE:	CATEGORY:	APPLIES TO:
Facebook, YouTube, Twitter, Google+, LinkedIn, IPR	Earned	2. Connect	2. Audience/Traffic	Website Social Email Mobile

ANSWERS QUESTION:

How many people subscribe to our content?

DEFINITION:

Number of unique people who "follow" or "subscribe" to your content over a reporting period, usually by clicking a "subscribe" or "follow" button, or "Like." Content can be of any type such as social network accounts of brands or people, videos, channels, blogs, RSS feeds, email newsletters or updates, and so on. Subscribing to content allows people to stay up to date with it.

People who undo or cancel their following or subscribing are often referred to as "unfollows," "unsubscribers," or "unlikes."

TECH NOTES:

Analytic products typically report the change in total subscribers by subtracting subscribers lost from subscribers gained for a selected date range.

ARF COMMENTS:

Subscriptions may be considered a basic measure of engagement, as they reflect a desire by visitors to stay connected with your brand, page, or content.

On Facebook, subscribers, which they call "Followers," have the capability to select which type of content from your page they want to see in their News Feed. Generally, pages for celebrities, brands, journalists, artists, public figures, and other "interesting people" often have Subscribe buttons. Individuals who are friends are automatically subscribed to each other's updates and can select which ones to see, or not. Individuals can have non-friends subscribe to their home page and receive public posts by opting-in for a subscribe button. Page owners with subscribe buttons can see who subscribes to their pages.

On a cautionary note, marketplaces have developed where brands can purchase subscribers. Make sure that you understand how your brand's subscribers or followers were acquired, evaluate them, and make adjustments accordingly.

Many brands seek to increase their numbers of Followers or Subscribers. The value of Followers, whether on Facebook, Twitter, LinkedIn, or other social networks, is very much an issue. Large Followings play into the conventional mass media notion that audience size matters. According to that view, Tweets or similar status updates from "influential" people that they share with their networks create earned impressions that reach people who are likely to value the content because of the sender's implied endorsement. Followings, however, can be purchased, and not all Tweets or status updates are seen or read, so larger does not necessarily mean better. Ev Williams, founder and board member of Twitter, discounts the value of the number of Followers. Instead he, and many other industry voices, advocate for a measure of an individual's online influence and distribution power, which will enable brands to target influential Tweeters or social media posters whose reputations encourage people to read their updates and amplify them (Mashable 2012). Larger follower sizes do not necessarily mean that a brand will have more engagement. A study of the 100 brands with the largest Twitter followings revealed that the 25 brands with the highest engagement levels, as measured by average retweets per post, had follower levels over one million, but so did 80 percent of the lesser engaged brands (Nestivity 2013).

Analysis of Subscribers or Followers should always take Unsubscribes and Unfollows into account, so that the dynamics and retention of Subscribers and Followers can be grasped and interpreted within the context of site goals. For example, high churn rates might be acceptable for sites that do not need to have an enduring relationship with people, whereas it is likely to be detrimental for sites that strive to retain users and engender loyalty. Along these lines, studying the behavior of Subscribers/Followers and Unsubscribers/Unfollowers may reveal differences that can help brands enhance their experience.

CITED RESEARCH:

Mashable (2012). Former Twitter CEO Says Network Needs a Better Metric Than Follower Count (http://goo.gl/bhFZV).

Nestivity (2013). The Most Followed Brands on Twitter Are Not the Most Engaged: A Study of Top Brands on Twitter (http://goo.gl/n5bb5).

SEE ALSO:

Like

Unfollow/Unsubscribe

Influencer

Form Submissions*

AUTHORITY:	MEDIA:	STAGE:	CATEGORY:	APPLIES TO:
comScore, Millward Brown Digital	Owned	2. Connect	7. Conversion	Website Social Mobile

ANSWERS QUESTION:

How many forms were submitted on our site?

DEFINITION:

The total number of successful form submissions, over a reporting period.

TECH NOTES:

comScore and other analytics vendors also compute related measures: Average Time Spent, Failures, and Abandonments.

Average Time Spent: The average duration in seconds that browsers have spent on a form before successfully submitting or abandoning it, over a reporting period.

Failures: The number of unsuccessful form submissions where the information in the form was not successfully sent to the server, over a reporting period.

Abandonments: The total number of times browsers abandoned a form without trying to submit it over a reporting period.

ARF COMMENTS:

Form Submissions answer the question: How many forms were filled out and submitted to our site?

Form Submissions are conversion events and may be used as a measure of engagement. Trends in submissions may be helpful for understanding the effectiveness of marketing or advertising strategy, or the site in motivating visitors to complete a form submission. In conjunction with average time spent, failures, and abandons, analysis may pinpoint issues that can be used to optimize form submissions.

CITED RESEARCH:

None

SEE ALSO:

Conversion Funnel
Conversion Rate
Form Abandonments

Frequency*

AUTHORITY:	MEDIA:	STAGE:	CATEGORY:	APPLIES TO:
Nielsen, comScore, Facebook	Paid Owned	1. Capture	1. Advertising	Website Social Email Mobile

ANSWERS QUESTION:

How many times did a person see a specific ad or other piece of content?

DEFINITION:

The number of times a person or home is exposed to a piece of content, or ad over a specified time period. Most often, frequency concerns exposure to advertising impressions.

Frequency is often averaged across people or homes, rather than reported by individual. Average frequency is used in calculating Gross Rating Points (GRPs).

TECH NOTES:

None

ARF COMMENTS:

Frequency is one of the traditional measures used in media planning, along with Reach and GRPs. When planning for frequency, the planner estimates the number of repetitions an ad needs in order to achieve a communications goal, such as raising awareness to a target level. For this reason, many digital ad serving platforms provide the ability to set an upper limit on the frequency of exposures an individual will receive over a specified time period; this is called a Frequency Cap.

Nielsen's Hess and Gaiser (2013) argue that while it is desirable to get as much unduplicated reach as possible in a media plan, advertisers "should also be aware that Digital can play important roles in building campaign Frequency in order to help attain Effective Frequency levels" (the number of exposures required to trigger a response).

CITED RESEARCH:

Hess, Mike and Tristan Gaiser (2013). Frequency: Don't Overlook It as Part of Digital's Toolkit. Nielsen (available from author Mike Hess at Nielsen).

SEE ALSO:

Ad Impression
Gross Ratings Points (GRP)
Reach

Friends of Fans (Facebook)

AUTHORITY:	MEDIA:	STAGE:	CATEGORY:	APPLIES TO:
Facebook	Earned	1. Capture	2. Audience/Traffic	Social

ANSWERS QUESTION:

What is the maximum number of people we could reach through people who Like our page?

DEFINITION:

The number of unique people who are friends with fans.

TECH NOTES:

The number of Friends of Fans will vary over time because Pages may increase Fans through their marketing and/or experience Unlikes which reduces the number of Friends of Fans.

ARF COMMENTS:

Friends of Fans represent a much larger set of consumers than Fans. The collective audience is often considered a measure of potential reach. In fact, that number may mislead. Analysts such as Baekdal (2012) point out that not all Friends of Fans will be exposed to a brand impression because of Facebook's EdgeRank algorithm. EdgeRank "decides" which posts to place on a Friend's timeline, when, and in what order. Not everyone with the potential to see, will see.

However, the Friends of Fans who do see a brand impression have value to a brand. comScore research illustrates that Friends of Fans are more likely than the average Internet visitor to visit a store, website, or purchase a product or service, but somewhat less so than people who Like a page.

CITED RESEARCH:

Baekdal, Thomas (2012). Facebook Insights: Debunking Friends of Fans (http://goo.gl/aSfS5).
comScore (2011). The Power of Like: How Brands Reach and Influence Fans through Social Marketing (http://goo.gl/Mi46Y).
Facebook (2013). Updating Page Insights (http://goo.gl/X5f29E).

SEE ALSO:

Fan (Facebook)
Likes—Page (Facebook)
Reach—Page (Facebook)

Gross Ratings Points (GRP)*

AUTHORITY:	**MEDIA:**	**STAGE:**	**CATEGORY:**	**APPLIES TO:**
comScore, Millward Brown Digital, Nielsen	Paid	1. Capture	1. Advertising	Website Social Email Mobile

ANSWERS QUESTION:

How much advertising weight did we purchase?

DEFINITION:

The Gross Ratings Points (GRP) measures the size of the duplicated audience. It is the product of the Audience Reach and the Average Frequency of exposure to a piece of content, usually an ad.

A single Gross Rating Point is equal to 1% of the total or target audience.

Note: Nielsen states that this definition is comparable to Nielsen television ratings [Impressions/US Pop Base].

TECH NOTES:

When the audience is defined in targeting terms, such as Women 18–49, the audience reach and average frequency may be calculated on that demographic basis. These are called Targeted Rating Points, or TRPs.

The Making Measurement Make Sense (3MS) initiative proposes that Viewable Impressions be used to compute GRPs. According to their website, these GRPs will also reflect age, gender, and ethnicities, with the ability to add other demographic and behavioral targeting variables. The base for GRP calculation will be the total US population, not TV households (3MS 2012).

GRPs may be computed for specific sites or combined to reflect the media buy.

ARF COMMENTS:

The GRP has long been a standard measure in media planning and buying. It is widely considered a measure of advertising "weight." The sum of GRPs for a media buy often exceeds 100%.

In digital media, the "viewability" of an ad impression has become an important topic as the industry comes to realize that not all ad impressions have an opportunity to be seen, and thereby create questions about the calculation of GRPs. Please read the entry for "Viewable Impression" for details and discussion.

comScore, Millward Brown Digital, and Nielsen are three measurement companies that have added Viewability to their counting and computing of GRPs. comScore also accounts for factors in addition to viewability that lead to mis-targeting, such as ads being delivered to the wrong audience or geography, ads served on inappropriate content, or ads served "fraudulently" to non-humans (e.g., spiders, bots, crawlers, or other automated visitors).

Digital GRPs are expected to allow cross-platform comparisons, so that TV can be compared to online, for example. According to the 3MS initiative, "eventually all GRPs will be calculated off a person's universe as all media go digital.

Media planners and buyers need to understand the basis for impression measurement and the accuracy of the GRP measures they are using in order to purchase media schedules efficiently and to evaluate post-buy performance.

CITED RESEARCH:

3MS (2012). FAQs (http://goo.gl/o3m2Q)
comScore (2012). For Display Ads, Being Seen Matters More than Being Clicked. (http://goo.gl/vycS4)

SEE ALSO:

Ad Impression
Frequency
Reach

Hit

AUTHORITY: Farris et al.

MEDIA: Owned

STAGE: 1. Capture

CATEGORY: 2. Audience/Traffic

APPLIES TO:
Website
Social
Mobile

ANSWERS QUESTION:

How many hits did our site receive over a reporting period?

DEFINITION:

Count of the number of files served to visitors on the web. Because web pages often contain multiple files, hits is a function not only of pages visited, but also the number of files on each page.

TECH NOTES:

Hits count all the files served per page including text, data, graphics, and multimedia.

ARF COMMENTS:

Hits have been supplanted by Page Views and are seldom used today, the key reason being that the number of hits are influenced by the number of elements displayed on a page and how the page was put together by a designer. As Farris et al. state, "As marketing on the Internet has become more sophisticated, better measures of Web activity and traffic have evolved [than hits]. Currently it is more common to use page views as the measure of traffic at a Web location. Page views aim to measure the number of times a page has been displayed to a user. It thus should be measured as close to the end user as possible" (Farris et al., 2006,). Although Page Views have largely replaced Hits, Page Views are also being questioned.

CITED RESEARCH:

Farris, Paul W. et al. (2006). Marketing Metrics, pp. 289–290. Hoboken: John Wiley & Sons.

SEE ALSO:

Page View

In-Unit Click

AUTHORITY:	MEDIA:	STAGE:	CATEGORY:	APPLIES TO:
IAB, Digital Analytics Association, Mobile Marketing Association	Paid Owned	2. Connect	5. Engagement/ Interaction	Website Social Mobile

ANSWERS QUESTION:

How many clicks did our ad receive that took a visitor to another page within our site?

DEFINITION:

The action of following a link within an advertisement, often a rich media unit, but does not result in a transfer from the publisher's site (as a click-through does). In-unit clicks allow the user to "drill down" for more information or interaction. Sometimes called a clickin.

TECH NOTES:

In-unit click-throughs should be tracked and reported as a 302 redirect at the ad server and should filter out robotic activity (IAB).

According to the Digital Analytics Association, "click-throughs measured on the sending side (as reported by your ad server, for example) and on the receiving side (as reported by your web analytics tool) often do not match. Minor discrepancies are normal, but large discrepancies may require investigation" (
See their Web Analytics Definitions Version 4: http://goo.gl/6H3C3).

ARF COMMENTS:

In-unit clicks are used to gauge an advertisement's effectiveness for direct response, display advertising, and in-ad engagement. See Click-Through Rate for a detailed discussion.

CITED RESEARCH:

None

SEE ALSO:

Click-Through
Click-Through Rate (CTR)

Incoming Links (Backlinks)

AUTHORITY:	MEDIA:	STAGE:	CATEGORY:	APPLIES TO:
Wikipedia, Google	Owned	1. Capture	2. Audience/Traffic	Website

ANSWERS QUESTION:

Which sites are linking to our website and specific web pages?

DEFINITION:

Also known as backlinks, inbound links, inlinks, and inward links, are links coming to a website or web page. In basic link terminology, a backlink is any link received by a web node (web page, directory, website, or top level domain) from another web node.

TECH NOTES:

On Facebook, links will be counted if they are follow-able. If they are no-follow, as they are on Profile pages and pages that require logging in, they are not counted.

ARF COMMENTS:

Backlink analysis has been essential for Search Engine Optimization (SEO). The number, quality, and authority of links to a website or web page help search engines determine relevance, popularity, importance, and ranking. High quality incoming links aid in generating targeted traffic.

Several SEO practitioners provide useful guides to the value of backlinks and how to optimize them: Springboard (http://goo.gl/pLfL2) and Kronik Media (http://goo.gl/TYiyu) are two. There are also many books on SEO available, such as *Search Engine Optimization: An Hour a Day* by Jennifer Grappone (http://goo.gl/hNBoK).

However, Google's Matt Cutts recently advised the industry that backlinks will play a lesser role in Google's algorithm, with greater weight given to engagement factors such as bounce rate, time on site, and semantic content analysis (reported in Jamierot 2013).

CITED RESEARCH:

Grappone, Jennifer and Gradiva Couzin (2011). Search Engine Optimization: An Hour a Day. 3rd Edition. Sybex (http://goo.gl/hNBoK).

Jamierot, Markus (2013). Google Disregard Backlinks as Ranking Factors (http://goo.gl/X6dTb).

SEE ALSO:

Referral Traffic
Source

Influencer*

AUTHORITY:	MEDIA:	STAGE:	CATEGORY:	APPLIES TO:
WOMMA, IPR	Earned	2. Connect	6. Amplification/ Endorsement	Social

ANSWERS QUESTION:

What are Influencers and how do they work for brands?

DEFINITION:

WOMMA, the Word of Mouth Marketing Association, defines a Key Influencer as: a person or group of people who possess greater than average potential to influence due to attributes such as frequency of communication, personal persuasiveness, or size of and centrality to a social network, among others.

Influencers operate online and offline. About 10% of the population are considered Influencers (Keller & Fay 2012).

WOMMA defines five types of Influencer: Advocate (unpaid), Ambassador (formal relationship with brand), Citizen (ordinary person with Influence), Professional/Occupational (authorities), and Celebrity (name recognition, often serves as advocate or ambassador).

Note: Influence is the ability to cause or contribute to a change in opinion or behavior.

TECH NOTES:

None

ARF COMMENTS:

The notion of the Influential originated in research by Katz and Lazarsfeld (1955) on personal influence. Essentially, their research concluded that "influentials" are responsible for influencing everyone else. Influentials are influenced by media, editorial content, their own research, their experiences, and other ways they discover and learn. For many in our industry, the idea that brands should influence the small number of Influentials (about 10% of the population) who, in turn, will "do your work" (spread the message to Followers) has become the dominant mental and executional model for Influencer marketing (Watts 2007). Studying the economic impact of WOM, word-of-mouth research firm Keller Fay (2012), reported findings from a study of Condé Nast magazine readers which established that a recommendation from an Influencer had about four times the economic impact as a recommendation from the average reader—a result later confirmed in a separate study by McKinsey which utilized a different methodology. A new line of research within the Influential model looks at the network structure, particularly the relationship between influencers and a firm's target consumers. Early findings reveal that the most valuable Influencers to a brand are those who provide exclusive influence to a group of target consumers. These consumers are not influenced by other online Influencers. In many instances, Influencers do not have exclusive relationships with consumers. The most effective Influencers in that situation are those with a small or a large number of competitors, but not a middling number (Katona 2013).

This dominant mental model has its challengers, among them Duncan Watts, who has argued that while the Influentials hypothesis appears to make sense and conform to experience (we want to see that someone or a small group caused something to happen first), the Influentials hypothesis has not really been empirically supported and, according to his research, Influentials do not matter as much as believed. Watts' work focuses on computer modeling the spread of ideas through social networks. Spread occurs not from Influencers to their Followers, but rather depends on whether or not the network structure permits innovations to spread. Large "cascades" of new ideas are primarily "driven by easily influenced individuals influencing other easily influenced individuals." Although Influencers can and sometimes do play a role, it is usually modest. Mark Earls takes a similar view albeit from a different tradition, anthropology, arguing that new ideas are spread by people noticing and copying what others do. Earls explored this notion in his book *Herd* (2009), which he later expanded upon with colleagues (Bentley, et al. 2011). Research methods, such as predictive analytics, for studying these nontraditional Influencer models are emerging and becoming commercialized, which may increase their acceptance and utilization (Haring 2013). Jim Rutenberg (2013) provides one case study, outlining how the 2012 Obama campaign targeted easily persuaded voters to help Obama win.

Each type of Influencer model offers brands different options to spread their messages and generate WOM. Although the conventional Influencer model holds sway, brands should also determine if creating cascades among the easily influenced in the spirit of Watts and Earls is appropriate for them. Whichever is chosen, the Influencer strategy should be tied to brand objectives and key performance indicators.

CITED RESEARCH:

Bentley, Alex, et al. (2011). *I'll Have What She's Having: Mapping Social Behavior.* Cambridge: MIT Press.

Earls, Mark (2009). *Herd: How to Change Mass Behaviour by Harnessing Our True Nature.* Hoboken: John Wiley & Sons.

Haring, Arjin (2013). *Why Marketers Should Focus on Persuadables* (http://goo.gl/ILgw9).

Katona, Zsolt. *Competing for Influencers in a Social Network* (July 1, 2013). Available at SSRN:http://goo.gl/qcYih1.

Katz, E and Paul Felix Lazarsfeld (1955). *Personal Influence: the Part Played by People in the Flow of Mass Communications.* New York: Free Press.

Keller, E. and Brad Fay (2012). *The Face-to-Face Book: Why Real Relationships Rule in a Digital Marketplace.* New York: Free Press.

Rutenberg, Jim (2013). *Data You Can Believe In: The Obama Campaign's Digital Masterminds Cash In.* (http://goo.gl/YwudG).

Watts, Duncan (2007). *Who Are the Influentials? What Are They Good For?* (paper presented at ARF Word of Mouth Session).

SEE ALSO:

Brand Advocate

Interactions—In Ad

AUTHORITY:	MEDIA:	STAGE:	CATEGORY:	APPLIES TO:
Patel & Flores	Paid	2. Connect	5. Engagement/ Interaction	Website Social Email Mobile

ANSWERS QUESTION:

How did visitors interact with our ad or app over a reporting period?

DEFINITION:

The number of visitors who interacted within a rich media ad or app. Interactions include mouse rollovers, hovers, games played within rich media ad units, mapping, click to call, video plays, and related activities, but do not include clicking on the ad.

TECH NOTES:

Analytics packages may account for interactions differently. Be certain that you understand which interactions are captured, how they are measured, and how they are reported, and concentrate on those that are most meaningful for your objectives.

ARF COMMENTS:

Interacting within rich media units has been a staple of online advertising for years and is increasingly available on mobile handsets and tablet devices. The IAB and The Open Rich Media for Mobile Advertising specifications group is establishing standards.

In-ad interactions promote user involvement and engagement with advertising. As interactivity increases, the long-used click-through may become less relevant as a success metric and may be replaced by measures that are specific to an ad's functionality and the device used to view and engage with it. [See: "PointRoll" (2011).]

Studies have established correlations between interactions and branding impact. Microsoft's "Dwell on Branding" study (http://goo.gl/w1r8v), done in collaboration with Eyeblaster and comScore, demonstrates that greater levels of online engagement lead to uplifts in measurable brand benefits. On the print side, research comparing static ads in a print publication to interactive ads for the same title in an iPad publication demonstrated greater effectiveness of the digital ads on engagement, message involvement, and attitude towards the ad across the advertisements studied that were encountered while browsing. When ads were force-exposed, lifts in those metrics were seen, along with an additional lift in purchase intention.

Yet Millward Brown and Google's study of roughly 4,300 rich media creative units argues that the size of the impacts are not meaningful. Their research, which examined the impact of interactions on branding, measure "weak positive relationships between ad interaction rates and both awareness and brand favorability, and a negative relationship with message association." They concluded that ad behaviors are not good predictors of brand impact, and cautioned that the fun and involvement of interacting with the ad may work against the ad unit delivering brand messages. In-market branding success, they suggest, may be better predicted by copy testing (see Mallon and Bruner 2009).

However, the world of rich media ad interaction continues evolving and is moving from an online to a mobile and tablet experience. Gauging the impact of interactions should take into account the type of ad unit, types of interactions, ad context, and platform to assess effectiveness in ways that are meaningful for a brand.

On Facebook, interactions with ads create stories that may appear on friends' timelines, which then act as earned media.

CITED RESEARCH:

Mallon and Bruner (2009). "Can Rich Media Metrics Predict Branding Impact?" (http://goo.gl/hpsXH).

Microsoft Advertising (2010). "Dwell on Branding" study (http://goo.gl/MlN7Z).

PointRoll (2011). PointRoll Mobile Research Reflects Differences in Consumer Behavior by Device, Driving Ad Engagement; Interaction Rates Increase on iPhone, Brand Time Grows on iPad" (http://goo.gl/r4TV7).

Wang, Alan (2011). Digital Ad Engagement: Perceived Interactivity as a Driver of Advertising Effectiveness (http://goo.gl/Ew3Hk).

SEE ALSO:

Click-Through

Click-Through Rate (CTR)

In-Unit Click

IP Address

AUTHORITY:	MEDIA:	STAGE:	CATEGORY:	APPLIES TO:
Wikipedia	Paid Owned Earned	1. Capture	2. Audience/Traffic	Website Social Mobile

ANSWERS QUESTION:

What is the IP address of a visitor's device?

DEFINITION:

A numerical label assigned to each device (e.g., computer, printer) participating in a computer network that uses the Internet Protocol for communication. Sometimes called an IP number, it is captured to identify visits.

An IP Address serves two principal functions: host or network interface identification and location addressing. Its role has been characterized as follows: "A name indicates what we seek. An address indicates where it is. A route indicates how to get there."

TECH NOTES:

Internet Protocol numbers are assigned to a host either anew at the time of booting, or permanently by fixed configuration of its hardware or software. Persistent configuration is also known as using a static IP number. In contrast, in situations when the computer's IP number is assigned newly each time, this is known as using a dynamic IP number.

IP addresses are binary numbers, but they are usually stored in text files and displayed in human-readable notations, such as 172.16.254.1 (for IPv4), and 2001:db8:0:1234:0:567:8:1 (for IPv6).

The Internet Assigned Numbers Authority (IANA) manages the IP address space allocations globally and delegates five regional Internet registries (RIRs) to allocate IP address blocks to local Internet registries (Internet service providers) and other entities.

ARF COMMENTS:

IP addresses are used to identify Unique Visitors (browsers) to sites. IP addresses may be used for audience targeting. Each IP address contains information about its user type—home, business, education, government, or wireless, According to Slavin (2012) targeting can be very fine grained because there are approximately 1.5 million home zones and 5 million business zones. Each home zone is about 77 times more precise than a zip code—averaging 145 people (Slavin 2012).

CITED RESEARCH:

None

SEE ALSO:

Cookie

Visit (Session)

Key Content Downloads (Coupons, Recipes, Apps, etc.)*

AUTHORITY:	MEDIA:	STAGE:	CATEGORY:	APPLIES TO:
Patel & Flores	Owned	2. Connect	7. Conversion	Website Social Mobile

ANSWERS QUESTION:

Which of our content files were downloaded, and how many times?

DEFINITION:

The number of content or file downloads that contribute to purchase, such as coupons, recipes, apps, songs, white papers, or brochures, for example.

TECH NOTES:

It is also important to count the number of download failures to learn if there is a problem with the file, a file transfer issue, or browser problem.

ARF COMMENTS:

Numbers of downloads can indicate the popularity of a giveaway to connect with consumers. Often the promotional materials are part of a program to spur another action. For this reason, it is important to compute ratios of what happened next. For example, was the app installed after being downloaded (registration data can be used), were further inquiries made after a white paper download (check the CRM database), or did sales of an ingredient increase after a certain recipe or usage was promoted? As these examples suggest, evaluating the impact of content downloads requires additional data from other corporate systems or resources.

When making downloads available to share, companies should have tracking capability. Sharing rates are another indicator of interest and also provide opportunities to communicate with or advertise to the person receiving the download.

CITED RESEARCH:

None

SEE ALSO:

Brochure Downloads
Coupon Downloads
Key Performance Indicator (KPI)
Recipe Downloads
Song Downloads

Key Performance Indicator (KPI)*

AUTHORITY:	MEDIA:	STAGE:	CATEGORY:	APPLIES TO:
Kaushik, Wikipedia	Paid	1. Capture	9. Ad Effectiveness	Website
	Owned	2. Connect		Social
	Earned	3. Close		Email
		4. Keep		Mobile

ANSWERS QUESTION:

What is a Key Performance Indicator?

DEFINITION:

A KPI is a key performance indicator that measures progress against one or more defined business objectives and strategy. Metrics, either quantitative or qualitative, are collected and evaluated to judge achievement of KPIs.

TECH NOTES:

None

ARF COMMENTS:

For example, an important key performance indicator for an online shop might be a sales increase of 15%. Conversion rate or average order value might be two metrics used to assess that KPI. For a website seeking to increase its user base while retaining prior visitors, the KPI could be a measured through a combination of New Visitors or Returning Visitors.

CITED RESEARCH:

None

SEE ALSO:

Like*

AUTHORITY:	MEDIA:	STAGE:	CATEGORY:	APPLIES TO:
Facebook, YouTube	Earned	2. Connect	6. Amplification/ Endorsement	Social

ANSWERS QUESTION:

How many Likes did our ad or content receive?

DEFINITION:

A "Like" is a way of registering enjoyment or interest of an ad or content without leaving a comment. Likes are typically registered by clicking a Like button that a site or network makes available.

The opposite of a Like is a "Dislike" or "Unlike."

TECH NOTES:

Analytics services frequently report Likes or their equivalents as a trend. Segmenting Likes can be very helpful to understanding which sources your Likes come from. Facebook, for example, offers sources such as, but not limited to, ads, search, mobile, or page.

ARF COMMENTS:

The Like button originated on Facebook, and is available today on a variety of social networks such as Pinterest, YouTube, Instagram, and LinkedIn. Some networks use variants. For example, Google + calls it a Plus One (+1); some others may use the "thumbs up/thumbs down" sign. Many social networks enable brand content to be Liked from outside their network. Likes work differently on Facebook than other networks because they are used to create stories that may show up in friends' News Feeds and, by doing so, increase the number of a brand's earned impressions and reach.

Likes are typically reported at a point in time. Analyzing trends in Total Likes, New Likes, and Unlikes (or their equivalents) may be helpful to understand the appeal of specific content and be used to optimize the type of content that brands make available.

Facebook Likes are frequently studied to determine their advertising and economic value to brands. In addition to counting Likes, it is also important to understand the motivations people have for Liking a particular brand. UPS (2013) researched people who Like retail brands in the US, discovering that 60% said it was because "the retailer occasionally offers special promotions to Facebook fans," and 47% said "the retailer incentivized me to 'Like' its Facebook page/application." These are the types of tactics that appeal to frequent brand users and/or deal seekers. Although retailing is just one category, research by Karen Nelson-Field (2012) shows that many brand Likers (fans) in a variety of categories are heavy users who are important for volume, but less so for brand growth. She offers that \ brands targeting growth should focus less on getting 'loved' and more on being seen by light buyers. comScore's studies in "The Power of Like" series (2012) reports that the earned media impressions that Likes generate from a brand's page increase Reach of the brand message and have an impact on purchase. This may be one way that brands can reach light buyers on Facebook. (See earned impressions for a discussion about their effectiveness.)

However, for global social networks such as Facebook, peoples' motivations for Liking can vary around the world. Adobe (2013) research shows that US consumers tend to Like brands they regularly buy or which offer promotions— supporting the UPS findings on retailers mentioned above. But consumers in the UK, France, Germany, Japan, South Korea, and Australia Like brands for another reason: They aspire to buy the brand.

To develop and execute successful strategy, brands need to move beyond merely counting Likes and gain insight into who is liking them, why, and where.

CITED RESEARCH:

Adobe (2013). Click Here: The State of Online Advertising (http://goo.gl/e75Z2).

comScore (2012). The Power of Like 2: How Social Marketing Works (http://goo.gl/eY4Os).

comScore (2012). The Power of Like Europe: How Social Marketing Works for Retail Brands (http://goo.gl/awndP).

comScore (2012). The Power of Like CPG (http://goo.gl/gCbnZ).

Nelson-Field, Karen et al. (2012). "What's Not to Like?" Can a Facebook Fan Base Give a Brand the Advertising Reach it Needs?" Journal of Advertising Research, Vol. 52, No. 2, pp. 262-269.

UPS (2013). UPS Pulse of the Online Shopper (https://thenewlogistics.ups.com/retail/comscoresurvey2013/. Registration required for download)

SEE ALSO:

Earned Impression

Likes - Page (Facebook)

Unlikes - Page (Facebook)

Likes—Page (Facebook)

AUTHORITY:	MEDIA:	STAGE:	CATEGORY:	APPLIES TO:
Facebook	Earned	2. Connect	5. Engagement/ Interaction	Social

ANSWERS QUESTION:

How many people Like our brand Page?

DEFINITION:

The number of unique people (Fans) who have clicked the Facebook "like" button on your brand Page. Liking is a way make a connection with a brand page.

Facebook allows people to "unlike" a page. Facebook's revised Page Insights reports Net Likes, which is the number of Likes minus the number of Unlkes.

When users connect to a Page, it will appear in their timelines and they will appear on the Page as a person who likes that Page. The Page will also be able to post content into their News Feed. A Like creates a story.

TECH NOTES:

Not all liking has to be done via explicit clicking on brand page. A user can like a brand via an ad or via the 'pages you may like' story that sometimes appears in a user's News Feed.

Facebook reports metrics at the Page and Post levels. It is very important to make sure that you use the right ones for your analytic task. Post-level metrics are typically reported on a lifetime basis, whereas Page-level metrics are typically reported for daily, weekly and 28-day periods.

ARF COMMENTS:

A "like" is considered a measure of brand engagement .

Brands on Facebook often seek to have large numbers of Likes in order to generate as large a reach as they can. Also important is understanding why people like brands. Researching people who Like retail brands, UPS (2013) discovered that 60% said it was because "the retailer occasionally offers special promotions to Facebook fans," and 47% said "the retailer incentivized me to "like" its Facebook page/application." These are the types of tactics that appeal to frequent brand users and/or deal seekers. Although retailing is just one category, research by Karen Nelson-Field (2012) shows that many brand Likers (fans) in a variety of categories are heavy users who are important for volume, but less so for brand growth. She offers that brands should focus less on getting 'loved' and more on being seen by light buyers. It is important to know your audience and their motivations for liking.

comScore's studies in "The Power of Like" series (2012) reports that the earned media impressions that Likes generate from a brand's page (they create "stories" that appear on Friend's newsfeeds), increase reach of the brand message and have an impact on purchase. This may be one way that brands can reach light buyers on Facebook. See Earned Impressions for a discussion about their effectiveness. On a cautionary note, marketplaces have emerged that enable brands to purchase Likes. For brands analyzing Likes and their value to the brand, it is very important to understand how the Likes were acquired.

Facebook offers star ratings to reviews to business pages. Star ratings may provide better indications of consumer sentiment towards a brand Page than a Like does, because the Like does not have gradations and people Like a page for many reasons including endorsement, support, interest, sympathy or even a feeling of dislike. Brands should keep tabs on the availability, use and requirements of the star rating system by following Facebook or the blogs and news sources that cover Facebook developments closely. This is important because the ratings on each Page may eventually become mandatory and people will consult them, just as they do for Yelp, Foursquare or Angie's List (Etherington 2013), and because ratings may require brands to consider and adopt new marketing strategies.

CITED RESEARCH:

comScore (2012). The Power of LIke 2: How Social Marketing Works (http://goo.gl/eY4Os).

comScore (2012). The Power of Like Europe: How Social Marketing Works for Retail Brands (http://goo.gl/awndP).

comScore (2012). The Power of Like CPG. (http://goo.gl/gCbnZ).

Etherington, Darrell (2013). A Like Is Not Enough: Facebook Tests Star Ratings Displayed On Pages (http://goo.gl/w09wnG).

Facebook (2013). Updating Page Insights. (http://goo.gl/X5f29E).

Facebook (2013). Like (definition). (http://goo.gl/gulSi).

Nelson-Field, Karen et al. (2012). What's Not to "Like?" Can a Facebook Fan Base Give a Brand the Advertising Reach it Needs? Journal of Advertising Research, Vol. 52, No. 2, pp. 262–269.

UPS (2013). UPS Pulse of the Online Shopper (https://thenewlogistics.ups.com/retail/comscoresurvey2013/. Registration required for download).

SEE ALSO:

Fan (Facebook)

New Likes—Page (Facebook)

Sponsored Story (Facebook)

Story (Facebook)

Unlikes—Page (Facebook)

Mentions*

AUTHORITY:	MEDIA:	STAGE:	CATEGORY:	APPLIES TO:
ARF	Earned	2. Connect	6. Amplification/ Endorsement	Social

ANSWERS QUESTION:

How many mentions did our brand receive in social media?

DEFINITION:

The total number of times a brand, company, or person was mentioned in social media, over a reporting period. Mentions may be included in tweets (@mentions), or written into posts, status updates, conversations, or comments.

Note: Not all mentions can be counted because access to them may be restricted due to privacy settings.

TECH NOTES:

Brands may use one or more tools to capture, aggregate, and analyze mentions. One key to meaningful counting is to define the search queries as precisely as possible. It is especially important to parse out the various meanings of words to increase the likelihood that only the mentions of interest to your brand are retrieved. For example, it's important to separate out the various meanings of common words that are also brand names, such as Dove, Dollar, or Visa, for example, and also to distinguish between similar sounding names, such as Carmax (automobiles) and Carmex (the blister cream). As mentioned above it is vital to be as complete as possible, making sure that variants and common misspellings are accounted for. Not doing so risks missing some number of mentions (Rappaport 2011).

ARF COMMENTS:

The counting of brand mentions, and those of competing brands, is common for companies or agencies involved in competitive analysis or reputation management. Such counts may be used to compute impressions or share of voice measures.

The value of mention counts by themselves is arguable. Mentions take on more meaning when placed in the context of brand objectives, the contexts in which they appear in, the social activities in which they are expressed, the people involved (such as influencers), the sentiment around them, and their reach and frequency (comScore (2011).

CITED RESEARCH:

comScore (2011). The Power of Like: How Brands Reach and Influence Fans through Social Marketing. (http://goo.gl/Mi46Y).
Rappaport, Stephen D. (2011). Listen First. Turning Social Media Conversations into Business Advantage. Hoboken: John Wiley & Sons.

SEE ALSO:
Comments
Reviews

Mobile App Downloads

AUTHORITY:	**MEDIA:**	**STAGE:**	**CATEGORY:**	**APPLIES TO:**
Webtrends	Owned	2. Connect	7. Conversion	Mobile

ANSWERS QUESTION:

How many times was our app downloaded?

DEFINITION:

Count of the number of times a specific app was downloaded during a reporting period.

TECH NOTES:

None

ARF COMMENTS:

The total number of downloaded mobile apps can indicate the upper limit of active users an app can have at any one time, according to Webtrends (Rickson 2010).

This metric is helpful in understanding the appeal of an app. As is the case with many metrics, see the Notes for Page Views, Visitors (Unique Visitors), and Time Spent on Site, for example; analyzing a group of measures jointly can lead to valuable insights. For example, comparing the ratios of Downloads to New App Users with the Active User Rate can reveal if app usage is building over time or if it is declining or being abandoned.

Experienced mobile apps marketers state that generating brand awareness for an app and encouraging downloads requires the app to be one of the most free or paid apps, and to be in the Top 25 for its category. Certain categories, like FMCG, have many apps from many companies, so standing out is difficult. For this reason, apps often need to be advertised and promoted (eMarketer 2010).

Downloads are a common conversion action on many Sites. Analyzing downloads as part of a conversion funnel may help brands understand their contribution to a larger brand or site goal.

CITED RESEARCH:

Rickson, E. (2010). "Top Metrics for Mobile Apps: Measure What Matters" (http://goo.gl/n6NfV).

eMarketer (2010). "Best Practices: Mobile Marketing & App Strategies for Food Brands" (http://goo.gl/Wb7PC).

SEE ALSO:

Active User Rate

Unique App Users

Mobile Browser Version

AUTHORITY:	MEDIA:	STAGE:	CATEGORY:	APPLIES TO:
comScore	Owned	1. Capture	2. Audience/Traffic	Mobile

ANSWERS QUESTION:

Which mobile browsers were used to visit our mobile website?

DEFINITION:

The mobile browser version used by the browser, for example, Safari 5.x, Android Browser 2.x, Opera Mini 6.x.

TECH NOTES:

None

ARF COMMENTS:

Mobile Browser Version counts and their percent distribution reveal the popularity of mobile browsers accessing a site. These metrics may be useful for optimizing the mobile website experience for users with different browsers and capabilities, such as that which is done for convention websites. Trending the data over time can reveal patterns suggesting site improvements or changes tied to shifts in browser usage.

CITED RESEARCH:

None

SEE ALSO:

Phone Brand
Phone Type
Mobile Operating System

Mobile Operating System

AUTHORITY:	MEDIA:	STAGE:	CATEGORY:	APPLIES TO:
comScore	Owned	1. Capture	2. Audience/Traffic	Mobile

ANSWERS QUESTION:

Which mobile operating systems accessed our mobile website?

DEFINITION:

The type of mobile phone operating system used by a mobile phone, for example, iOS, Android, or Windows Mobile.

TECH NOTES:

None

ARF COMMENTS:

Mobile phone operating systems counts and their percent distribution reveal the popularity of operating systems for accessing a site. These metrics may be useful for optimizing the mobile website experience for users with different devices, operating systems and their capabilities. Trending the data over time can reveal patterns suggesting site improvements or changes tied to shifts in mobile operating systems usage.

CITED RESEARCH:

None

SEE ALSO:

Phone Brand
Phone Type
Mobile Browser Version

Mouseover

AUTHORITY:	MEDIA:	STAGE:	CATEGORY:	APPLIES TO:
IAB	Paid	2. Connect	5. Engagement/ Interaction	Website Social

MOBILE ANSWERS QUESTION:

How long did visitors mouseover or hover on our ad?

DEFINITION:

The process by which a user places his/her mouse over a media object, without clicking. The mouse may need to remain still for a specified amount of time to initiate some actions. Also called Hover. Usually measured for rich media ads as time spent interacting.

TECH NOTES:

Often presented in rich media reports that list average interaction times.

ARF COMMENTS:

CITED RESEARCH:

None

SEE ALSO:

Click

Rich Media Interactive Impressions

Negative Feedback from Users—Post (Facebook)

AUTHORITY:	MEDIA:	STAGE:	CATEGORY:	APPLIES TO:
Facebook	Earned	2. Connect	5. Engagement/ Interaction	Social

ANSWERS QUESTION:

How many unique people expressed a negative action regarding our post?

DEFINITION:

The number of unique people who have given negative feedback to your page, such as hiding it, unliking it, or marking it as spam.

Note: Facebook also reports the number of times people took a negative action on your post (Post Negative Feedback).

TECH NOTES:

Facebook offers segmentation for both metrics by the type of negative feedback. Facebook reports metrics at the Page and Post levels. It is very important to make sure that you use the right ones for your analytic task. Post-level metrics are typically reported on a lifetime basis, whereas Page-level metrics are typically reported for daily, weekly, and 28-day periods.

ARF COMMENTS:

Approximately 1 out of 50 post views gets a negative response (Kanter 2013). Understanding negative feedback can be helpful to optimize Post content. Detecting patterns of hiding indicates the types of content that users are apparently not interested in, and spam patterns indicate those that are less desired or irrelevant. Negative Feedback may affect your ads. Facebook states that "Ads that receive excessive negative feedback may be removed. Excessive negative feedback or poor performance is often a sign that an ad is poorly targeted, contains suggestive images and language, or relates to sensitive topics."

CITED RESEARCH:

Kanter, Beth (2013). How to Use Negative Feedback on Facebook to Improve Your Content Strategy (http://goo.gl/vk05E).

SEE ALSO:

Negative Feedback from Users—Page (Facebook)
Unfollow/Unsubscribe

Negative Feedback from Users—Page (Facebook)

AUTHORITY:	MEDIA:	STAGE:	CATEGORY:	APPLIES TO:
Facebook	Earned	2. Connect	5. Engagement/ Interaction	Social

ANSWERS QUESTION:

How many unique people generated a negative action on our Page?

DEFINITION:

The number of unique people who have given negative feedback to your Page, such as unliking or hiding, for a reporting period.

Note: Facebook also reports the number of times people took a negative action on your page (Page Negative Feedback).

TECH NOTES:

Facebook offers segmentation for both metrics by the type of negative feedback. Facebook reports metrics at the Page and Post levels. It is very important to make sure that you use the right ones for your analytic task. Post-level metrics are typically reported on a lifetime basis, whereas Page-level metrics are typically reported for daily, weekly, and 28-day periods.

ARF COMMENTS:

Four types of actions count as negative feedback:
- Hide: hides a single specific post from the user's newsfeed
- Hide All: hides all the posts by that page from the user's newsfeed. This used to be known as "unsubscribing."
- Unlike Page: "unfan" the page
- Report spam: user thinks your page is spam

Approximately 1 out of 50 post views gets a negative response. Brands experiencing negative feedback are wise to find the reasons why and correct them in order to optimize the content quality, reach, and effectiveness of their pages and posts (Kanter 2013). This metric is useful for optimizing content and content strategy. Learning which posts or content types lead people to express negative feedback enables brands to fix or eliminate problematic materials, potentially stemming defections and reducing interaction rates. Negative Feedback may affect your ads. Facebook states that "Ads that receive excessive negative feedback may be removed. Excessive negative feedback or poor performance is often a sign that an ad is poorly targeted, contains suggestive images and language, or relates to sensitive topics."

CITED RESEARCH:

Kanter, Beth (2013). How to Use Negative Feedback on Facebook to Improve Your Content Strategy (http://goo.gl/vk05E).

SEE ALSO:

Unfollow/Unsubscribe
Unlikes—Page (Facebook)
Unsubscribe Rate—Page (Facebook)

New App Users*

AUTHORITY:	MEDIA:	STAGE:	CATEGORY:	APPLIES TO:
Webtrends	Owned	2. Connect	2. Audience/Traffic	Mobile

ANSWERS QUESTION:

How many new app users used our mobile app?

DEFINITION:

Count of the number of users that first used a specific app during a reporting period.

TECH NOTES:

None

ARF COMMENTS:

This metric is helpful in understanding the appeal of an app and also for gauging if the app audience is growing or shrinking. As is the case with many metrics [see the Notes for Page Views, Visitors (Unique Visitors) and Time Spent on Site, for example], analyzing a group of measures jointly can lead to valuable insights. For example, comparing New App Users with the Active User Rate can reveal if app usage is building audience reach over time, stagnant, declining, or being abandoned.

CITED RESEARCH:

Rickson, E. (2010). "Top Metrics for Mobile Apps: Measure What Matters" (http://goo.gl/n6NfV).

SEE ALSO:

Active User Rate
Mobile App Downloads
Unique App Users

New Likes—Page (Facebook)

AUTHORITY:	MEDIA:	STAGE:	CATEGORY:	APPLIES TO:
Facebook	Earned	2. Connect	2. Audience/Traffic	Social

ANSWERS QUESTION:

How many new Likes did our page generate?

DEFINITION:

The number of new unique people who have Liked your Page.

Note: People who Like a Page are called Fans.

TECH NOTES:

Facebook Page Insights provides demographic segmentation to understand where the Likes are coming from, such as Gender, Age, Country, City, Language, and segmentation by sources, including On Page, Timeline, Mobile, On Hover, and Ads.

ARF COMMENTS:

▌ See Likes—Page (Facebook) for discussion.

CITED RESEARCH:

None

SEE ALSO:

Likes—Page (Facebook)
Unlikes—Page (Facebook)

New Visitor

AUTHORITY:	MEDIA:	STAGE:	CATEGORY:	APPLIES TO:
comScore, Digital Analytics Association, Google, Millward Brown Digital	Owned	1. Capture	2. Audience/Traffic	Website Social Mobile

ANSWERS QUESTION:

How many Unique Visitors came to our site for the first time during a reporting period?

DEFINITION:

The number of Unique Visitors with activity including a first-ever visit to a site during a reporting period.

Note: Yahoo! calls these "First Time Visitors." comScore calls them "New Browsers."

TECH NOTES:

According to the Digital Analytics Association, "A visitor can only be counted as a New Visitor" if it is the first time to your site. It is not possible for a visitor be counted as both a New Visitor and Return Visitor in the same reporting period. Some tool providers may define New Visitors differently. Ask your tool provider how these metrics are computed."

See Visitors (Unique Visitors) for more technical detail.

ARF COMMENTS:

New Visitors can be useful to gauge the effectiveness of an ad or content for driving traffic to a site, landing page, or destination. Comparing the behavior of New Visitors to Repeat Visitors or Returning Visitors can reveal patterns that enable site owners to optimize the experience for each group and conversion rates for actions, such as registration, downloads, or transactions. Additionally, comparing trends in New Visitors to Repeat Visitors or Returning Visitors may reveal if the site is building audience and expanding reach, and its abilities to stimulate additional visits. Interpreting the trends must be done within the context of business goals and strategy.

Brands that have a blog as part of their social media efforts should keep in mind that most corporate blog readers are first-time visitors who are delivered through organic search engine results. Many have very small core readerships. For this reason, corporate blogs should be optimized for first-time visitors (Compendium 2010).

CITED RESEARCH:

Compendium (2010). Corporate Blogging and Social Media Trends Survey. Reported by MarketingProfs.com (http://goo.gl/d5VWN).

SEE ALSO:

New Visitor (Percent)
Repeat Visitors
Return Visitor
Unique Visitors (Unique Browsers)

New Visitor (Percent)*

AUTHORITY:	MEDIA:	STAGE:	CATEGORY:	APPLIES TO:
Google, Digital Analytics Association	Owned	1. Capture	2. Audience/Traffic	Website Social Mobile

ANSWERS QUESTION:

What percentage of our visitors are new visitors?

DEFINITION:

The percentage of Unique Visitors with activity including a first-ever visit to a site during a reporting period.

Note: Yahoo! calls these "First Time Visitors."

TECH NOTES:

According to the Digital Analytics Association, "A visitor can only be counted as a New Visitor" if it is the first time to your site. It is not possible for a visitor be counted as both a New Visitor and Return Visitor in the same reporting period. Some tool providers may define new visitors differently. Ask your tool provider how these metrics are computed."

Cookie deletion may overstate the number of new visitors over a reporting period. See the entry for Cookie for a detailed discussion.

ARF COMMENTS:

The metric may be useful to gauge the effectiveness of an ad or content for driving traffic to a site, landing page, or destination. Comparing the percentages of New Visitors to Repeat Visitors or Returning Visitors can reveal patterns that enable site owners to optimize the experience for each group and conversion rates for actions, such as registration, downloads, or transactions.

CITED RESEARCH:

None

SEE ALSO:

New Visitor
Unique Visitors (Unique Browsers)

Organic Impressions—Posts (Facebook)

AUTHORITY:	MEDIA:	STAGE:	CATEGORY:	APPLIES TO:
Facebook	Earned	1. Capture	1. Advertising	Social

ANSWERS QUESTION:

How many times were our posts seen organically in news feeds, tickers, or on the page itself?

DEFINITION:

The number of times your post was seen in News Feed or ticker or on visits to your page. These impressions can be by people who have liked your page. Organic impressions are unpaid impressions.

TECH NOTES:

Facebook reports metrics at the Page and Post levels. It is very important to make sure that you use the right ones for your analytic task. Post-level metrics are typically reported on a lifetime basis, whereas Page-level metrics are typically reported for daily, weekly, and 28-day periods.

ARF COMMENTS:

Organic Impressions are a type of earned impression. See the entry on Earned Impressions for current research. Regarding Facebook it is important to note that Facebook's EdgeRank algorithm has reduced organic impressions in many cases prompting brands to utilize or increase paid advertising to generate targeted levels of impressions. Brands should understand the differences between paid and organic impressions on Facebook, evaluate how your brand posts are performing, and how to optimize them to achieve your impression objectives.

CITED RESEARCH:

None

SEE ALSO:

Total Impressions—Page (Facebook)

Organic Reach—Page (Facebook)

AUTHORITY:	MEDIA:	STAGE:	CATEGORY:	APPLIES TO:
Facebook	Earned Owned	1. Capture	2. Audience/Traffic	Social

ANSWERS QUESTION:

How many people saw any of our content organically on Facebook?

DEFINITION:

Organic reach is the number of unique people, fans or non-fans, who saw any content published by your brand page through unpaid distribution, over a reporting period. Organic reach is concerned only with unpaid distribution.

TECH NOTES:

Stories may or may not appear in a user's News Feed because of an optimization algorithm called Edge Rank. This computation takes into account many factors, including but not limited to, the age of the post, the type of interaction (such as Like or Comment), and information about each person. Facebook changes Edge Rank from time to time. Brands should keep up with changes to determine impacts to their pages and posts.

Facebook reports metrics at the Page and Post levels. It is very important to make sure that you use the right ones for your analytic task. Post-level metrics are typically reported on a lifetime basis, whereas Page-level metrics are typically reported for daily, weekly, and 28-day periods.

ARF COMMENTS:

Facebook's EdgeRank has reduced organic reach in many cases prompting brands to utilize or increase paid advertising to generate targeted levels of reach. The key takeaway is to understand the differences between paid and organic reach on Facebook, how your brand pages are performing, and how to optimize them to achieve your reach objectives. Brands are competing for their share in users' news feeds and every one should give themselves the best chances for appearing in them (Facebook Business 2013; Facebook for Business 2014).

CITED RESEARCH:

Facebook (2013). Updating Page Insights (http://goo.gl/X5f29E).
Facebook Business (2013). What Increased Content Sharing Means for Businesses (http://goo.gl/XRZokL).
Facebook for Business (2014). Organic Reach on Facebook: Your Questions Answered (http://goo.gl/sGblSG)

SEE ALSO:

Reach
Total Reach—Page (Facebook)

Organic Reach—Post (Facebook)

AUTHORITY:	MEDIA:	STAGE:	CATEGORY:	APPLIES TO:
Facebook	Earned Owned	1. Capture	2. Audience/Traffic	Social

ANSWERS QUESTION:

What is the organic reach of our page post?

DEFINITION:

Organic reach is the number of unique people who saw a page post in their news feeds, ticker, or on your page's Wall.

TECH NOTES:

Stories may or may not appear in a user's News Feed because of an optimization algorithm called Edge Rank. This computation takes into account many factors, including but not limited to, the age of the post, the type of interaction (such as Like or Comment), and information about each person. Facebook changes Edge Rank from time to time. For many brands organic reach levels have been declining. Brands should keep up with changes to determine impacts to their pages and posts and adjust their strategies for achieving targeted reach levels as appropriate.

Facebook reports metrics at the Page and Post levels. It is very important to make sure that you use the right ones for your analytic task. Post-level metrics are typically reported on a lifetime basis, whereas Page-level metrics are typically reported for daily, weekly, and 28-day periods.

ARF COMMENTS:

▌ See Organic Reach—Page (Facebook) for discussion.

CITED RESEARCH:

None

SEE ALSO:

Organic Reach—Page (Facebook)
Total Reach—Post (Facebook)

Page

AUTHORITY:	MEDIA:	STAGE:	CATEGORY:	APPLIES TO:
Digital Analytics Association	Paid Owned Earned	1. Capture	1. Advertising	Website Social Mobile

ANSWERS QUESTION:

What is a Page?

DEFINITION:

A page is an analyst-definable unit of content. It specifies which types of files or file requests count as a page.

TECH NOTES:

According to the Digital Analytics Association, "Most web analytics tools allow the client to specify what types of files or requests qualify as a "page." Certain technologies including (but not limited to) Flash, AJAX, media files, downloads, documents, and PDFs do not follow the typical page paradigm but may be definable as pages (and their access counted as a page view) in specific tools.

ARF COMMENTS:

CITED RESEARCH:

None

SEE ALSO:

Hit

Page View

Page (Facebook, LinkedIn)

AUTHORITY:	MEDIA:	STAGE:	CATEGORY:	APPLIES TO:
Facebook, LinkedIn	Owned	1. Capture	1. Advertising	Social

ANSWERS QUESTION:

What is a Facebook Page or LinkedIn Company Page?

DEFINITION:

Facebook Pages are for businesses, organizations and brands to share their stories and connect with people. Page owners can customize pages by adding content such as apps, posting stories, and hosting events.

LinkedIn Corporate Pages are for businesses or organizations that describe their brands, products and services, or job opportunities.

TECH NOTES:

Only the official representative of an organization, business, celebrity, or band is permitted to create a Facebook Page. Similarly LinkedIn Company Pages have admins.

ARF COMMENTS:

Brands use Pages to create a presence within Facebook or LinkedIn.

Facebook measures are computed at the Page Level, which reflects activity on the Page, and at the Post Level, which reflects activity generated by a specific entry on the page. Page activity is reported through Facebook Page Insights and through a provided data export facility. Insights reports such metrics as Likes, Reach, Number of Posts, Followers and People Engaged. The data export contains these metrics and many more, such as Post Consumptions and Lifetime Negative Feedback. A complete guide to Page Insights is available (Facebook 2013). Data are available to Page Admins.

LinkedIn Company Pages offer analytics, too. "Follower Insights" reports measures such as followers, impressions, and new followers in the last seven days. "Page Insights" shows information such as page views, Unique Visitors, page clicks over the last seven days, page views by tab, and page visitor demographics. A complete list is available on LinkedIn (2013). Data are available to Page Admins.

Both companies are continually developing their metrics; it is important to stay up to date with the changes, improvements, and additions they offer by consulting Facebook and Facebook commenters, such as TechCrunch.

Facebook offers five-point star ratings and reviews for business pages. These ratings, previously available only on Facebook's mobile site, should "encourage more people to rate a business, making it eligible to appear in News Feed and help others discover a business they didn't know about previously. For businesses themselves, this also leads to greater brand awareness" Adding star ratings may also enable Facebook to compete more directly with Angie's List, Foursquare, and Yelp for finding local businesses and evaluating them from the ratings and comments consumers leave. Additionally, star ratings may provide finer sentiment information than the Facebook Like (Etherington 2013).

CITED RESEARCH:

Etherington, Darrell (2013). A Like Is Not Enough: Facebook Tests Star Ratings Displayed On Pages (http://goo.gl/w09wnG).

Facebook (2013.). About Page Insights (http://goo.gl/53U4Z).

LinkedIn (2013). Follower and Page Insights for Company Pages (http://goo.gl/Lqx2l).

SEE ALSO:

Page

Page Post (Facebook)

Page Exit Rate

AUTHORITY:	MEDIA:	STAGE:	CATEGORY:	APPLIES TO:
Yahoo!, Google	Owned	2. Connect	3. Site Navigation/Site Performance	Website Social Mobile

ANSWERS QUESTION:

Which pages did visitors exit from?

DEFINITION:

Page Exit Rate is the percentage of visitors leaving a site after visiting a specific page. In mobile, this may be called Screen Exit Rate.

Note: Page Exit Rate and Bounce Rate, both of which measure the pages viewed to leave a site, are often confused.

TECH NOTES:

To understand the difference between exit and bounce rates for a particular page in your site, Google states that three things need to be kept in mind:

1. For all page views to the page, the exit rate is the percentage that were the last in the session.
2. For all sessions that start with the page, bounce rate is the percentage that were the only one of the session.
3. The bounce rate calculation for a page is based only on visits that start with that page.

ARF COMMENTS:

Page Exit Rate is often thought of as identifying the pages that prompt visitors to leave a site, which can be considered problem pages. As Kaushik (2010) points out, the analytic issue is that everyone has to leave a site, and there's no way of knowing from this metric if their visit was a success or a failure. For example, if someone purchases a product and then goes to another page and leaves, that is not a failure of the last page. Bounce rate, he argues, is better for diagnosing problems because it measures the people who visit a particular page, do not click or interact with it, and then leave.

However, Page Exit Rate can be helpful for some sites, typically e-commerce sites, that are organized by one or more conversion funnels. Studying the exit rates of key pages along the funnel path may reveal pages that are detracting from reaching the conversion goal. That rate is usually called the "abandonment rate."

CITED RESEARCH:

Kaushik, Avinash (2010). Web Analytics 2.0. Sybex.

SEE ALSO:

Abandonment Rate
Bounce Rate (Website or Social Network)
Conversion Funnel

Page Load Times*

AUTHORITY:	**MEDIA:**	**STAGE:**	**CATEGORY:**	**APPLIES TO:**
Google	Owned	1. Capture	3. Site Navigation/Site Performance	Website Social Mobile

ANSWERS QUESTION:

How long does it take a specific page to load?

DEFINITION:

Page load time (latency) measures how quickly pages load in different browsers, and often by geographic areas, traffic sources, visitor type, operating system or screen resolution. Commonly reported as an average over a reporting period.

TECH NOTES:

None

ARF COMMENTS:

Analyzing Page Load times allows you to identify which pages load the fastest and which ones are slower. Segmenting analysis of Page Load Times by geographic areas, traffic sources, visitor type, operating system, plugin, or screen resolution may provide additional insight into the user experience. Correlating Page Load Times with events of interest, such as exits or conversions, may help identify problem pages that can be optimized.

Long loading times contribute to page abandonment and affects shopper behavior. Pages with long load times decrease repeat shopping, site loyalty, and customer satisfaction. A one-second delay in page response can reduce conversions by 7% (KissMetrics 2012). Slow loading times is one of the "most serious issues a brand's customer encounters" when interacting on a mobile device" (Charlton 2013).

CITED RESEARCH:

Charlton, Graham (2013). Companies Struggling with Mobile Optimisation: report (http://goo.gl/FJjrB).
KissMetrics (2012). How Loading Time Affects Your Bottom Line (http://goo.gl/hvGDI).

SEE ALSO:

Page View

Page Post (Facebook)

AUTHORITY:	MEDIA:	STAGE:	CATEGORY:	APPLIES TO:
Facebook	Owned	1. Capture	1. Advertising	Social

ANSWERS QUESTION:

What is a Facebook Page Post?

DEFINITION:

A Page Post is content that is added to a Facebook Page. Content can include text, status updates, links, photos, videos, file uploads, event, questions, and any other type that Facebook allows. Facebook Page Posts are considered sponsored content.

TECH NOTES:

Facebook reports metrics at the Page and Post levels. It is very important to make sure that you use the right ones for your analytic task. Post-level metrics are typically reported on a lifetime basis, whereas Page-level metrics are typically reported for daily, weekly, and 28-day periods.

ARF COMMENTS:

Facebook recently upgraded the ability for page owners to target Page Posts, TechCrunch reports. In the past, posts could only be targeted to people who Liked a page, their location, and languages.

Targeting refinements include targeting by such factors as, but not limited to, gender, age, Interests, relationship status, education, connections, Likes, birthdays, and many other characteristics.

These new targeting criteria enable page owners to display more relevant posts by tailoring content to different people who Like a page. For example, Chevrolet might push their econo-cars to college students but offer discounts on SUVs to people in their 30s and 40s.

CITED RESEARCH:

TechCrunch (2012). Facebook Unleashes Powerful Marketing Tool: Page Post Targeting By Age, Gender, Likes, and More (http://goo.gl/ERh3J).

SEE ALSO:

Page (Facebook, LinkedIn)

Page View (Facebook)

AUTHORITY:	MEDIA:	STAGE:	CATEGORY:	APPLIES TO:
Facebook	Owned	2. Connect	4. Media Consumption	Social

ANSWERS QUESTION:

How many times did our page display on a particular day?

DEFINITION:

Page View on Facebook is the number of times each of your Page tabs (ex: Timeline, Info Tab) was viewed on each day.

Note: Facebook also reports Page Views from Unique Users - which is the number of users logged into Facebook on each day, and from users who are logged out.

TECH NOTES:

None

ARF COMMENTS:

Facebook Pages are defined somewhat differently from website pages. Web pages are defined by analysts; what constitutes a page may differ from site to site. Facebook Pages are treated as whole units.

CITED RESEARCH:

None

SEE ALSO:

Page View

Page View, Logged-in (Facebook)

Page View, Logged-in (Facebook)

AUTHORITY:	MEDIA:	STAGE:	CATEGORY:	APPLIES TO:
Facebook	Owned	2. Connect	4. Media Consumption	Social

ANSWERS QUESTION:

How many people who viewed our page were logged-in to Facebook at the time?

DEFINITION:

Daily Page Views from users logged into Facebook, provided for Total Page Views and Unique Users.

TECH NOTES:

Facebook Pages are defined somewhat differently from website pages. Web pages are defined by analysts; what constitutes a page may differ from site to site. Facebook Pages are treated as whole units.

ARF COMMENTS:

In most cases, the number of Page Views from logged-in Unique Users will be less than the number of Total Page Views of logged-in Facebook users. This metric may be helpful when comparing the behavior or logged-in vs. non-logged-in users for optimizing the brand page.

CITED RESEARCH:

None

SEE ALSO:

Page View

Page View*

AUTHORITY:	MEDIA:	STAGE:	CATEGORY:	APPLIES TO:
Digital Analytics Association, Google, comScore, Nielsen, IAB, Yahoo!	Paid Owned	2. Connect	4. Media Consumption	Website Social Mobile

ANSWERS QUESTION:

Which pages on our site are viewed most often?

DEFINITION:

The number of times a page was viewed. In mobile, a Page View is often called a Screen View.

Page Views are counted each time a page is displayed, which may be its first time, a repeat, such as by clicking forward or backward buttons or a link, or from a user's local cache.

TECH NOTES:

A page is defined by an analytics package or analysts who "specify what types of files or file requests count as a page." Counting of page views may be distorted by automated systems that click links and generate views. When counting page views, make certain that automated activity is filtered out, otherwise inaccuracies will result. Additionally, some newer display technologies and some file types "do not follow the typical page paradigm, but may be definable as pages in specific [vendor] tools." Check with your analytics supplier to learn how to make counting page views as accurate as possible (Digital Analytics Association).

comScore provides additional Page View metrics that reveal information about Page display. These include: First Page View—the first page requested after a person enters your site, and Repeated Page View—the second, third, fourth time, etc., that a page was requested within the same visit by using navigation links within your site or the Back, Forward, and Refresh button on the web browser.

Some platforms, such as Facebook, cache preview images for applications, which can mean that page views are not counted until a user clicks through to an application canvas page.

ARF COMMENTS:

Page or Screen Views are generally considered a top-level measure of the popularity of website content and the ability of people to navigate a site. Many sites, especially those with CPM advertising models, seek to increase the number of page views because they potentially expose more ads to site visitors. However, there are times when minimizing the number of page views is desirable, such as when giving product support or closing sales transactions, for example. Interpreting page views must be done in the context of the business issue and decisions that need to be made.

CITED RESEARCH:

None

SEE ALSO:

Average Page Views Per Visit
Cost per Thousand (CPM) Impressions

Page Views per Visit*

AUTHORITY:	MEDIA:	STAGE:	CATEGORY:	APPLIES TO:
Google, Digital Analytics Association, Yahoo!	Owned	2. Connect	4. Media Consumption	Website Social Mobile

ANSWERS QUESTION:

What is the average number of pages viewed each visit, over a specific time frame?

DEFINITION:

The average number of page views in a reporting period divided by number of visits in the same reporting period. In mobile applications, Page Views are often called Screen Views.

TECH NOTES:

A page is defined by an analytics package or analyst who "specify what types of files or file requests count as a page." Counting of page views may be distorted by automated systems that click links and generate views. When counting page views, make certain that automated activity is filtered out, otherwise inaccuracies will result. Additionally, some newer display technologies and some file types "do not follow the typical page paradigm, but may be definable as pages in specific [vendor] tools" (Digital Analytics Association). Check with your analytics supplier(s) to learn how to make counting page views as accurate and comparable as possible.

ARF COMMENTS:

Especially important with this metric, and other ratio measures Kaushik explains (2010), is to look at trends in the underlying numbers. Even though Page Views per Visit may seem relatively constant over time, the ratio may mask changing fundamentals, such as increases or decreases in the number of Visits and/or Page Views. The only way to know that is to see the raw data. Check your analytics package to learn how to get at them.

In early Internet days, Page Views were considered a measure of audience engagement. That view is largely obsolete today because of the rise of dynamic nature of pages, their ability to create rich experiences, and interest in the interactions visitors have with content. Observers like Kaushik and Belkin (2008) have opined that "the Page View is dead" for these very reasons and that the industry will move on to metrics that better measure the user experience. While that does not seem to be the case yet, considering alternatives may be worthwhile for brands offering a less page-centric experience.

CITED RESEARCH:

Kaushik, Avinash (2010). Web Analytics 2.0. Sybex.

Belkin, Matt (2008). Measuring Visitor Engagement Take Two: Unique Visitors and Page Views. Adobe Digital Marketing Blog (http://goo.gl/sDRFx).

SEE ALSO:

Page View

Visit (Session)

Paid Impression—Page (Facebook)

AUTHORITY:	MEDIA:	STAGE:	CATEGORY:	APPLIES TO:
Facebook	Paid	1. Capture	1. Advertising	Social

ANSWERS QUESTION:
How many Paid Impressions did our ads generate on Facebook?

DEFINITION:
Count of the number of times your ad was served on Facebook, for a reporting period. On Facebook mobile apps, an ad is counted as served the first time it's viewed. On all other Facebook interfaces, an ad is served the first time it's placed in someone's News Feed or each time it's placed in the right column of Facebook.

TECH NOTES:
According to Facebook's Patrick Kemp (2013) not all paid impressions on Facebook have an associated brand page. Ad units shown in users' News Feeds must have an associated brand page, but right-hand-side ad units may or may not have an associated brand page.

Facebook reports metrics at the Page and Post levels. It is very important to make sure that you use the right ones for your analytic task. Post-level metrics are typically reported on a lifetime basis, whereas Page-level metrics are typically reported for daily, weekly, and 28-day periods.

ARF COMMENTS:
In late 2012, Facebook research of 50 packaged goods advertisers revealed that ad impressions, not clicks, stimulate offline sales. Partnering with loyalty card database firm Datalogix, they showed that 99 percent of sales were from view-throughs—people who saw ads but didn't interact with them. That finding was consistent with a Nielsen study which showed that there's virtually no correlation between clicks on ads and either brand metrics or offline sales. However, focusing on clicks may make sense for direct-response campaigns where there is a clear conversion funnel.

The Facebook research also illustrated the value of reaching a broad audience and controlling frequency, confirming points made separately by Ehrenberg-Bass research (2012). When reach expanded and frequency was optimized at lower levels, ROI improved between 70% and 40%, respectively (Ha 2012; Chacos 2012).

The applicability of these findings for non-CPG brands has not yet been demonstrated, although that is likely to change as more studies are conducted. But they do support the strategy of continuous reach and lower frequency in general.

CITED RESEARCH:
Chacos, Brad (2012). Facebook: For Ads, Clicks Aren't All That Counts (http://goo.gl/t78q5).

Ha, Anthony (2012). Facebook's Brad Smallwood Offers More Data on Ad Effectiveness, Says Datalogix Partnership Isn't a Privacy Risk (http://goo.gl/Qm3UU).

Kemp, Patrick (2013). Personal communication.

Nelson-Field, Karen et al. (2012). What's Not to "Like?" Can a Facebook Fan Base Give a Brand the Advertising Reach it Needs? Ehrenberg-Bass Institute, J. Advertising Research, Vol. 52, No. 2, 2012.

Facebook for Business (2014). Organic Reach on Facebook: Your Questions Answered (http://goo.gl/sGbISG)

SEE ALSO:
Ad Impression
Paid Reach-Post (Facebook)
Social Impressions (Facebook)
Sponsored Story (Facebook)

Paid Impressions—Post (Facebook)

AUTHORITY:	MEDIA:	STAGE:	CATEGORY:	APPLIES TO:
Facebook	Paid	1. Capture	1. Advertising	Social

ANSWERS QUESTION:

How many impressions did our paid advertising generate?

DEFINITION:

The number of impressions of your page post through paid distribution, over its lifetime. People may see multiple impressions of the same post. On Facebook mobile apps, an ad is counted as served the first time it's viewed. On all other Facebook interfaces, an ad is served the first time it's placed in someone's News Feed or each time it's placed in the right column of Facebook.

Note: Facebook offers a related metric, Unique Paid Post Impressions, that reports the number of people who saw your Page Post through paid distribution.

TECH NOTES:

Facebook reports metrics at the Page and Post levels. It is very important to make sure that you use the right ones for your analytic task. Post-level metrics are typically reported on a lifetime basis, whereas Page-level metrics are typically reported for daily, weekly, and 28-day periods.

ARF COMMENTS:

▌ See Paid Impressions—Page for discussion.

CITED RESEARCH:

None

SEE ALSO:

Paid Impression—Page (Facebook)
Paid Reach-Post (Facebook)
Total Impressions— Post (Facebook)

Paid Reach—Page (Facebook)

AUTHORITY:	MEDIA:	STAGE:	CATEGORY:	APPLIES TO:
Facebook	Paid	1. Capture	2. Audience/Traffic	Social

ANSWERS QUESTION:

What is the number of people reached by our Facebook page's ad?

DEFINITION:

The total number of unique people who were shown your post as a result of ads, for a reporting period.

TECH NOTES:

Facebook provides measures at the Page and Post levels. Make sure that you are using the one most appropriate for your analytic needs. Post-level metrics are typically reported on a lifetime basis, whereas Page-level metrics are typically reported for daily, weekly, and 28-day periods.

ARF COMMENTS:

comScore and Facebook research indicates that paid Facebook ads provide opportunities for brands to extend the reach of their socially-enabled brand content "significantly beyond the audience they are able to reach with organic media alone." They also found that brands with the largest fan bases (greater than 20 million fans) benefit "significantly" from using ads to extend reach. Lastly, their research showed that the paid audiences reached on Facebook represent segments that are active in-category buyers and shoppers (Polich et al. 2012).

CITED RESEARCH:

Polich, Adrienne et al (2012). Understanding Paid and Earned Reach on Facebook (http://goo.gl/HLrCe).

SEE ALSO:

Paid Impressions-Page (Facebook)
Reach*

Paid Reach—Post (Facebook)

AUTHORITY:	MEDIA:	STAGE:	CATEGORY:	APPLIES TO:
Facebook	Paid	1. Capture	2. Audience/Traffic	Social

ANSWERS QUESTION:

What is the number of people reached by our Facebook post?

DEFINITION:

The number of unique people who received impressions of your page post through paid distribution, for a reporting period. The reach number might be less than the impressions number since one person can see multiple impressions.

TECH NOTES:

Facebook reports metrics at the Page and Post levels. It is very important to make sure that you use the right ones for your analytic task. Post-level metrics are typically reported on a lifetime basis, whereas Page-level metrics are typically reported for daily, weekly, and 28-day periods.

ARF COMMENTS:

comScore and Facebook research (Polich 2012) concludes that "the relative sizes of the paid and organic portions of each post's audience are to a large extent determined by a brand's decisions, such as how the brand chooses to target a given post, when the content is posted, and whether the brand uses paid media to boost a post into news feed or the right-hand side. There are cases where the paid reach exceeds organic reach, and vice versa, because of different page posting and ad strategies. Keep in mind that since this research was published, organic reach levels have been steadily declining and are expected to drop further. Competition among stories for exposure, the people's News Feeds and Facebook's EdgeRank algorithm, which aims to display only the most relevant stories to a person, are the factors responsible for lowered organic reach levels. Consequently, brands now purchase advertising to achieve their desired reach levels.

Their data suggest that "brands can and should tune their posting thoughtfully, choosing to invest in paid amplification for some posts to address a broad audience through advertising, while utilizing other posts primarily to address their connected fans and friends of fans. For brands who have invested in the creation of content, this represents a potentially big lever to amplify and extend the life of content."

CITED RESEARCH:

Polich, Adrienne et al. (2012). Understanding Paid and Earned Reach on Facebook (http://goo.gl/HLrCe).

SEE ALSO:

Paid Impressions-Page (Facebook)
Total Reach—Post (Facebook)

Pay Per Click (PPC)

AUTHORITY:

MEDIA:
Paid

STAGE:
1. Capture

CATEGORY:
1. Advertising

APPLIES TO:
Website
Social
Email
Mobile

ANSWERS QUESTION:
What is the amount we are paying per click?

DEFINITION:
See Cost per Click (CPC)

TECH NOTES:
None

ARF COMMENTS:

CITED RESEARCH:
None

SEE ALSO:

People Engaged—Post (Facebook)

AUTHORITY:	**MEDIA:**	**STAGE:**	**CATEGORY:**	**APPLIES TO:**
Facebook	Paid Owned	2. Connect	5. Engagement/ Interaction	Social

ANSWERS QUESTION:

How many unique people liked, commented on, or shared our post?

DEFINITION:

The people who have liked, clicked on, commented on, or shared your posts.

TECH NOTES:

None

ARF COMMENTS:

People Engaged measures the ability of posts to promote interaction and by whom, and to compare the engagement levels across posts. Brands can leverage this metric to optimize post content in ways that help achieve brand objectives. Facebook has been moving towards measures that more precisely capture actions which are presumably more relevant to advertisers. People Engaged is a good example of this direction, focusing only on four types that imply meaningful engagement, instead of any type as is the case with Engaged Users.

CITED RESEARCH:

None.

SEE ALSO:

Actions (Facebook)
Engaged Users—Post (Facebook)
Story (Facebook)

People Talking About This—Page (Facebook)

AUTHORITY:	MEDIA:	STAGE:	CATEGORY:	APPLIES TO:
Facebook	Earned	2. Connect	6. Amplification/ Endorsement	Social

ANSWERS QUESTION:

How engaged are people with our page?

DEFINITION:

People Talking About This, commonly referred to as PTAT, was deprecated by Facebook in 2014 and will eventually be removed from Page Insights. PTAT was a summary engagement measure that combined several metrics into one.

To better see how people interact with a page's content, the PTAT metrics have been split into separate elements: Page Likes, People Engaged (the number of unique people who have clicked on, liked, commented on, or shared your posts), Page tags and mentions, Page check-ins and other interactions on a Page.

TECH NOTES:

None

ARF COMMENTS:

As a compound metric that is composed from several other metrics, People Talking About This was challenging to interpret because it was hard to pinpoint reasons for rises or declines in PTAT scores. Facebook recommends that you use the individual metrics listed above in the definition above, to evaluate your Page posting strategy and engagement. Merely relying on the total figure may not be sufficiently diagnostic (Kaushik 2012).

CITED RESEARCH:

Kaushik, Avinash (2012). Facebook Advertising/Marketing: Best Metrics, ROI, Business Value (http://goo.gl/dgPjV).

SEE ALSO:

People Engaged—Post (Facebook))

Story (Facebook)

People Talking About This—Post (Facebook)

AUTHORITY:	MEDIA:	STAGE:	CATEGORY:	APPLIES TO:
Facebook	Earned	2. Connect	6. Amplification/ Endorsement	Social

ANSWERS QUESTION:

How many Unique people created stories from our page post?

DEFINITION:

People Talking About This, commonly referred to as PTAT, was deprecated by Facebook in 2014 and will eventually be removed from Page Insights. PTAT was a summary engagement measure that combined several metrics into one.

Facebook is breaking PTAT into elements that will now be reported separately, which are Post Likes, People Engaged, and other interactions on a Post.

TECH NOTES:

None

ARF COMMENTS:

This metric may be helpful to understanding the user engagement with individual posts on a page and the word of mouth that engagement generates. In combination with the type of actions taken the create stories, brands can compare posts and gain insights for optimizing them. Paid advertising on Facebook may broaden reach and promote engagement (comScore 2012).

As a compound metric that is composed from several other metrics, People Talking About This was challenging to interpret because it was hard to pinpoint reasons for rises or declines in PTAT scores. Facebook recommends that you use the individual metrics listed above in the definition above, to evaluate your posting strategy and engagement.

CITED RESEARCH:

Kaushik, Avinash (2012). Facebook Advertising/Marketing: Best Metrics, ROI, Business Value (http://goo.gl/dgPjV).

SEE ALSO:

People Engaged—Post (Facebook)
Story (Facebook)

Phone Brand

AUTHORITY:	MEDIA:	STAGE:	CATEGORY:	APPLIES TO:
comScore	Owned	1. Capture	2. Audience/Traffic	Mobile

ANSWERS QUESTION:

Which phone brands accessed our mobile website?

DEFINITION:

The brand name of a mobile phone—for example, Apple, Samsung, Nokia, or Blackberry—accessing a mobile website, over a reporting period.

TECH NOTES:

None

ARF COMMENTS:

Phone brand counts and their percent distribution reveal the popularity of manufacturer handsets accessing a site. These metrics may be useful for optimizing the mobile website experience for users with different devices and capabilities. Trending the data over time can reveal patterns suggesting site improvements or changes tied to shifts in usage by different handset brands.

CITED RESEARCH:

None

SEE ALSO:

Phone Type
Mobile Operating System

Phone Type

AUTHORITY: **MEDIA:** **STAGE:** **CATEGORY:** **APPLIES TO:**

comScore   Owned   1. Capture   2. Audience/Traffic   Mobile

ANSWERS QUESTION:

Which phone types accessed our mobile website?

DEFINITION:

The type of mobile phone—for example, Apple iPhone, Samsung Galaxy S3, Nokia Lumina, or Blackberry 9800—accessing a mobile website.

TECH NOTES:

None

ARF COMMENTS:

Phone Type counts and their percent distribution reveal the popularity of handsets accessing a site. These metrics may be useful for optimizing the mobile website experience for users with different devices and capabilities. Trending the data over time can reveal patterns suggesting site improvements or changes tied to shifts in handset usage.

CITED RESEARCH:

None

SEE ALSO:

Phone Brand
Mobile Browser Version
Mobile Operating System

Pinners

AUTHORITY:	MEDIA:	STAGE:	CATEGORY:	APPLIES TO:
Pinterest	Earned	1. Capture	2. Audience/Traffic	Social

ANSWERS QUESTION:

How many Unique people pinned something from our website?

DEFINITION:

The number of Unique people who pinned from a brand's website, over a reporting period.

TECH NOTES:

None

ARF COMMENTS:

Pinners may be thought of as a type of engaged user. Trends in Pinners can suggest the appeal of a brand's website content for their visitors who are also Pinterest users.

CITED RESEARCH:

None

SEE ALSO:

Repinners

Unique Visitors (Unique Browsers)

Pins

AUTHORITY:	MEDIA:	STAGE:	CATEGORY:	APPLIES TO:
Pinterest	Earned	2. Connect	1. Advertising	Social
	Paid		6. Amplification/ Endorsement	

ANSWERS QUESTION:

How many things were pinned from our website, over a reporting period?

DEFINITION:

The number of things pinned from a site over a reporting period.

TECH NOTES:

None

ARF COMMENTS:

Pins are a type of amplification, in which users bookmark content from a site and place it on their pinboards. Brands analyzing pins may gain insight into the type of content that Pinterest users find interesting, which can assist with optimizing content.

To help brands make their pins more appealing, Pinterest offers Rich Pins, which include extra information right on the pin. At press time five types of Rich Pins were available: product, movie, recipe, article, and place.

Pinterest offers advertising in the form of Promoted Pins. These are "Pins businesses pay for so that more people will see them. They show up in search results and in the Everything, Popular and category feeds. Promoted Pins work just like regular Pins, only they have a special "promoted" label." Promoted Pins are paid ad impressions.

Pinterest modified their privacy policy in late 2014 in order to target Promoted Pins more effectively based on users' interests and on information that advertisers have shared. Privacy policy changes will also enable Pinterest to report the number of times their Promoted Pins are showing, and the types of actions that people took after clicking on a Promoted Pin. Pinterest appears to be building an advertising platform similar to that of Facebook or Twitter.

CITED RESEARCH:

None

SEE ALSO:

Ad Impression
Repins

Playlist Average Playing Time

AUTHORITY:	MEDIA:	STAGE:	CATEGORY:	APPLIES TO:
comScore	Owned	2. Connect	4. Media Consumption	Website Social Mobile

ANSWERS QUESTION:

How long was our playlist listened to, on average?

DEFINITION:

The total time a playlist was streamed (represented in HH:MM:SS) divided by all starts for that playlist.

A playlist is a sequence of audio and/or video tracks, called clips. These can be programs, episodes of a program, or advertising messages.

TECH NOTES:

None

ARF COMMENTS:

Playlist Average Play Time is primarily a measure of media consumption, buy may be considered an engagement metric. When interpreted in the context of completions it may paint a picture of the depth of engagement. This measure may be helpful to optimize playlist composition and creation.

CITED RESEARCH:

None

SEE ALSO:

Playlist Completions
Playlist Starts

Playlist Completions

AUTHORITY:	MEDIA:	STAGE:	CATEGORY:	APPLIES TO:
comScore	Owned	2. Connect	5. Engagement/ Interaction	Website Social Mobile

ANSWERS QUESTION:

How many times was our playlist listened or viewed through to the end?

DEFINITION:

The total number of times a playlist was completely played over a reporting period. Typically a threshold is set at which a playback is considered fully played, such as 90%.

A playlist is a sequence of audio and/or video tracks, called clips. These can be programs, episodes of a program, or advertising messages.

TECH NOTES:

None

ARF COMMENTS:

Playlist Completions may be considered a measure of the depth of viewer/listener engagement, especially when interpreted in the context of related metrics such as starts, repeated starts, stops, and average playing time. This metric may be helpful to optimize playlist composition and creation.

CITED RESEARCH:

None

SEE ALSO:

Playlist Average Playing Time
Playlist Starts

Playlist Starts

AUTHORITY:	MEDIA:	STAGE:	CATEGORY:	APPLIES TO:
comScore	Owned	2. Connect	5. Engagement/ Interaction	Website Social Mobile

ANSWERS QUESTION:

How many times was our playlist listened to or watched?

DEFINITION:

The total number of times of first and repeated playlist starts, over a reporting period.

A playlist is a sequence of audio and/or video tracks, called clips. These can be programs, episodes of a program, or advertising messages.

TECH NOTES:

None

ARF COMMENTS:

A basic level of interaction. The depth of engagement may be assessed from related metrics: playlist completions and average playing time. Metric may be used to optimize the types of playlists offered.

CITED RESEARCH:

None

SEE ALSO:

Playlist Average Playing Time
Playlist Completions

Program Completion Rate

AUTHORITY:	MEDIA:	STAGE:	CATEGORY:	APPLIES TO:
comScore	Owned	2. Connect	5. Engagement/ Interaction	Website Social Mobile

ANSWERS QUESTION:

Of all the times a program was started, what is the percentage of programs that played all the way through?

DEFINITION:

The total number of times a program has been played completely as a percentage of the total number of starts for that program.

A program is the name of a radio or television show, such as *Modern Family*.

TECH NOTES:

None

ARF COMMENTS:

Program Completion Rate is primarily an interaction measure. Analyzing trends in Program Completion Rate may be helpful to optimize program selection.

CITED RESEARCH:

None

SEE ALSO:

Program Starts
Program Stops

Program Completions

AUTHORITY:	MEDIA:	STAGE:	CATEGORY:	APPLIES TO:
comScore	Owned	2. Connect	5. Engagement/ Interaction	Website Social Mobile

ANSWERS QUESTION:

How many times was our program listened or viewed through to the end?

DEFINITION:

The total number of times a program was completely played over a period of time. Typically a threshold is set at which a playback is considered fully played, such as 90%.

A program is the name of a radio or television show, such as *Modern Family*.

TECH NOTES:

ARF COMMENTS:

Program Completions is a basic interaction measure. By analyzing patterns in Program Completions, the metric may be helpful for optimizing program selection and length.

CITED RESEARCH:

None

SEE ALSO:

Program Completion Rate
Program Repeated Completions
Program Starts
Program Stops

Program Repeated Completions

AUTHORITY:	MEDIA:	STAGE:	CATEGORY:	APPLIES TO:
comScore	Owned	2. Connect	5. Engagement/ Interaction	Website Social Mobile

ANSWERS QUESTION:

How many times was our program repeated and listened or viewed through to the end?

DEFINITION:

The total number of times a program was repeated and completely played over a period of time. Typically a threshold is set at which a playback is considered fully played, such as 90%.

A program is the name of a radio or television show, such as *Modern Family*.

TECH NOTES:

None

ARF COMMENTS:

Primarily a measure of interaction, analyzing Program Repeated Completions may be used to help optimize program selection and length.

CITED RESEARCH:

None

SEE ALSO:

Program Repeated Starts

Program Repeated Starts

AUTHORITY:	MEDIA:	STAGE:	CATEGORY:	APPLIES TO:
comScore	Owned	2. Connect	5. Engagement/ Interaction	Website Social Mobile

ANSWERS QUESTION:

How many times was our program repeatedly watched or listened to?

DEFINITION:

The total number of times of first and repeated program starts, over a period of time.

A program is the name of a radio or television show, such as *Modern Family*.

TECH NOTES:

None

ARF COMMENTS:

Program Repeated Starts is a basic interaction measure. Depth of engagement may be detected by analyzing related metrics such as Program Completions. This metric may be helpful for optimizing program selection.

CITED RESEARCH:

None

SEE ALSO:

Program Completions
Program Starts

Program Starts

AUTHORITY:	MEDIA:	STAGE:	CATEGORY:	APPLIES TO:
comScore	Owned	2. Connect	5. Engagement/ Interaction	Website Social Mobile

ANSWERS QUESTION:

How many times was our program watched or listened to?

DEFINITION:

The total number of times of first and repeated program starts, over a period of time.

A program is the name of a radio or television show, such as *Modern Family*.

TECH NOTES:

None

ARF COMMENTS:

Program Starts is a basic interaction measure. Analyzing related metrics, such as program completions and average playing time, can suggest the depth of engagement. This metric may be helpful in optimizing program selection.

CITED RESEARCH:

None

SEE ALSO:

Program Completions
Program Repeated Starts
Program Stops

Program Stops

AUTHORITY:	MEDIA:	STAGE:	CATEGORY:	APPLIES TO:
comScore	Owned	2. Connect	5. Engagement/ Interaction	Website Social Mobile

ANSWERS QUESTION:

How many times was our program stopped?

DEFINITION:

The total number of times of a program was stopped because the browser hit "Stop," or the end of the program was reached, over a period of time.

A program is the name of a radio or television show, such as *Modern Family*.

TECH NOTES:

None

ARF COMMENTS:

Program Stops is a basic measure of interaction. In combination with related program metrics, such as Program Starts and Program Completions, degree of engagement may be revealed. Analyzing which programs were stopped, and when, this metric may help with optimizing programs.

CITED RESEARCH:

None

SEE ALSO:

Program Completions
Program Starts

Reach*

AUTHORITY:	MEDIA:	STAGE:	CATEGORY:	APPLIES TO:
comScore, IAB, Millward Brown Digital, Nielsen	Paid	1. Capture	2. Audience/Traffic	Website Social Email Mobile

ANSWERS QUESTION:

What is the percentage of the target audience that had the opportunity to see a specific ad at least once, over a reporting period?

DEFINITION:

The number of individuals in the target audience that will have the opportunity to see a specific online or mobile advertisement at least once, usually expressed as a percentage of a defined universe over a reporting period.

TECH NOTES:

Cookie deletion poses challenges to computing reach and frequency because it can overestimate reach and understate frequency (comScore 2011). When calculating reach and frequency, factor cookie deletion in to generate reasonable numbers.

The Digital Analytics Association has a proposed social media standard definition for Reach: "Reach represents the total number of unique people who had an opportunity to see an ITEM or a valid reproduction of that ITEM across any digital media." In their definition: "An ITEM of content is a post, micro-post, article or other instance appearing for the first time in digital media." The word ITEM replaces such terms as "clip," "post," or other "unclear terms." ITEMs contain one or more MENTIONS, which can refer to a brand, organization, campaign, or entity that is being tracked. DAA points out that the REACH metric "assumes an ideal environment where one can quantify individual people across platforms using social media monitoring tools, social platforms, and/or panel-based measurement solutions. However, in reality each tool, platform, and solution may have a unique method of calculating REACH and each might introduce duplication and error." (Capitalization in original.)

ARF COMMENTS:

Reach is one of the most fundamental advertising measures. Advertisers consider both net reach and "unduplicated reach," which is a measure of how many people were reached at least once. Reach and exposure frequency form the basis of much media planning and buying. Planners seek to balance reach and frequency, and purchase enough advertising weight, expressed in Gross Rating Points (GRPs), to achieve specific brand objectives. The topic of reach, frequency, and GRPs is too broad to cover here, but there are several very good books on media planning that cover the relevant details, strategies and issues. Baron and Sissors (2010), now in its 7th edition, is one of the important standard works in the field.

Social networks may compute Reach for different types of impressions. Facebook, for example, computes reach for total, paid, and organic impressions at the Page and Post levels.

CITED RESEARCH:

Baron, Roger and Jack Sissors (2010). Advertising Media Planning, 7th Edition. McGraw-Hill.

comScore (2011). The Impact of Cookie Deletion on Site-Server and Ad-Server Metrics in Australia: An Empirical comScore Study (http://goo.gl/t1D6d).

Digital Analytic Association (2013). Proposed Social Media Standard Definitions for Reach and Impressions, from the Digital Analytics Association (http://goo.gl/FQugv).

SEE ALSO:

Ad Impression
Frequency
Gross Ratings Points (GRP)
Target Impressions

Recipe Downloads

AUTHORITY:	MEDIA:	STAGE:	CATEGORY:	APPLIES TO:
Patel & Flores	Owned	2. Connect	7. Conversion	Website Social Mobile

ANSWERS QUESTION:

How many recipes were downloaded?

DEFINITION:

The number of recipe downloads over a reporting period.

TECH NOTES:

None

ARF COMMENTS:

Downloads are a common conversion action on many Sites. Analyzing downloads as part of a conversion funnel may help brands understand their contribution to a larger brand or site goal.

Numbers of downloads can indicate the popularity of a giveaway to connect with, and provide service to, consumers. Often the promotional materials are part of a program to spur another action. For this reason, it is often useful to look at measures the download may have influenced. For example, was the app installed after being downloaded (registration data can be used), were further inquiries made after a white paper download on the site or through another channel (check the CRM database), or did sales of an ingredient increase after a certain recipe or usage was promoted? As these examples suggest, evaluating the impact of content downloads may require additional data from the site and other corporate systems or resources. For example, Kraft's "Real Women of Philadelphia" site promoted cooking with Philadelphia Cream Cheese and offered recipes and contests. By tracking supermarket sales, Kraft determined that the initiative was bringing about the desired sales increases.

CITED RESEARCH:

None

SEE ALSO:

Key Performance Indicator (KPI)

Referral Traffic*

AUTHORITY:	MEDIA:	STAGE:	CATEGORY:	APPLIES TO:
Digital Analytics Association, Facebook, Google, IAB, Twitter, Millward Brown Digital, Mobile Marketing Association, Yahoo!	Owned	1. Capture	2. Audience/Traffic	Website Social Mobile

ANSWERS QUESTION:

Where is our site traffic coming from?

DEFINITION:

Referral Traffic is any visitor who arrived at the site via one of three methods: through internal links, external links, or search links:

1. Internal—a link that is internal to the website or to a web property within the website
2. External—a link that is outside the website or social network
3. Search—a link that was generated from a keyword search

Every referral to a site has a Channel (sometimes called Medium) and Source.

TECH NOTES:

According to the Digital Analytics Association, "Each hit to a website has a referrer. However there are several situations where the referrer value is empty or null. These include when the referrer value in the request header is not specified, or when the URL is directly entered or selected from a list of bookmarks. These are often reported as "No Referrer" or "Direct Navigation."

In Facebook, external referrers are listed and counted for an individual page. Twitter reports clicks on links within Tweets that send traffic to external sites.

ARF COMMENTS:

Understanding the quality of the referred traffic helps: 1) determine if marketing or advertising strategy is working as expected, and 2) in managing and growing relevant site traffic that attracts targeted visitors, prospects, and buyers, and for setting advertising rates. Traffic that is high in number but not relevant to advertisers will not have much commercial value. For example, a company posts a video on YouTube with the intent of driving traffic to its site. Analyzing referral traffic will reveal the effectiveness of the YouTube video.

To gauge referral traffic quality, routinely monitor and compare conversion outcomes from the different referral sources. That analysis can also serve to help with optimization, weeding out the low-quality referring sources and maximizing the high-quality ones.

It's important to recognize, comScore's Gian Fulgoni advises, that referral traffic "reflects direct navigation from one site to another. It doesn't reflect the overall/latent influence of the referring property. For example, while Facebook generally accounts for less than 1% of the referring traffic to retailer websites, its overall influence on consumer e-commerce buying is far greater" (Fulgoni 2013).

CITED RESEARCH:

Fulgoni, Gian (2013). Personal communication.

SEE ALSO:

Channel
Direct Traffic Visitors
Search Traffic
Source

Repeat Visitors

AUTHORITY:	MEDIA:	STAGE:	CATEGORY:	APPLIES TO:
Digital Analytics Association, IAB, Millward Brown Digital	Owned	2. Connect	2. Audience/Traffic	Website Social Mobile

ANSWERS QUESTION:

Are people coming back to our website, app, or brand page within a certain time period, and how many?

DEFINITION:

Unique visitors who have accessed a site, app, or brand page two or more times within a specific reporting period.

TECH NOTES:

See Visitors (Unique Visitors) for the notes.

IAB's definition of Return Visits is more similar to the Repeat Visitor definition than the Return Visitor definition. IAB's "Social Media Metrics Definitions" defines Return Visits as "the average number of times a user returns to a site or application over a specific time period."

ARF COMMENTS:

Repeat Visitors can indicate if website content is bringing users back and retaining their interest. For e-commerce sites, the number of repeat visits may reveal how many visits are required to make (or lose) the sale. Further, tracking the time between visits—minutes, hours, or days—can be helpful in terms of understanding the length of the sales process. For e-commerce it is important to keep in mind that people shopping for a product or service will be visiting a number of sites, coming back to compare, and so forth. For this reason, e-commerce sites should provide repeat visitors with shortcuts and services that support and smooth the transaction. Dainow (2005) provides a good overview of the value of Repeat Visitors for e-commerce sites.

Sites that are interested in retaining audiences over time may also be interested in the Returning Visitor metric, which measures whether or not people visit over a span of reporting periods.

CITED RESEARCH:

Dainow, Brandt (2005). Defining Unique Visitors (http://goo.gl/qxvSu, accessed January 3, 2013).

SEE ALSO:

Return Visitor
Visit (Session)
Unique Visitors (Unique Browsers)

Repinners

AUTHORITY:	MEDIA:	STAGE:	CATEGORY:	APPLIES TO:
Pinterest	Owned	1. Capture	2. Audience/Traffic	Social

ANSWERS QUESTION:

How many unique people repinned our pins, over a reporting period?

DEFINITION:

The number of unique people who repinned a brand's pins on Pinterest, over a reporting period.

TECH NOTES:

None

ARF COMMENTS:

Repinners expand the reach of a brand's pins. Brands analyzing trends in repinners may gain insight into the type of content that Pinterest users find interesting enough to place on their own pinboards.

CITED RESEARCH:

None

SEE ALSO:

Pinners

Repins

AUTHORITY:	MEDIA:	STAGE:	CATEGORY:	APPLIES TO:
Pinterest	Earned	2. Connect	6. Amplification/ Endorsement	Social

ANSWERS QUESTION:

How many times were pins on our website repinned, over a reporting period?

DEFINITION:

The number of times pins for a brand's website were repinned on Pinterest, over a reporting period.

TECH NOTES:

None

ARF COMMENTS:

Repins expand the reach of a brand's content. Brands analyzing Repins may gain insight into the type of content that Pinterest users find interesting and notable enough to Pin on their page; understanding trends may assist with optimizing content.

CITED RESEARCH:

None

SEE ALSO:

Pins

Return Visitor*

AUTHORITY:	MEDIA:	STAGE:	CATEGORY:	APPLIES TO:
comScore, Digital Analytics Association, IAB, Millward Brown Digital, Yahoo!,	Owned	2. Connect 3. Close 4. Keep	2. Audience/Traffic	Website Social Mobile

ANSWERS QUESTION:

How many visitors came back to our site in this reporting period who visited in an earlier reporting period?

DEFINITION:

The number of Unique visitors with activity consisting of a visit to a site during a reporting period, who also visited the site prior to the reporting period. comScore calls this a "Returning Browser." Nielsen has a similar measure called "Retention Rate" that is based on monthly periods.

TECH NOTES:

See Visitors (Unique Visitors) for the notes.

ARF COMMENTS:

Return Visitors are often confused with Repeat Visitors. The difference is that Return Visitors are Unique Visitors who return across two or more time periods, whereas Repeat Visitors are Unique Visitors who return within a single time period. The Return Visitors metric is a measure of engagement and ongoing interest. Paying attention to the ratio of New Visitors to Returning Visitors can indicate the appeal of a site, and also indicate if it is growing by attracting new visitors and retaining their interest. Tracking return visitors over time through the connect, close, and keep stages may indicate the ability of a site to retain visitors and its ability to engender loyalty.

When visitors return, it is helpful to track what actions they take, how those compare with New Visitors, and how Return Visitor actions relate to brand strategy. For example, if Return Visitors and New Visitors use the site differently, those differences may suggest ways to optimize the experience of each visitor. Strategically, product marketers, such as auto companies, may want to see progress along the path to purchase, from information seeking, making comparisons, configuring options, locating dealers, and on to scheduling test drives, for example. Makers of fast-moving consumer goods may be interested in comparing the actions New vs. Return Visitors take, such as downloading content, commenting, or participating in contests, as ways to measure changes in engagement levels over time. Whatever the category, brands should evaluate the value of Return Visitors in the context of their objectives and strategies.

CITED RESEARCH:

None

SEE ALSO:

Repeat Visitors
Visit (Session)
Unique Visitors (Unique Browsers)

Retweets

AUTHORITY:	MEDIA:	STAGE:	CATEGORY:	APPLIES TO:
Twitter	Earned	2. Connect	6. Amplification/ Endorsement	Social

ANSWERS QUESTION:

How many times was a specific Tweet retweeted?

DEFINITION:

Represents the number of retweets for an individual Tweet. A retweet is a reposting of someone else's Tweet.

TECH NOTES:

Retweet rates are frequently included in Twitter management tools and the Twitter API. Several free and paid tools count retweets.

ARF COMMENTS:

Retweeting is a form of pass-along readership. It is often used to compute the reach of a Tweet (by adding up the followers in the retweeter's networks), and also as a measure of engagement. Retweets may be exposed on third-party networks that agree to post them, such as Facebook. As with comments and reviews, it is important to make sure the retweets are authentic, not spam, and not a result of automated activity. Retweet rates factor into measures of online influence and are sometimes manipulated to raise the profile of an individual, brand, or company.

When a retweet contains information about a brand or company, in the Tweet or appended link, it contains a "mention" and may also be considered and counted as an earned impression.

In addition to simply counting retweets, social media marketers typically analyze retweets of authors to identify people who have sizable followings that value what they say and pass along what they write. (Keep in mind that brands or their agencies may enlist and pay celebrities and prominent people to retweet posts to their followers, so it is important to understand the source of the retweets.) This simple measure of online influence may be used to identify advocates, detractors, and brand ambassadors, who can then be communicated with in ways that help promote a brand through Twitter. Several services provide measures of online influence that are derived more complexly, such as Klout (www.klout.com), as well as straightforwardly presenting metrics for reach, velocity, engagement, and demand. Using them requires understanding what they measure, their relevance, and applicability to your brand.

CITED RESEARCH:

None

SEE ALSO:

Earned Impression
Follower (Twitter)

Revenue Over Email Delivered*

AUTHORITY:
Experian Marketing Services

MEDIA:
Owned

STAGE:
3. Close

CATEGORY:
8. E-Commerce

APPLIES TO:
Email

ANSWERS QUESTION:

What is the average amount of revenue earned for each delivered email?

DEFINITION:

Average amount of revenue earned for each delivered email.

TECH NOTES:

None

ARF COMMENTS:

Revenue per email is useful for evaluating the sales effectiveness of an individual email or campaign. The key is being able to identify revenue generated by email. For pure-play e-commerce providers, revenue numbers are often captured by a tracking program that can integrate with an email system or provider. Omnichannel retailers need to make sure that relevant revenues from all their outlets are rolled-up.

Using A/B tests, revenue per email may be helpful in deciding which email executions are working the hardest for a brand, and can be used to optimize. This metric can place standard email metrics in context. For example, Email A may generate more Opens, yet Email B may generate fewer Opens but higher sales (Jennings 2011).

CITED RESEARCH:

Jennings, Jeane (2011). The Value of Calculating Revenue per Email (http://goo.gl/JxuZO).

SEE ALSO:

Average Order Value
Bounce—Email
Email Delivered

Reviews (product)*

AUTHORITY:	MEDIA:	STAGE:	CATEGORY:	APPLIES TO:
ARF	Earned	2. Connect	6. Amplification/ Endorsement	Website Social Mobile

ANSWERS QUESTION:

How many reviews did a product receive over a specific time period?

DEFINITION:

The number of reviews a product receives over a specified time period.

TECH NOTES:

Product reviews often include a rating, typically on a scale of 1 to 5, with 5 being the most positive.

ARF COMMENTS:

The number of reviews products receive can be an indicator of interest and engagement. As with comments to blog posts, the number of product reviews may be distorted by so-called review spam, a type of review posted by people paid to write positive reviews—a common practice—and spam automatically placed on review sites by bots and other automated agents. It is extremely important to make sure that the reviews are authentic, clean, and unduplicated. A number of companies are working on these issues to improve the quality of reviews that appear on sites.

Interpreting and listening to reviews is not so simple as "positive=good, negative=bad." Research shows that people read reviews critically. "Helpful" reviews are often stronger purchase motivators than happy, 5-star reviews. Other characteristics that influence sales from reviews are: the mix of objective and subjective statements, the characteristics of the reviewer, the amount of coverage a product gets, sentiment, and the passage of time. Rappaport provides a systematic review of this literature (2011).

Apart from sales, reviews can have an impact on stock price. Negative reviews that issue shortly after a product's release have been show to depress a company's stock price, but positive reviews have no impact (Belsky 2012).

CITED RESEARCH:

Belsky, Gary (2012). Why Product Reviews May Be the Next Big Thing for Investors (http://goo.gl/jRXgy).

Rappaport, Stephen D. (2011). Listen First: Turning Social Media Conversations into Business Advantage, Hoboken: John Wiley & Sons.

SEE ALSO:

Comments

Rich Media Interactive Impressions

AUTHORITY:	MEDIA:	STAGE:	CATEGORY:	APPLIES TO:
Google DoubleClick	Paid	1. Capture	1. Advertising	Website
Millward Brown Digital				Mobile

ANSWERS QUESTION:

How many impressions did our rich media ad generate?

DEFINITION:

The number of impressions that occur when a user interacts with a Rich Media ad. Interactive impressions are captured when the user: clicks an exit link; makes the ad display full-screen; mouses over the ad for at least one continuous second; or expands the ad, for a reporting period.

IAB's Measurement Council defines rich media ads as: "those with which users can interact as opposed to solely animation, and they include such formats as transitionals and various over-the-page units such as floating ads, page take-overs and tear-backs." Their measurement guidelines are primarily applicable to Internet media companies, ad serving organizations, and rich media vendors.

TECH NOTES:

Similar to general Internet ad impressions, an ad impression or Rich Media is defined as: A measurement of responses from a rich media ad delivery system to an ad request from the user's browser, which is filtered from robotic activity and is recorded at a point as late as possible in the process of delivery of the creative material to the user's browser—therefore closest to the actual opportunity to see by the user (IAB 2007).

In the rich media area, where advertising creative is more process-resource intensive for Internet users, servers, and publishers, the number of redirects in the transaction stream can impact the accuracy of ad counting due to latency. All parties are encouraged to consider this latency when considering the structure of rich media serving arrangements.

Client-initiated counting is required. Client-initiated counting is based on activity (content or ad requests, formatting, and redirects) originating at the Internet user's browser and involves more than one Internet round-trip before counts can be recorded. The initial Internet round-trips are generally to request and return general content and advertising content, and subsequent round-trips can facilitate counting using calls, redirects, beacons, etc.

ARF COMMENTS:

Rich media format ads may include static or animated GIF or JPEG images, Flash, HTML 5, or video. They can provide a personalized, interactive experience for people. Overall, rich media ads have been shown to positively impact online Ad Awareness, Message Association, Aided Brand Awareness, Brand Favorability, and Purchase Intent. Differences in effect vary by the elements included. Rich media ads with video, for example, outperform all executions on these branding measures except Message Association, whereas GIF or JPEG treatments excel at Message Association (DoubleClick 2009).

Rich media is becoming popular in mobile apps. The IAB and its Mobile Marketing Center of Excellence released the "Mobile Rich-Media Ad Interface Definitions" or MRAID 2.0. These new guidelines "will enable greater consistency when it comes to the delivery of a range of rich media ad formats, including the new IAB Mobile Rising Stars units, allowing agencies to be able to quickly and easily run creative across applications from different publishers, rather than needing to rewrite the programming behind their ad creative several times for a single campaign. The combination of common rich media mobile ad formats, and a standardized way to program those ads "under the hood," will help the industry scale to levels that were previously impossible.

CITED RESEARCH:

IAB (2007). Rich Media Measurement Guidelines (http://goo.gl/KN84S).

DoubleClick (2009). The Brand Value of Rich Media and Video Ads (http://goo.gl/OoSQN).

IAB (2012). Mobile Rich Media Ad Interface Definitions (MRAID) (http://www.iab.net/mraid).

SEE ALSO:

Ad Impression

Screen View

AUTHORITY:	MEDIA:	STAGE:	CATEGORY:	APPLIES TO:
	Owned	2. Connect	4. Media Consumption	Mobile

ANSWERS QUESTION:

How many screen views were recorded over a certain period of time?

DEFINITION:

Screen View is the mobile equivalent of a Page View.

TECH NOTES:

None

ARF COMMENTS:

❚ See Page View or Page Views per Visit for details.

CITED RESEARCH:

None

SEE ALSO:

Page View

Screen Views per Visit

AUTHORITY:

MEDIA:
Owned

STAGE:
2. Connect

CATEGORY:
4. Media
Consumption

APPLIES TO:
Mobile

ANSWERS QUESTION:

How many screen views did our mobile site receive over a reporting period?

DEFINITION:

Screen Views per Visit is the mobile equivalent of a Page Views per Visit, for a reporting period.

TECH NOTES:

None

ARF COMMENTS:

▌ See Page Views per Visit for details.

CITED RESEARCH:

None

SEE ALSO:

Page Views per Visit

Search Traffic

AUTHORITY:	MEDIA:	STAGE:	CATEGORY:	APPLIES TO:	Social
Google, Millward Brown Digital	Owned	1. Capture	2. Audience/ Traffic	Website	Mobile

ANSWERS QUESTION:

Which search engines are sending traffic to our site?

DEFINITION:

Search Traffic is the number of visits that arrives via a search engine, through organic or paid search links for a reporting period.

TECH NOTES:

Analytics software does not always name all referring search engines. For example, by default Google Analytics identifies only a select list of websites as search engine referrals in reports; all others are aggregated under the heading of Referring Sites. Facebook reports Search Traffic with its list of External Referrers to a Page.

ARF COMMENTS:

When analyzing search traffic, analytics packages and measuring services usually report the top referring search terms. These are the most-used words and phrases people type into search engines to find your content. One best practice in search engine optimization and search engine marketing is to use consumer language, not marketer-speak. Marketers sometimes focus on words that differentiate and distinguish their brand or reflect their internal language (Plummer et al. 2007).

Breaking out traffic generated from organic results and paid search links is an important analysis to perform, as it can indicate the pulling power of a brand's website content and its paid search advertising. Segmenting the traffic reports by site usage or e-commerce performance may reveal differences that reflect on the quality of organic and paid sources. Understanding these quality differences may lead to optimizing the site for each visitor type, and for deciding on which search sources to invest in. Search engine traffic is one type of Referral Traffic.

CITED RESEARCH:

Plummer, Joseph et al. (2007). The Online Advertising Playbook. Hoboken: John Wiley & Sons.

SEE ALSO:

Referral Traffic

Source

Sentiment*

AUTHORITY:	MEDIA:	STAGE:	CATEGORY:	APPLIES TO:
ARF	Earned	2. Connect	6. Amplification/ Endorsement	Social

ANSWERS QUESTION:

What is the opinion expressed towards my brand?

DEFINITION:

Among marketers, sentiment is generally thought of as the opinion expressed towards a brand, its products, services, or experiences, or actions in social media conversations, reviews, and ratings. Sentiment is calculated by the various techniques of sentiment analysis, which include natural language processing, computational linguistics, and text analytics. Sentiment analysis may be conducted at different levels including: all documents in a collection, individual documents, sentence, phrase, or specific feature (named entity, topic, or concept). Most sentiment is reported as positive, negative, or neutral, but technical advances are bringing about measures that reflect the emotional states of writers in social media such as sadness, happiness, anger, or love. Sentiment analysis is also called opinion mining.

TECH NOTES:

None

ARF COMMENTS:

Sentiment analysis offers brands the potential capability to harvest consumer opinions and better understand them for a variety of purposes, such as—but not limited to—branding, discovering new opportunities, product development and improvement, reputation management, competitive analysis, advertising and communications, and short-term market or sales predictions.

Even with the progress being made commercially and academically, sentiment scoring, while valuable, remains imperfect. Brands seeking guidance from sentiment need to understand the sentiment scores they are presented, the documents on which they are based, the methods used to derive them, and the fit of particular sentiment methods to brand objectives and decisions.

Sentiment scoring depends heavily on the quality of the data set compiled used for analysis and its purity. It is truly a case of "garbage in, garbage out." Great care needs to be paid to making sure that the document set collects the range of a brand's conversations, captures enough of them for meaningful analysis at the brand and topic levels, eliminates spam, and separates out irrelevant results. For example, distinguishing Visa the credit card from "visa" the travel document is crucial to determining sentiment for the credit card. If the travel document was included the accuracy of the sentiment scoring would be way off and the results misleading. Consider, too, at which marketing or sales stage the conversations occur: Conversations do not necessarily reflect all the stages, as is often assumed. ARF (2012) research on the role of social media in the purchase process discovered that 75% of conversations relating to packaged meats take place after the purchase. In contrast, 60% of conversations about small cars mostly happen before the purchase—when people are defining the problem, researching brands, and evaluating competitors. The point here is that conversations do not necessarily span the purchase process, and when brands are talked about differs for categories. Brands need to know when their products are talked about in order to understand what the sentiment scores are reflecting.

Despite its intuitive appeal, it is imperative not to assume that positive sentiment associates with beneficial business outcomes and vice versa. Sometimes negative sentiment can have positive impacts, as it may for lesser-known brands (Rappaport 2011). Gauge the value of sentiment by triangulating it with other measures of business performance, such as sales, customer satisfaction, returns, consumer interactions, or branding measures. Sentiment analysis authority Seth Grimes advises to "always look beyond the numbers to business impact" (quoted in Falls 2012).

CITED RESEARCH:

ARF (2012). Digital/Social Media in the Purchase Decision Process. (White Paper available from ARF. Fee for non-members.)

Grimes, Seth (2012). Social Media Sentiment: Competing on Accuracy. Getting to the truth on measuring sentiment in online conversations (http://goo.gl/INCcO4).

Rappaport, Stephen D. (2011). Listen First: Turning Social Media Conversations into Business Advantage. Hoboken: John Wiley & Sons.

SEE ALSO:

Conversation

Share of Active Days

AUTHORITY:	MEDIA:	STAGE:	CATEGORY:	APPLIES TO:
Nielsen	Owned	2. Connect	2. Audience/Traffic	Website Social Mobile

ANSWERS QUESTION:

When people go on the web, what percent of visits go to our site?

DEFINITION:

The number of days individuals visited a website, expressed as a percentage of the total number of days they were active on the web for the specified reporting period.

TECH NOTES:

None

ARF COMMENTS:

Share of Active Days is a metric of visitor loyalty to a website. This metric benefits from trend analysis that may reveal patterns in visitation, seasonality, and so forth. Interpreting the metric should take advertising and marketing strategy into account.

CITED RESEARCH:

None

SEE ALSO:

Retention Rate

Share of Streams

AUTHORITY:	MEDIA:	STAGE:	CATEGORY:	APPLIES TO:
Nielsen	Owned	2. Connect	4. Media Consumption	Website Social Mobile

ANSWERS QUESTION:

What is the relative popularity of our streaming video or audio files?

DEFINITION:

The number of streams for a specific audio or video file as a percentage of total streams for a defined reporting period, expressed as a percentage.

TECH NOTES:

None

ARF COMMENTS:

Share of Streams measures the popularity of video and audio files that brands make available to site visitors. Understanding share may help with optimizing the types of files and content that visitors find most appealing.

CITED RESEARCH:

None

SEE ALSO:

Views, Videos

Sharing*

AUTHORITY:	MEDIA:	STAGE:	CATEGORY:	APPLIES TO:
ARF	Earned	2. Connect	6. Amplification/ Endorsement	Social

ANSWERS QUESTION:

How often is our content, ad, or app being shared with friends, contacts, or connections?

DEFINITION:

Sharing is the ability to publish or transfer content, ads or apps, usually to a website or social network, and give access to it. Sharing is one of the features integral to social media. Sites that permit sharing may be dedicated to certain types of content such as videos (e.g., YouTube), photos (Flickr), or music, or be more general, such as, but not at all limited to, Facebook, Pinterest, Instagram, or LinkedIn, Twitter, corporate sites, blogs, or review sites. Sharing is also accomplished in email through email forwards.

Sharing is usually facilitated by a link, button, widget, or forwarding feature. Several solutions exist that enable site or network owners to add multiple sharing options that transfer the content, ad, or app and typically provide tracking options. Because much sharing is done by simple copying and pasting, some companies offer solutions that capture and track such URLs without the need for a button. Once shared, functions are typically available that allow for liking, commenting, and further sharing.

TECH NOTES:

None

ARF COMMENTS:

Analyzing sharing is helpful to understanding which of your content is appealing. Sharing generates Earned Impressions and potentially expands the reach of brand content. Sharing is often valued for the implicit endorsement it carries from senders to their networks or friends. One study supporting this finding is of Moms by Share This and Digitas (Adotas 2013). Moms are more than three times as likely to share some type of content than the average sharing rate (30% vs. 10%, respectively), and their shared content generated about 8% more clicks per share. Their research makes an important point: It is not enough to know which links were shared and how many times; it is also important to learn how often recipients read the stories that are shared.

33 Across's study on sharing and reading (2013) examined sharing across 500 of "the world's largest publishers." They examined sharing in 24 categories such as science, parenting, consumer technology, entertainment, and celebrities. Their findings revealed that the relationship between sharing rate and reading is not necessarily a direct one. Science articles have the highest sharing rate but only a 9% clickback rate (the average is 24% across categories)—people want to show they're smart but aren't necessarily interested in what their reader thinks. The opposite example is seen in Men's media articles. They are seldom shared, about 1%, but their clickback rates are almost 50%, indicating high interest from recipients. Their study identifies three motivational types for sharing: 1) ego-driven, the dominant type, as having high share rates but low clickback rates like Science, 2) practical sharing, so-called for its emphasis on how-tos, tips, reviews, and such, have moderate share and clickback rates, and 3) water-cooler sharing; a typical category is celebrity and entertainment, which has low share rates—ostensibly because there's so much coverage of pop culture (like the Kardashians), but high clickback rates, reflecting that once shared there's still a lot of interest. One implication of this research is that if people are sharing to promote their personal brand, sharing strategy might benefit by enabling ego-sharers to communicate themselves along with the content (Martin 2013).

The types of content shared differs across social networks, as does the type of content that is shared. The top five categories on Facebook are Apparel, Jewelry, Electronics, Sports, and Children, whereas on Twitter they are: Apparel, Health, Entertainment, Electronics, and Gifts (AddShoppers 2013). Understanding sharing requires knowledge of the site, content type, people, and their motivations.

Advertisers, agencies, and media companies exhibit a growing interest in analyzing sharing, and not merely counting them. Subjecting sharing to high-octane analytics can reveal consumer interests and patterns, and be used to develop profiles that may be helpful for important brand tasks, some of which include consumer insight, content development and offerings, social network analysis (e.g., who is sharing what with whom, when, through which media, with what effect, role of influencers), marketing strategy, advertising targeting, creative, and media planning— e.g., deciding which outlets to use (MediaPoondi 2013). Social TV is one area where sharing is being combined with TV. Media brands like ESPN have combined with Twitter to show video clips on Twitter (Wall Street Journal 2013).

While sharing is something that people do and is enabled by online media, brands can help shape sharing in ways that benefit consumers and help the brand achieve its communications objectives. Relating sharing to specific outcomes may help brands recognize the value of their sharing strategy and provide guidance for its optimization.

CITED RESEARCH:

33 Across (2013). Content Sharing Motivated Primarily by Ego (http://goo.gl/kdJqS).

AddShoppers (2013). Social Sharing Does Lead to Sales (http://goo.gl/6yDDF).

Adotas (2013). Wired To Share: New Research From ShareThis and Digitas Reveals Important Insights Into Digital Sharing Behavior of Moms (http://goo.gl/z8uTK).

Martin, Ben (2013). Do Brands Understand What Motivates Sharing? (http://goo.gl/xyZ3E).

MediaPoondi (2013). SMG and ShareThis Announce 'Social Quality Index' Integration Into comScore Media Metrix Interface (http://goo.gl/Yt4G0).

Wall Street Journal Online (2013). ESPN, Twitter Expand Tie-up (http://goo.gl/yWFl1).

SEE ALSO:

Engagement

Social Click Rate

AUTHORITY:	MEDIA:	STAGE:	CATEGORY:	APPLIES TO:
Facebook	Paid	2. Connect	5. Engagement/ Interaction	Social

ANSWERS QUESTION:

How many clicks did our ads get that had social context?

DEFINITION:

Social Clicks divided by Social Ad Impressions over a reporting period, usually expressed as a percentage.

TECH NOTES:

None

ARF COMMENTS:

Social Click-Through Rate can be interpreted as a measure of the influence individuals have on their friend's propensity to click on an ad they Like or interact with.

CITED RESEARCH:

See the entry for Social Impressions.

SEE ALSO:

Click-Through Rate (CTR)
Social Impressions (Facebook)
Social Clicks

Social Clicks

AUTHORITY:	MEDIA:	STAGE:	CATEGORY:	APPLIES TO:
Facebook	Earned	2. Connect	5. Engagement/ Interaction	Social

ANSWERS QUESTION:

How many clicks did our Facebook ad receive from friends?

DEFINITION:

The number of times an ad was clicked with social context (i.e., with information about a viewer's friend(s). On Facebook for example, when Jane Doe Likes an ad that creates a story. The story may appear in a friend's News Feed. If the friend clicks on the ad, that is a Social Click.

Social clicks are most often associated with Facebook, but are not limited to Facebook.

TECH NOTES:

None

ARF COMMENTS:

Social clicks measure the interactions with an ad that one of their friends has endorsed in some way.

Researchers and brands are investigating the effectiveness of social clicks. One study of social clicks on Facebook concluded that "users are less likely to click on sponsored stories when more friends endorse the brand. Firms may not get value from social influence when promoting their brand through a platform such as Facebook. However, they may still get value from the ability of the platform to target individuals with similar preferences" (Agarwal & Hosanager 2012). This finding needs to be replicated, but appears to have some support from research showing that, for large CPG brands advertising on Facebook, 99% of offline sales were correlated with Facebook advertising view-throughs, not clicks (Ha 2012). Learning more about the value of social clicks is important because it will help clarify the role of endorsements and influence in social networks.

CITED RESEARCH:

Agarwal, Ashish and Kartik Hosanager (2012). Social Advertising: Does Social Influence Work? (http://goo.gl/UqkMo).

Ha, Anthony (2012). Facebook's Brad Smallwood Offers More Data on Ad Effectiveness, Says Datalogix Partnership Isn't a Privacy Risk (http://goo.gl/Qm3UU).

SEE ALSO:

Ad Impression
Click-Through Rate (CTR)
Social Click Rate
Social Impressions (Facebook)
Sponsored Story (Facebook)

Social Impressions (Facebook)

AUTHORITY:	MEDIA:	STAGE:	CATEGORY:	APPLIES TO:
Facebook	Paid	1. Capture	1. Advertising	Social

ANSWERS QUESTION:

How many impressions of our ad included social context?

DEFINITION:

The number of times a paid ad was shown to a viewer that includes stories about the viewer's friends created by engagement with the advertiser's Page, Events, or Applications.

TECH NOTES:

Social Impressions appear in Facebook's Advertising Performance Report.

ARF COMMENTS:

Social impressions are a hybrid, combining paid media formats with earned media. With social impressions a viewer's friends see an implied endorsement. Nielsen and Facebook research provides early evidence that social impressions are effective. They studied three types of exposure on reach and branding metrics. The exposure types were: organic impressions (stories that were generated by interacting with an ad that appear in friend's newsfeeds), paid advertising impressions, and social impressions. The branding metrics were awareness, recall, and purchase intent.

For reach, Nielsen and Facebook found that social impressions exhibited a comparable level of reach to paid ads. For the branding measures, social impressions occupied a middle ground between paid ads alone, which generated the lowest scores, and organic impressions, which generated the highest scores. Nielsen concludes that the power of social and organic impressions comes from paid advertising that drives engagement and generates stories.

Note: As of this writing, only Facebook offers this type of impression but similar offerings may be made available by other social networks.

CITED RESEARCH:

Nielsen and Facebook (2010). Advertising Effectiveness: Understanding the Value of a Social Media Impression (http://goo.gl/BJ5P6).

SEE ALSO:

Paid Ad Impression (Facebook)
Ad Impression
Earned Impression
Sponsored Story (Facebook)

Social Percentage (Facebook)

AUTHORITY:	MEDIA:	STAGE:	CATEGORY:	APPLIES TO:
Facebook	Paid	1. Capture	6. Amplification/ Endorsement	Social

ANSWERS QUESTION:

What percentage of our ads have a social element?

DEFINITION:

Social percentage is the percent of paid ad impressions that are social.

TECH NOTES:

Social Impressions appear in Facebook's Advertising Performance Report.

ARF COMMENTS:

CITED RESEARCH:

None

SEE ALSO:

Ad Impression (Facebook)

Ad Impression

Song Downloads

AUTHORITY:	MEDIA:	STAGE:	CATEGORY:	APPLIES TO:
	Owned	2. Connect	7. Conversion	Website Social Mobile

ANSWERS QUESTION:

How many songs were downloaded?

DEFINITION:

The number of song downloads over a specific period of time.

TECH NOTES:

None

ARF COMMENTS:

Downloads are a common conversion action on many sites. Analyzing downloads as part of a conversion funnel may help brands understand their contribution to a larger brand or site goal.

Numbers of downloads can indicate the popularity of a giveaway to connect with, and provide service to, consumers. Often the promotional materials are part of a program to spur another action. For this reason, it is often useful to look at measures the download may have influenced. For example, was the app installed after being downloaded (registration data can be used), were further inquiries made after a white paper download on the site or through another channel (check the CRM database), or did sales of an ingredient increase after a certain recipe or usage was promoted? As these examples suggest, evaluating the impact of content downloads may require additional data from the site and other corporate systems or resources. For example, Kraft's "Real Women of Philadelphia" site promoted cooking with Philadelphia Cream Cheese and offered recipes and contests. By tracking supermarket sales, Kraft determined that the initiative was bringing about the desired sales increases.

CITED RESEARCH:

None

SEE ALSO:

Key Content Downloads (Coupons, Recipes, Apps, etc.)

Source

AUTHORITY:	MEDIA:	STAGE:	CATEGORY:	APPLIES TO:
comScore	Owned	1. Capture	2. Audience/Traffic	Website Social Email Mobile

ANSWERS QUESTION:

Which sources within online media channels are visitors using to arrive at our site?

DEFINITION: .

A specific group within a channel that delivers traffic to your website. Examples include: Google, Yahoo, Twitter, Pinterest, and Facebook, newsletters, and direct (people who typed your URL into their browser or from a bookmark).

A channel is an online media type through which you attract browsers to your website. Examples include: Cost-per-Click (also called PPC, pay-per-click), RSS (Really Simple Syndication), Email, and Social Media

TECH NOTES:

None

ARF COMMENTS:

Understanding the sources used to reach your site provides guidance for gauging the strategy ("Is Facebook working as we would like?"), and the relative abilities of different sources to direct traffic. Channel and Source analysis is helpful for optimizing traffic—and the right traffic—to a site.

CITED RESEARCH:

None

SEE ALSO:

Channel
Referral Traffic

Sponsored Story (Facebook)

AUTHORITY:	MEDIA:	STAGE:	CATEGORY:	APPLIES TO:
Facebook	Paid	1. Capture	1. Advertising	Social Mobile

ANSWERS QUESTION:

What is a sponsored Story?

DEFINITION:

Sponsored stories were a form of Facebook advertising that combined an action taken a person took with a brand, and delivered that information as an ad to that person's friends in their newsfeeds.

TECH NOTES:

None

ARF COMMENTS:

Facebook eliminated the sponsored Story as separate ad unit in 2014. However, the social network has made it possible for advertisers to retain social context by allowing stories about the social actions friends have taken (liking, checking-in and son on) to appear next to all ads shown in the sidebar.

CITED RESEARCH:

None

SEE ALSO:

Ad Impression

Paid Impression—Page (Facebook)

Story (Facebook)

Story (Facebook)

AUTHORITY:
Facebook, comScore

MEDIA:
Earned

STAGE:
2. Connect

CATEGORY:
5. Engagement/ Interaction

APPLIES TO:
Social

ANSWERS QUESTION:

How many Facebook Stories were created by people who interacted with our page, app, or event?

DEFINITION:

The number of stories created about your page.

A Facebook story is created when: someone connects with a page, app, or Event. Stories may be created when a person takes action, such as: Likes a page; posts to a page Wall; Likes, comments on or shares a post; answers a question on a page; responds to an event; uses an app; mentions a page; tags a page in a photo; checks in at a place; or recommends a place. Stories may appear in the News Feeds of friends.

A story is an earned impression.

Note: If you are interested in the number of stories created for each action type, Facebook offers the Post Stories by Action Type metric. If the number of unique people creating stories about your post is of interest, Facebook offers Post Storytellers by Action Type.

TECH NOTES:

Stories may or may not appear in a user's News Feed because of a prioritization algorithm called Edge Rank. This computation takes into account the age of the post, the type of interaction (such as Like or Comment), and the frequency of interaction. When Facebook rolls out a new product or service, such as when it launched Place Check-Ins, they are often weighted higher than other types, making them more likely to show up. Facebook changes Edge Rank from time to time. Brands should keep up with changes to determine impacts to their pages and posts.

ARF COMMENTS:

Stories from friends become visible in the News Feed or on a friend's wall. Stories may also appear to Fans and Friends of Fans.

Facebook users can control which of their interactions are shared and that may generate stories. For this reason, the number of stories shared may not be equal to the number of interactions.

Stories from friends, when mentioning brands, businesses, or organizations, are a type of earned impression.

CITED RESEARCH:
None

SEE ALSO:
Earned Impression

Streams per Unique Viewer*

AUTHORITY:	MEDIA:	STAGE:	CATEGORY:	APPLIES TO:
Nielsen, comScore	Owned	2. Connect	4. Media Consumption	Website Social Mobile

ANSWERS QUESTION:

How many streams did Unique Viewers initiate over a reporting period?

DEFINITION:

Count of the number of streams initiated by Unique Viewers on a single measured source, over a reporting period.

Nielsen also supplies a related metric: Total Streams per Unique Viewer, that reports the average number of streams viewed by a Unique User over all measured properties.

TECH NOTES:

None

ARF COMMENTS:

Streams per Unique Viewer measures consumption. Trends in this metric may be helpful in understanding the appeal of the streaming content, but needs to be interpreted in light of the content strategy and business goals.

CITED RESEARCH:

None

SEE ALSO:

Views, Videos

Tab Views, Total (Facebook)

AUTHORITY:	MEDIA:	STAGE:	CATEGORY:	APPLIES TO:
Facebook	Owned	2. Connect	2. Audience/Traffic	Social

ANSWERS QUESTION:

Which Facebook Tabs were viewed on our page?

DEFINITION:

The number of times each of a page's tabs was viewed. Tabs available to view include: Timeline, Photos, Events, Information, and Others. Note: Facebook may add, delete, or modify these tab names.

TECH NOTES:

None

ARF COMMENTS:

Total Tab Views indicates how people are navigating a page; trends tell which tabs are most used. Facebook allows six tabs to be displayed. This metric can help optimize the number of tabs and identify which ones are most effective and should appear.

CITED RESEARCH:

None

SEE ALSO:

Page (Facebook, LinkedIn)

Target Audience*

AUTHORITY:	MEDIA:	STAGE:	CATEGORY:	APPLIES TO:
IAB, ARF	Paid	1. Capture	1. Advertising	Website Social Email Mobile

ANSWERS QUESTION:

Who are we targeting with our online advertising?

DEFINITION:

The intended audience for an ad, usually defined in terms of specific demographics or combinations of them (age, sex, income, geography, etc.), product purchase behavior, product usage, or media usage. Target audiences may also be defined by other factors such as affinity, psychographics, interests, and characteristic of devices used to access content.

TECH NOTES:

None

ARF COMMENTS:

Online targeting capabilities vary by publisher. It is essential to understand the specific targeting abilities for each network or site contemplated for an online media plan.

Explanations and case examples of various online targeting approaches are found in *The Online Advertising Playbook* (Plummer et al. 2007). These include targeting by conventional criteria such as by demographics, geography, and daypart, and ones that utilize visitors' online actions that are used for behavioral targeting and re-targeting, as well as by shared interests or affinities. Additional targeting criteria can include characteristics of devices used to access content and advertising, such as type (e.g., desktop, mobile, tablet), their operating systems, browser versions, carriers, or manufacturers.

comScore research on impression delivery shows that campaigns with "very basic demo targeting objectives" performed well. The best results were seen for single demo targeting, such as age, and then declined as two or three demos were combined. Their study offers intriguing evidence that targeting "behavioral segments"—the heaviest consumers (top 50%) of topic-specific web content, such as sports, food, cars, personal electronics, or travel, resulted in more accurate impression delivery than demographic targeting in some categories, such as automotive and a CPG. comScore's deeper analysis revealed that the automotive audience over-indexed in the financial products and family and parenting categories, suggesting that identifying overlaps of interest may aid in developing more relevant advertising in this and other categories (Abraham et al. 2012). Sites and services that require registration and log-ins, such as Facebook, Google+, or Twitter, for example, enable the creation of rich, detailed profiles provide advertisers with the potential to target advertising with very fine precision.

CITED RESEARCH:

Plummer, Joseph et al. (2007). The Online Advertising Playbook. Hoboken: John Wiley & Sons.

Abraham, Linda et al. (2012). Changing How the World Sees Digital Advertising. comScore (http://goo.gl/vld9h, free to download, registration required).

SEE ALSO:

Impressions
Target Impressions

Target Impressions

AUTHORITY:	**MEDIA:**	**STAGE:**	**CATEGORY:**	**APPLIES TO:**
comScore	Paid	1. Capture	1. Advertising	Website
				Social
				Email
				Mobile

ANSWERS QUESTION:

How many impressions were served to our target audience for a particular media buy?

DEFINITION:

The number of impressions in the media buy served to a particular target audience at that site.

TECH NOTES:

None

ARF COMMENTS:

▌ See the discussion of GRP and Ad Impression and Viewable Impression for detailed discussion.

CITED RESEARCH:

None

SEE ALSO:

Ad Impression
Frequency
Gross Ratings Points (GRP)
Reach
Viewable Impression

Time Spent Viewing, Average*

AUTHORITY:	MEDIA:	STAGE:	CATEGORY:	APPLIES TO:
comScore, Millward Brown Digital, Nielsen, Google DoubleClick, YouTube	Owned	2. Connect	4. Media Consumption	Website Social Mobile

ANSWERS QUESTION:

What is the average length of time a specific video stream is played per viewer, for a reporting period?

DEFINITION:

The average amount of time a specific video stream is viewed per viewer, expressed in minutes, over a defined reporting period.

Note: comScore calls this measure "Minutes per Viewer." Google DoubleClick reports a similar measure as "Video View Time," which is expressed in seconds. Nielsen calls it "Time Spent Viewing per Viewer."

Analytics vendors differ in their measurement approaches. Some vendors, like YouTube, do not count auto-plays. Others, such as comScore, count auto-plays and user-initiated plays that ran for at least three seconds

TECH NOTES:

None

ARF COMMENTS:

Average Time Spent Viewing, a consumption metric, may be considered a measure of engagement with specific video(s). The length of time watched needs to be evaluated in line with the length of the video. The time spent measure may gain additional context when analyzed along with video start rate, completion rate, user interaction rates, search behavior, and purchase data. Additionally, video is often used for branding. For this reason, studying the impacts of video on brand awareness is valued and often done by advertisers and agencies.

CITED RESEARCH:

None

SEE ALSO:

Estimated Minutes Watched
Time Spent Viewing, Total
Unique Viewers
Views, Videos

Time Spent Viewing, Total

AUTHORITY:	MEDIA:	STAGE:	CATEGORY:	APPLIES TO:
comScore, Millward Brown Digital, Nielsen, YouTube	Owned	2. Connect	4. Media Consumption	Website Social Mobile

ANSWERS QUESTION:

How long were our videos viewed?

DEFINITION:

The total time spent watching video(s) over a defined reporting period. Can be from any measured source.

Note: comScore names this metric "Total Minutes."

TECH NOTES:

Streams may be specific to a specific channel or aggregated across channels, depending on the analytical requirements.

comScore's video product manager Dan Piech (2013) points out that when multiple videos are being consumed simultaneously by a viewer, the durations of all video consumption should be added to the total minutes.

ARF COMMENTS:

Total Time Spent Viewing measures overall consumption. Trends in this metric over time may reflect changing interest in the video content brands make available for viewing. Examining the performance of individual videos and channels as contributors to the total, in the context of content strategy and business goals, may be helpful to optimizing video content and sources.

CITED RESEARCH:

Piech, Dan (2013). Personal communication.

SEE ALSO:

Estimated Minutes Watched
Time Spent Viewing, Average
Views, Videos

Time to Purchase*

AUTHORITY:	MEDIA:	STAGE:	CATEGORY:	APPLIES TO:
Facebook, Google, Millward Brown Digital	Owned	3. Close	8. E-Commerce	Website Social Email Mobile

ANSWERS QUESTION:

How many days and visits does it take for a visitor to purchase an item from our website?

DEFINITION:

The number of days and number of visits it takes to purchase, starting from the most recent campaign through the completed transaction (Google).

Facebook has a similar but slightly different metric called Conversions by Conversion Time. Facebook reports show the number of conversions organized by the time of the conversion event (e.g., purchase time), categorized by the length of time between a user's view or click on a Facebook Ad and the conversion (i.e., 0–24 hours, 1–7 days, 8–28 days).

TECH NOTES:

None

ARF COMMENTS:

This metric reveals how long it takes customers to make the decision to purchase, and how many visits to your site it takes to induce them to purchase. This information can help with revenue forecasting or with optimizing the site. Taking the former, for example, brands or products with regular sales cycles or seasonality can combine that knowledge with overall sales forecasts to make reasonable predictions about expected revenue. For sites whose customers visit several times before they purchase, brands might think about optimizing the site in ways that make it easier to reach transaction pages or make product or price comparisons. Many analytic packages offer a similar measure.

CITED RESEARCH:

None

SEE ALSO:

Conversion
Conversion Funnel

Top Viewed Pages*

AUTHORITY:	MEDIA:	STAGE:	CATEGORY:	APPLIES TO:
	Owned	2. Connect	4. Media Consumption	Website Social Mobile

ANSWERS QUESTION:

Which are the top viewed pages on our site?

DEFINITION:

A rank ordering of pages by the number of Page Views they generate over a reporting period.

TECH NOTES:

None

ARF COMMENTS:

Top Viewed Pages identifies those pages that are generating the most views. The metric can take on added value when segmented by different types of users (e.g., New Visitors, Returning Visitor), the source of traffic, or relevant page measures such as Time Spent on Page. Doing so can help gauge whether or not the pages most viewed are the brands in line with marketing and advertising strategy, which can then be adjusted accordingly. Additionally, Kaushik (2010) points out that this metric when combined with Top Entry Pages explain why people look at the pages they do.

CITED RESEARCH:

Kaushik, Avinash (2010). Web Analytics 2.0. Sybex.

SEE ALSO:

Entry Page (Top Entry Pages)
Page View

Total Impressions—Page (Facebook)

AUTHORITY:	MEDIA:	STAGE:	CATEGORY:	APPLIES TO:
Facebook	Paid Owned	1. Capture	1. Advertising	Social

ANSWERS QUESTION:

How many impressions did our page generate?

DEFINITION:

The number of impressions seen of any content associated with your page. These include paid impressions and organic (unpaid) impressions.

TECH NOTES:

Facebook reports metrics at the Page and Post levels. It is very important to make sure that you use the right ones for your analytic task. Post-level metrics are typically reported on a lifetime basis, whereas Page-level metrics are typically reported for daily, weekly, and 28-day periods.

ARF COMMENTS:

None

CITED RESEARCH:

None

SEE ALSO:

Ad Impression *

Total Impressions—Post (Facebook)

AUTHORITY:	MEDIA:	STAGE:	CATEGORY:	APPLIES TO:
Facebook	Paid Owned	1. Capture	1. Advertising	Social

ANSWERS QUESTION:

How many impressions did our post generate?

DEFINITION:

Count of the number of impressions of your page post over its lifetime. These include paid impressions and organic impressions.

TECH NOTES:

Facebook reports metrics at the Page and Post levels. It is very important to make sure that you use the right ones for your analytic task. Post-level metrics are typically reported on a lifetime basis, whereas Page-level metrics are typically reported for daily, weekly, and 28-day periods.

ARF COMMENTS:

None

CITED RESEARCH:

None

SEE ALSO:

Ad Impression

Organic Impressions—Posts (Facebook)

Paid Impressions—Post (Facebook)

Total Reach—Page (Facebook)

AUTHORITY:	MEDIA:	STAGE:	CATEGORY:	APPLIES TO:
Facebook	Paid Owned	1. Capture	2. Audience/Traffic	Social

ANSWERS QUESTION:

How many Unique people saw any content associate with our page?

DEFINITION:

The number of Unique people who have seen any content associated with a Facebook Page through paid or organic (unpaid) distribution over a reporting period.

Total Reach is often less than the sum of Paid and Organic reach because it counts the number of Unique people exposed to your content, not the number of exposures to that Unique person.

TECH NOTES:

Facebook Page Insights report Reach by a variety of segments for understanding how people reached a brand page and demographics on who was reached. These data are also available through third-party tools that use the Facebook API.

Facebook reports metrics at the Page and Post levels. It is very important to make sure that you use the right ones for your analytic task. Post-level metrics are typically reported on a lifetime basis, whereas Page-level metrics are typically reported for daily, weekly, and 28-day periods.

ARF COMMENTS:

The Facebook platform enables content to reach people through paid and organic distribution. Facebook states that the sum of people reached through paid and organic channels may be greater than the total because people may see your content through more than one of these channels. They are counted once for each channel, but only once in the Total. It is important to understand that Facebook has an algorithm, called EdgeRank, that optimizes each Facebook user's news feed, presenting content that is likely to garner the most engagement. EdgeRank thus limits distribution, meaning that every piece of content does not reach every potential recipient, thus placing limits on organic reach.

On Facebook, reach includes Fans, Friends of Fans, and non-fans. Facebook does not include all Friends of Fans but a subset—the number of people that can be exposed organically.

According to comScore, Friends of Fans are important to reach because they may include prospects who are not reached through owned or paid media. Studying visits to Southwest Airlines' website, comScore (2011) compared three groups: Fans, Friends of Fans who were exposed to earned media, and the average site visitor from the Total Internet. comScore learned that Fans made the most visits, but that Friends of Fans visited about three times as often as average site visitor. In a separate study, comScore (2012) studied Fans and Friends of Fans for Starbucks and Target, matching their purchase levels. Comparing Facebook Fans and Friends of Fans who were reached by organic media impressions to those who were not, comScore found that the Fans and Friends of Fans exposed to organic media impressions exhibited higher purchase lifts than the unexposed groups.

For official brand pages on Facebook, Reach within Facebook is influenced by the frequency of posting, along with the appeal and quality of the content. comScore research provides early support for this notion of posting frequency. Their research reveals that Reach increases as posting frequency increases, rising from about 8% reach for one time per week to about 22% for brands posting daily.

comScore's research suggests that socially influenced brand exposures may be related with increasing brand engagement among a secondary circle of relationships. This is intriguing because it relates to theories of influence and persuasion, and deserves much further study.

CITED RESEARCH:

comScore (2011). The Power of Like: How Brands Reach and Influence Fans Through Social Media Marketing (http://goo.gl/U1D9W).

comScore (2012). The Power of Like 2: How Social Marketing Works (http://goo.gl/G4nO7).

Facebook (2013). Updating Page Insights. (http://goo.gl/X5f29E).

SEE ALSO:

Fan (Facebook)

Organic Reach—Page (Facebook)

Paid Reach—Page (Facebook)

Total Reach—Post (Facebook)

AUTHORITY:	MEDIA:	STAGE:	CATEGORY:	APPLIES TO:
Facebook	Paid Owned	1. Capture	2. Audience/Traffic	Social

ANSWERS QUESTION:

How many unique people saw our page post?

DEFINITION:

The total number of unique people who have seen your page post over its lifetime across paid and organic (unpaid) channels.

Total Reach is often less than the sum of Paid and Organic reach because it counts the number of unique people exposed to your content, not the number of exposures to that unique person.

TECH NOTES:

Stories may or may not appear in a user's News Feed because of an optimization algorithm called Edge Rank. This computation takes into account the age of the post, the type of interaction (such as Like or Comment), and the frequency of interaction. Facebook changes Edge Rank from time to time. Brands should keep up with changes to determine impacts to their pages and posts.

Facebook reports metrics at the Page and Post levels. It is very important to make sure that you use the right ones for your analytic task. Post-level metrics are typically reported on a lifetime basis, whereas Page-level metrics are typically reported for daily, weekly, and 28-day periods.

ARF COMMENTS:

▌ See Total Reach—Page (Facebook) for discussion.

CITED RESEARCH:

None

SEE ALSO:

Organic Reach—Post (Facebook)
Paid Reach—Post (Facebook)
Reach

Unduplicated Video Reach

AUTHORITY:	MEDIA:	STAGE:	CATEGORY:	APPLIES TO:
comScore	Owned	1. Capture	2. Audience/Traffic	Website Social Mobile

ANSWERS QUESTION:

How many unique people did our video reach?

DEFINITION:

Measurement services have developed methods for calculating unduplicated video reach. At the present time, unduplicated video reach may be calculated on different universe estimates. comScore's definitions cover the range and are used here to demonstrate the variety.

comScore defines Unduplicated Video Reach as three distinct measures. They are all percentages. Each one uses the number of Unique Viewers for a given entity (show or program), but differ in the population of interest: Unique Viewers on the Total Internet, Total Number of Internet Users on the Total Internet, and Total Number of Individuals in the Population.

1) Viewer Penetration: the percentage of the number of Unique Viewers for a given entity to the Total Number of Unique Viewers on the Total Internet for the reporting period

2) % Reach Web Pop: the percentage of the number of Unique Viewers for a given entity to the Total Number of Internet Users (not just video viewers) on the Total Internet for the reporting period,

3) % Reach Total Pop: the percentage of the number of Unique Viewers for a given entity to the Total Number of Individuals in the Population for the reporting period.

TECH NOTES:

Unique viewers are counted by time period. If the time period is seven days, each person who comes to visit during that time is counted once, no matter how many times they visit.

Unique Video Viewers may be specific to a specific channel or aggregated across channels, depending on the analytical requirements.

ARF COMMENTS:

▌ Understanding the reach patterns of different videos may help brands optimize the types of videos they offer.

CITED RESEARCH:

Piech, Dan (2013). Personal communication.

SEE ALSO:

Reach

Unfollow/Unsubscribe*

AUTHORITY:	MEDIA:	STAGE:	CATEGORY:	APPLIES TO:
Facebook, YouTube, Twitter, Google +, Experian Marketing Services	Earned	4. Keep	2. Audience/Traffic	Website Social Email Mobile

ANSWERS QUESTION:

How many people have unsubscribed from our content?

DEFINITION:

Number of unique people who unfollow or unsubscribe from your content over a reporting period. Unsubscribing or unfollowing is usually accomplished by clicking a link or button or using an opt-out method.

Note: For emails, unsubscribes/unfollows are computed on the basis of emails delivered.

TECH NOTES:

None

ARF COMMENTS:

Unsubscribes/unfollows can be considered measures of relevancy, engagement, and loyalty. Unsubscribes are a part of life for digital marketers and advertisers, the key is keeping them as low as possible. Unsubscribes potentially reduce reach.

Tracking Unsubscribers/Unfollowers may be helpful for understanding changes in interest in your page or content. It may also be used to optimize content by identifying its patterns of Subscribes and Unsubscribes.

On Facebook, Unfollow enables people to remove your page's updates from their News Feed. Page owners with Unfollow buttons can see who unsubscribes to their pages.

CITED RESEARCH:

None

SEE ALSO:

Email Unsubscribe Rate
Followers/Subscribers

Unique App Users*

AUTHORITY: **MEDIA:**   **STAGE:**   **CATEGORY:**   **APPLIES TO:**

Webtrends   Owned   1. Capture   2. Audience/Traffic   Mobile

ANSWERS QUESTION:

How many unique users does our app have?

DEFINITION:

Number of unique application users over a defined time period.

TECH NOTES:

None

ARF COMMENTS:

This metric reveals the reach of an app, counting how many people are using an app after downloading and installing it. Trends in Unique Application Users can detect whether the app audience is growing or shrinking. Interpretation depends on the goal and time period. Like many metrics, calculating ratios can be helpful. For example, computing the ratio of Unique Application Users to Total Downloads over a specified period may suggest how engaging and desirable an app may be. Additionally, analyzing which features are used or not used can be used to optimize the app for users.

CITED RESEARCH:

None

SEE ALSO:

Mobile App Downloads

Unique Clicks

AUTHORITY:	MEDIA:	STAGE:	CATEGORY:	APPLIES TO:
Google, Facebook, Experian Marketing Services, Yahoo!	Paid Owned Earned	2. Connect	5. Engagement/ Interaction	Website Social Email Mobile

ANSWERS QUESTION:

How many Unique people clicked on our ad?

DEFINITION:

The number of Unique users that clicked on an ad or link within a web content or email, for a reporting period.

TECH NOTES:

The Uniqueness of a Click is related to the time period established by the analyst. If the time period is one day, the Uniqueness will reset 24 hours after a person clicked a link. This means that if a Unique User clicked on a link five (5) times in one day, that would be counted as one (1) Unique Click. If that person clicked on the same link 24 hours later, two (2) Unique Clicks would be reported (one for each day). Uniqueness is tracked using a cookie.

ARF COMMENTS:

Unique Clicks provide advertisers and content owners with insight into the number of individuals clicking their links, instead of focusing on the total number of clicks. Trends in Unique Clicks may give insight into the ability of the advertising to generate audience and traffic to an advertiser-specified landing page or destination. Unique Clicks are reported by many analytics programs across a variety of digital channels, such as email, social networks, search advertising, and content marketing.

CITED RESEARCH:

None

SEE ALSO:

Click-Through
Click-Through Rate (CTR)
Unique Visitors (Unique Browsers)

Unique Program Viewers or Listeners

AUTHORITY:	MEDIA:	STAGE:	CATEGORY:	APPLIES TO:
comScore	Owned	1. Capture	2. Audience/Traffic	Website Social Mobile

ANSWERS QUESTION:

How many unique people watched or listened to some amount of our program?

DEFINITION:

The total number of unique browsers that have spent a minimum number of seconds playing programs.

comScore calls this metric "Browser Minimum Playing Time."

TECH NOTES:

None

ARF COMMENTS:

Unique Viewers may be useful for getting a general indication of interest in the program and determining audience reach. It may take on additional value when comparing a brand's own programs or against competitor programs. Should be evaluated along with related metrics that reveal the degree of interest and depth of engagement for individual programs.

CITED RESEARCH:

None

SEE ALSO:

Reach

Unique Visitors (Unique Browsers)

Unique Viewers*

AUTHORITY:	MEDIA:	STAGE:	CATEGORY:	APPLIES TO:
YouTube, Nielsen, comScore	Owned	2. Connect	2. Audience/Traffic	Website Social Email Mobile

ANSWERS QUESTION:

How many unique people viewed some portion of our video?

DEFINITION:

Count of the number of discrete individuals that viewed a video for any length of time, for a reporting period.

Note: Measurement companies usually require that a video be watched (consumed) for a minimum amount of time.

TECH NOTES:

Unique viewers are counted by time period. If the time period is seven-days, each person who comes to visit during that time is counted once, no matter how many times they visit.

It is important to know if your measurement service has a minimum viewing time and its length. In comScore's reporting, for example, the minimum viewing time counted is three seconds.

ARF COMMENTS:

Comparing trends in Unique Viewers for different videos a brand or site offers may give indications of the videos and content that are of greatest and least interest to viewers, which can be helpful for planning new content to offer and optimizing the catalog of videos made available.

CITED RESEARCH:

None

SEE ALSO:

Unique Visitors (Unique Browsers)

Unique Visitors (Unique Browsers)*

AUTHORITY:	MEDIA:	STAGE:	CATEGORY:	APPLIES TO:
Google, Facebook, comScore, Nielsen, IAB, Yahoo!, Microsoft	Paid Owned	1. Capture	2. Audience/Traffic	Website Social Mobile

ANSWERS QUESTION:

How many Unique Visitors came to our site over a reporting period?

DEFINITION:

Unique Visitors, sometimes just called Visitors, are defined in two different contexts:
1) web analytics, and 2) audience measurement.

Web Analytics—Unique Visitors, sometimes called Unique Browsers, counts the number of Unique cookies which requested one or more pages from a web server or social network site during a reporting period. This is a measure of traffic.

Audience Measurement—Unique Visitors determines the number of Unique people, rather than cookies or computers, who are exposed to specific content or media. This is a measure of audience reach. Note: Nielsen refers to this metric as "Unique Audience."

There are three (3) types of visitors: New Visitor, Return Visitor, and Repeat Visitor.

TECH NOTES:

The Unique Visitors metric does not count a browser twice during the time period. For example, over a seven-day period, if a browser visits a site five times in one week, that browser is counted only one time. If the browser returns on the eighth day, he or she is counted once again as a Unique Visitor.

In the web analytics context, the most accurate visitor-tracking systems generally employ persistent cookies to maintain tallies of distinct visitors. Accurate counts also depend on removing automated activity from crawlers, spiders, or robots. Filtering can be done by blocking IP addresses from known bots, by requiring registration or site login, using cookies, or using panel data.

The Digital Analytics Association advises that: "A unique visitor count is always associated with a time period (most often day, week, or month), and it is a "non-additive" metric. This means that unique visitors can not be added together over time, over page views, or over groups of content, because one visitor can view multiple pages or make multiple visits in the time frame studied. Their activity will be over-represented unless they are de-duplicated. The deletion of cookies, whether 1st party or 3rd party, will cause unique visitors to be inflated over the actual number of people visiting the site. Users that block cookies may or may not be counted as unique visitors, and this metric is handled in different ways depending on the analytics tool used. Ask your tool provider how blocked cookies are managed in their tool: it is important to understand how this impacts other metrics with regard to these visitors."

Analytics expert Kaushik (2009) strongly cautions about duplication in the Daily, Weekly, and Monthly Unique Visitors numbers. He advocates for "Absolute Unique Visitors," used in Google Analytics, because it removes duplication for any time period of interest. Check with your analytics vendor to learn how Unique Visitors are counted.

Cookie deletion is a common practice that can result in over-counting Unique Visitors (Nguyen 2011). See the entry on Cookie for a detailed discussion.

ARF COMMENTS:

A Unique Visitor often, but not always, reflects a person. Computers that are shared, for example, have multiple users, yet they typically appear as one Unique Visitor.

comScore VP Industry Analyst Andrew Lipsman (2013) points out the importance of understanding Unique Visitors in the two contexts: web analytics (site measurement) and audience measurement. Unique Visitors, he argues, is best used in the audience measurement context, and should refer to the number of "Unique people" who visit a website. Unique Browsers is preferred for web analytics. Lipsman's distinction is practical. It enables brands to analyze website performance in ways that are specific to site or advertising objectives. Check with your analytics vendor on how Unique Visitors and Unique Browsers are defined and reported.

Sites requiring login or registration for use, such as Facebook, Google +, or YouTube, can more accurately identify Unique Visitors as Unique Users. Sites with large numbers of logged-in users have the potential to shift advertising on those sites from the conventional cost-per-thousand model of buying impressions for delivery to a mass audience to delivering impressions one-by-one to individual people. This can be a major change to media planning and buying, which should be explored by brands advertising on large networks with high numbers of signed-in users.

Segmenting Visitors by sources of traffic or type of visitor (new, returning, repeat) is a capability offered by many analytics solutions. Using segments is a good way to learn about types of visitors and from where traffic is coming, such as direct traffic, search engines, website referral, or ad, and how relevant and targeted traffic is or isn't. The goal is to maximize valuable traffic and minimize that which is not. Track and trend visitors over time to reveal seasonality, spikes, and patterns. Further, monitoring the Click Stream that different visitors and visitors from various traffic sources take may be used to optimize their experience on a site or network.

Primarily a measure of Capture (from a web analytics perspective), segmenting visitors by Connect, Close, and Keep stages may furnish observations about their use of a site or network in different contexts that help a brand achieve its objectives and improve the user experience.

CITED RESEARCH:

Kaushik, Avinash (2009). Standard Metrics Revisited: #6: Daily, Weekly, Monthly Unique Visitors" (http://goo.gl/0Pvlq).

Kaushik, A. (2010). Web Analytics 2.0, Sybex.

Lipsman, Andrew (2013). Personal communication.

Nguyen, Joe (2011). Cookie Deletion: Why It Should Matter to Advertisers and Publishers (http://goo.gl/VhCkW).

SEE ALSO:

Cookie

New Visitor

Repeat Visitors

Return Visitor

Repeat Visitors

Unique Users

Unlike/Dislike*

AUTHORITY:	MEDIA:	STAGE:	CATEGORY:	APPLIES TO:
Facebook, YouTube	Earned	4. Keep	6. Amplification/ Endorsement	Social

ANSWERS QUESTION:

How many Unlikes is our content getting?

DEFINITION:

Unlike or Dislike is the opposite of a Like. Unliking or Disliking an ad or content no longer counts a user as a supporter. Because people may change their minds, most services offering an Unlike/Dislike button enable allow people to remove or cancel their Unlikes or Dislikes.

TECH NOTES:

None

ARF COMMENTS:

Unliking/ Disliking reflects popularity and, on networks like Facebook, potentially lowers the Reach of a Page. Unliking/Disliking may have marketing and branding impacts as well, since they are often reporting on a page or for a specific ad or content. Brands should discover why their ad, page, or page content is Unliked/Disliked— analyzing comments may be one way—and then take actions to optimize them to increase relevance, reach, and effectiveness.

CITED RESEARCH:

None

SEE ALSO:

Like

Unlikes—Page (Facebook)

Unlikes—Page (Facebook)

AUTHORITY:	MEDIA:	STAGE:	CATEGORY:	APPLIES TO:
Facebook	Earned	4. Keep	6. Amplification/ Endorsement	Social

ANSWERS QUESTION:

How many Unlikes is our page getting?

DEFINITION:

A Page Unlike is the opposite of a Page Like. Unliking a Page removes a user as a page supporter and they are no longer counted in the Page's statistics.

TECH NOTES:

Facebook reports metrics at the Page and Post levels. It is very important to make sure that you use the right ones for your analytic task. Post-level metrics are typically reported on a lifetime basis, whereas Page-level metrics are typically reported for daily, weekly, and 28-day periods.

ARF COMMENTS:

Unliking a Page removes the Like and also the Liker's "Friends of Fans" from the Page statistics. Unliking lowers the Reach of a Page, and may have marketing and branding impacts as a result. Brands should discover why their page or page content is Unliked, and then take actions to optimize them increase relevance, reach, and effectiveness.

CITED RESEARCH:

None

SEE ALSO:

Like
Likes—Page (Facebook)
Negative Feedback from Users—Page (Facebook)

Video—Audience Retention

AUTHORITY:	MEDIA:	STAGE:	CATEGORY:	APPLIES TO:
YouTube	Owned	2. Connect	5. Engagement/ Interaction	Social

ANSWERS QUESTION:

How long are people watching our video?

DEFINITION:

The trend in viewer drop-off over the length of a video.

TECH NOTES:

Video plays are usually recorded as events in the event tracking capabilities of analytics packages.

Many brands have channels of video on sites like YouTube or Crackle, as well as their own sites. Most analytic packages offer the ability to track individual videos and roll them up into groups or channels.

ARF COMMENTS:

Analyzing the trend in audience retention can pinpoint those spots in the video where users maintain, increase, or lose interest. Knowing this is helpful for optimizing interest and engagement for a brand's videos.

CITED RESEARCH:

None

SEE ALSO:

Engagement—Video
Event Tracking
Views (Video)

Viewable Impression*

AUTHORITY:	MEDIA:	STAGE:	CATEGORY:	APPLIES TO:
IAB, 3MS, Media Rating Council, comScore	Paid	1. Capture	1. Advertising	Website Social Email Mobile

ANSWERS QUESTION:

How many of the impressions our campaign delivered had an opportunity to be seen?

DEFINITION:

A "Viewable Impression" officially occurs when the ad content is loaded, rendered, and at least 50% of the ad surface area is within the visible area of a viewer's browser window on an in-focus web page for at least one continuous second following the rendering of the ad.

TECH NOTES:

The Media Rating Council (MRC) carefully studied the Viewable Impression and approved it as a currency for transacting business based upon them on March 31. 2014. The MRCs Viewable Impression guidelines were primarily designed for desktop browser-based advertising rather than mobile advertising. The MRC recommends that companies measuring mobile display ads consider the guidelines as they are currently drawn until such time as specific guidelines are designed for mobile. Additionally, the MRC, along with the Internet Advertising Bureau and Mobile Marketing Association, assumes that ad impressions which are served in an in-application environment are viewable (MRC 2014).

viewable (MRC 2014).

ARF COMMENTS:

Impression counting is a matter of great debate, especially as digital media and mobile advance technologically. Industry organizations and private companies are exploring new ways of counting. Foremost among these are recommendations to move away from "served" impressions to "viewable" impressions. Notably, a joint industry effort by IAB, ANA, and 4As called "Making Measurement Make Sense," abbreviated as 3MS, advocates for the shift towards viewable-based metrics including reach and gross rating points (see IAB 2011). In addition to more accurate online impression counting, the viewable impression is seen as a way to bring about more comparable measurement across media, especially television in which the opportunity to see (OTS) is a core component of the definition (Vollman 2013).

Several research companies offer viewable impression counting and have been accredited by the MRC, such as comScore, DoubleVerify, Google (for Display Network and DoubleClick for Advertisers), and RealVu (Mane 2013, Miller 2013).

However, there are counter-arguments for moving to a strictly "viewable" counting currency, such as that: ads at the bottom of the page are encountered after user reading and scrolling and may be more relevant; that certain behaviors such as clicks can be deemed indicative of viewability; and also factors like time spent with an ad and engagement levels may influence effectiveness more than simply visibility. Additionally some observers suggest that only counting viewable impressions may lead to higher prices and less inventory for brand marketers (see Allen 2012).

Brands and agencies that need to count advertising impressions need to understand the various approaches available by measurement companies and publishers, weigh their strengths and weaknesses, and select the method(s) that best fit their business needs.

CITED RESEARCH:

3MS (2013). FAQs (http://goo.gl/o3m2Q).

Allen, Larry (2012). We Need a New Way to Define Ad Impressions. The Business Insider, February 14 (http://goo.gl/dlK8d).

IAB (2011). 3MS Initiative Releases 5-part Digital Marketing Measurement Solution. September 19 (http://goo.gl/xQHuz).

Koegel, Kathryn (2012). Is An Online Ad Still an Ad if Nobody Saw It? Advertising Age, April 9 (http://goo.gl/CEdk1).

Mane, Sherrill (2013). Better Safe than Sorry (http://goo.gl/z14qX).

Media Ratings Council (2014). Viewable Ad Impressions Measurement Guidelines, Version 1.0 (Final). June 30 (http://goo.gl/1sLBdl)

Miller, Simon (2013). Media Measurement Auditing Body the Media Rating Council (MRC) Has Accredited Google's Viewability Measurement Product Active View (http://goo.gl/t3bgc).

Vollman, Andrea (2013). Personal communication.

SEE ALSO:

Ad Impression

Frequency

Gross Rating Points (GRP)

Reach

Views

AUTHORITY:	MEDIA:	STAGE:	CATEGORY:	APPLIES TO:
	Paid	1. Capture	1. Advertising	Website
	Owned			Social
	Earned			Email
				Mobile

ANSWERS QUESTION:

What is a View?

DEFINITION:

Often used as a synonym for "impression." See Ad Impression for details.

TECH NOTES:

None

ARF COMMENTS:

▌ Discussion about the various types of impressions are found in the entries listed in the "see also" section.

CITED RESEARCH:

None

SEE ALSO:

Ad Impression

Views, Videos*

AUTHORITY:
comScore, Millward Brown Digital, Google DoubleClick, YouTube

MEDIA:
Owned

STAGE:
2. Connect

CATEGORY:
4. Media Consumption

APPLIES TO:
Website
Social
Mobile

ANSWERS QUESTION:

How many times was our video viewed?

DEFINITION:

Count of the number of discrete instances of a video stream for a reporting period.

Analytics vendors differ in their measurement approaches. Some vendors, like YouTube, do not count auto-plays. Others, such as comScore, count auto-plays and user-initiated plays that ran for at least three seconds. YouTube defines a View as a playback of any duration. YouTube calls a playback of 30 seconds or more an "exhibition."

Note: comScore calls this metric "Videos."

TECH NOTES:

Video views are usually recorded as events in the event tracking capabilities of analytics packages. Video events can be defined as granularly as needed, but usually include: start, stop, pause, length of time played, exit point, rewind, and replay.

Analytics vendors sometimes require a minimum playing time for the view to be counted. For example, comScore defines that an individual must have consumed at least three seconds of a video to be counted. Additionally, check with your analytics vendor to understand how autoplays are treated.

ARF COMMENTS:

Counting video plays provides guidance on which videos are popular. Analytics packages often report them in lists, organized by most to least played. Understanding the types of video content that receive plays helps with optimizing the video assets of a site, with the aim of promoting more viewing and engagement.

Because views can be counted as started by autoplay or through a user event, it is important to make sure that the views you are counting are the type you want to count.

CITED RESEARCH:
None

SEE ALSO:
Estimated Minutes Watched
Time Spent Viewing, Average
Time Spent Viewing, Total
Unique Viewers

Viral Impressions—Page (Facebook)

AUTHORITY:	MEDIA:	STAGE:	CATEGORY:	APPLIES TO:
Facebook	Earned	1. Capture	6. Amplification/ Endorsement	Social

ANSWERS QUESTION:

How many impressions did our page generate virally?

DEFINITION:

The number of impressions of a story published by a friend about your page. Stories are generated by someone liking your page; posting to a page's Wall; Liking, commenting on, or sharing a page post; answering a posted Question; RSVPing to an event; mentioning a page, phototagging a page; or checking in at a place. Facebook once reported Viral impressions separately. They are included in Organic Impressions and no longer broken out independently.

TECH NOTES:

None

ARF COMMENTS:

None

CITED RESEARCH:

None

SEE ALSO:

Earned Impressions

Organic Impressions—Page (Facebook)

Total Impressions—Page (Facebook)

Viral Impressions—Post (Facebook)

AUTHORITY:	MEDIA:	STAGE:	CATEGORY:	APPLIES TO:
Facebook	Earned	1. Capture	6. Amplification/ Endorsement	Social

ANSWERS QUESTION:

How many viral impressions did our page post generate?

DEFINITION:

The number of impressions of your page post in a story generated by a friend, over a reporting period. Viral Impressions are now included in Organic Impressions and not reported separately.

TECH NOTES:

None

ARF COMMENTS:

None

CITED RESEARCH:

None

SEE ALSO:

Earned Impressions

Organic Impressions—Post (Facebook)

Total Impressions—Post (Facebook)

Viral Reach—Post (Facebook)

AUTHORITY:	MEDIA:	STAGE:	CATEGORY:	APPLIES TO:
Facebook	Paid	1. Capture	2. Audience/Traffic	Social

ANSWERS QUESTION:

How many people did our post reach through stories created by friends?

DEFINITION:

The number of unique people who saw your page post through sponsored page content, including viral stories, resulting from paid impressions.

Viral Reach is now included as part of Organic Reach. Page Admins not participating in the Preview will continue to have Viral Reach reported separately.

TECH NOTES:

Stories may or may not appear in a user's News Feed because of an optimization algorithm called Edge Rank. This computation takes into account the age of the post, the type of interaction (such as Like or Comment), and the frequency of interaction. Often, when Facebook rolls out a new product or service, such as when it launched Place Check-ins, they are weighted higher than other types, making them more likely to show up. Facebook changes Edge Rank from time to time. Brands should keep up with changes to determine impacts to their pages and posts.

ARF COMMENTS:

▌ See Organic Reach—Page (Facebook) for discussion.

CITED RESEARCH:

Facebook (2013). Updating Page Insights (http://goo.gl/X5f29E).

SEE ALSO:

Organic Reach—Post (Facebook)
Reach
Total Reach—Post (Facebook)

Viral Reach—Page (Facebook)

AUTHORITY:	MEDIA:	STAGE:	CATEGORY:	APPLIES TO:
Facebook	Earned	1. Capture	2. Audience/Traffic	Social

ANSWERS QUESTION:

How many unique people saw any of our Facebook brand page content through a friend's story?

DEFINITION:

Viral reach is the number of unique people who saw your page from a story published by a friend, over a reporting period.

Viral Reach is now included in Organic Reach and no longer separately reported.

TECH NOTES:

None

ARF COMMENTS:

None

CITED RESEARCH:

Facebook (2013). Updating Page Insights (http://goo.gl/X5f29E).

SEE ALSO:

Organic Reach—Page (Facebook)
Reach
Total Reach—Page (Facebook)

Virality/Engagement Rate—Post (Facebook)

AUTHORITY:	MEDIA:	STAGE:	CATEGORY:	APPLIES TO:
Facebook	Earned	2. Connect	6. Amplification/ Endorsement	Social

ANSWERS QUESTION:

What percentage of people who saw our post engaged with it by liking, sharing, commenting, or clicking?

DEFINITION:

Facebook (2013) explains that: "[Virality] doesn't include clicks in its measurement, which are a strong indicator of positive post engagement and a key piece in providing marketers with metrics around overall post quality. So moving forward, we're including clicks in this metric and renaming 'virality' to 'engagement rate' to be clearer in our definition."

TECH NOTES:

None

ARF COMMENTS:

Facebook renamed Virality to "Engagement Rate" because "Virality did not include clicks in its measurement, which Facebook considers a strong indicator of positive post engagement and a key piece in providing marketers with metrics around overall post quality." (Facebook 2013).

Engagement Rate indicates which posts on your page people interact with more, and by doing so suggests the types of posts that create stories and can expand your page's reach. Examining this metric in combination with Engaged Users and People Engaged may provide additional context for optimization.

Facebook has been moving towards measures that more precisely capture only those actions which are presumably more relevant to advertisers. Replacing Virality with Engagement Rate is a good example of this direction. Another example is the addition of People Engaged, a more focused measure of engagement types than the more general Engaged Users.

CITED RESEARCH:

Facebook (2013). Updating Page Insights (http://goo.gl/X5f29E).

SEE ALSO:

Engaged Users—Post (Facebook)
Reach—Page (Facebook)

Visit (Session)*

AUTHORITY:	MEDIA:	STAGE:	CATEGORY:	APPLIES TO:
Digital Analytics Association, comScore, Nielsen, IAB	Owned	1. Capture	2. Audience/Traffic	Website Social Mobile

ANSWERS QUESTION:

How many times did someone come to do something on our website?

DEFINITION:

A Visit is a series of requests from the same uniquely identified individual (a Unique Visitor) over a reporting period. A Visit is made up of one or more Page Views and often shows a track through a site. A Visit ends after a defined period of inactivity, often 30 minutes. A Visit is also called a session.

For social media and user-generated content, IAB defines a visit in a similar vein, but slightly differently to reflect its unique aspects: a single continuous set of activity attributable to a cookied browser or user (if registration-based or a panel participant) resulting in one or more pulled text and/or graphics downloads from a site.

TECH NOTES:

While most measurement services end a session after 30 minutes of inactivity, Google treats it differently. In Google's computation, if the browser is closed and the visitor returns within 30 minutes, the session will continue unless the source of traffic changes.

The Visits metric can be distorted by automated programs—robots, spiders, or crawlers—that visit websites to collect information, perform an action on the site, or index its content. Filtering that automated traffic out is essential for deriving meaningful counts of visits, as well as Hits, Visitors, Bounces, Page Views, Time on Site, and % New Visits.

While Page Views are usually requested, the Digital Analytics Association explains that Hits may be useful at times. "In the case of sites where interaction consists solely of file downloads, streaming media, Flash, or other non-HTML content, a request for this content may or may not be defined as a "page" in a specific web analytics program but could still be viewed as a valid request as part of a visit. The key is that a visitor interaction with the site is represented."

ARF COMMENTS:

The number of Visits during a reporting period may be greater than the number of Unique Visitors because a Unique Visitor may initiate more than one session over the time period being measured.

The number of Visits/Sessions is mainly used as a Capture measure of traffic to a website, where the main concern is learning how many times people come to your property. Analysts, like Kaushik (2012), recommend trend analysis over long periods of time so that one can understand overall growth, seasonality, and spikes.

Segmenting Visits/Sessions by types of engagement and/or actions taken (and type of visitor) may be helpful for understanding the relationship between Visits and targeted behaviors in the Connect and Close stages. For example, if a brand targets newsletter signup as a Connect behavior and learns that it takes three Visits on average for visitors to subscribe, the brand can judge whether that is acceptable and, if not, take steps to optimize the signup. In the Keep context, tracking Visits from Return Visitors may be construed as a measure of loyalty.

Visits can also be a useful tool for competitive analysis of one's website to others in its category or competitive set. Metrics like "share of visits" can be easily calculated, for example. Additionally, some observers feel that Visits can be a better metric than Page Views because pages can be undercounted.

CITED RESEARCH:

Kaushik, Avinash (2010). Web Analytics 2.0: The Art of Online Accountability and Science of Customer Centricity (Sybex).

SEE ALSO:

Average Time Spent on Site (Session Length)

Page Views per Visit

Visits—Buy Now Section

AUTHORITY:
Millward Brown
Digital, Patel & Flores

MEDIA:
Owned

STAGE:
3. Close

CATEGORY:
8. E-Commerce

APPLIES TO:
Website
Mobile

ANSWERS QUESTION:

How many visits to our site's Buy Now section are we attracting?

DEFINITION:

Represents the section of the website that displays retail outlets (offline/online) where products are available.

TECH NOTES:

Depending on marketing objectives, this metric can be computed on the basis of Visits alone, but also on the basis of Visits per Unique visitor.

ARF COMMENTS:

For e-commerce oriented sites, Visits to the Buy Now Section are often a step in the Conversion Funnel. The number of visits provide a measure of the effectiveness of advertising or site content to drive purchase consideration, and therefore has potential impacts on revenue and profitability.

Calculating a ratio of visits to purchases can give an indication of the site's ability to convert a shopper from a visitor to a buyer. However, relating purchases to Buy Now Section visits may require incorporating other data sources, especially when the purchases take place off your site. For this reason, treating the visit to this section as a conversion event and assigning it a dollar value can provide insight into the site's sales power.

Additionally, computing this metric on a Visits per Unique Visitor basis allows for more fine-grained understanding.

CITED RESEARCH:

None

SEE ALSO:

Conversion
Conversion Funnel
Conversion Rate
Visit (Session)
Unique Visitors (Unique Browsers)

Visits—Customer Service/Support Section

AUTHORITY:	MEDIA:	STAGE:	CATEGORY:	APPLIES TO:
Millward Brown Digital, Patel & Flores	Owned	2. Connect	5. Engagement/ Interaction	Website Mobile

ANSWERS QUESTION:

How many visits is the support section of our site getting?

DEFINITION:

Count of the number of visits to the sections of a website that offer customer service, product support, or technical support over a reporting period.

TECH NOTES:

Depending on marketing objectives, this metric can be computed on the basis of Visits alone, but also on the basis of visits per Unique Visitor.

ARF COMMENTS:

Count of Visits to Customer Service can provide indicators of customer problems and issues. Trending this data is very helpful. While spikes and drops in visits may indicate issues appearing or receding, it is vitally important to learn why the visits are coming in or not. Having a way to categorize the Count of Visits to Customer Service, such as with a checklist of reasons, provides valuable diagnostics as to where the problem(s) reside and suggest courses of actions to take or remedies to develop. Similarly, comparing visits and resolution measures (completions, time to resolution, satisfaction) can provide indicators of the quality of customer service.

Further, if the metric is calculated as Visits per Unique Visitor, different insights into support are possible. For example, a high number of Visits may indicate problems with the service or information provided.

CITED RESEARCH:

None

SEE ALSO:

Unique Visitors (Unique Browsers)
Visit (Session)

Visits—Store Locator Section

AUTHORITY:	MEDIA:	STAGE:	CATEGORY:	APPLIES TO:
Millward Brown Digital, Patel & Flores	Owned	3. Close	8. E-Commerce	Website Mobile

ANSWERS QUESTION:

How often was the store locator feature visited?

DEFINITION:

Count of the number of visits to the website section that offers store location features.

TECH NOTES:

Depending on marketing objectives, this metric can be computed on the basis of Visits alone, but also on the basis of Visits per Unique visitor.

ARF COMMENTS:

For brands with brick and mortar locations or who sell through online third-parties, visits to the Store Locator are often a step in the Conversion Funnel. The number of visits provide a measure of the effectiveness of advertising or site content to drive purchase consideration, and therefore has potential impacts on revenue and profitability. Visits to Store Locator section metrics may be made more useful by computing the ratio of this metric to store or third-party visits and sales, if they are available. For this reason, treating the visit to this section as a conversion event and assigning it a dollar value can provide insight into the site's sales power.

Further, if the metric is calculated as Visits per Unique Visitor, different insights into shopping are possible. For example, a high number of Visits may indicate problems with the information—it may be out of date, or it is not being presented in a way that is helpful.

CITED RESEARCH:

None

SEE ALSO:

Unique Visitors (Unique Browsers)
Visit (Session)

Viewpoints

Viewpoints on Measurement:
The Present and Its Futures

Leading authorities on measurement contributed 12 essays to this volume. We divided them into two groups: Viewpoints 1's four essays concern measurement and perspectives in today's media, marketing, and advertising environment; Viewpoints 2's eight pieces discuss emerging practices and the future for measuring. Over the last 15 years, our industry struggled to extend mass media principles into the digital realm. But these latter essays make it clear that a new way is needed: The longstanding mental models derived from those principles which shaped strategy and measurement for decades are being challenged, updated, or replaced with those designed for a more humanistic era, the era of humetrics. Both sets of essays provide valuable guidance for coping with today's needs and dealing effectively with ever more digital and social tomorrows.

Viewpoints 1:
Perspectives and Practices in Today's Measurement Landscape

Digital audience measurement and media delivery for the important purposes of media planning, buying, evaluating delivery, and gauging advertising effectiveness summarize the interests of these writers. They offer very practical guidance:

Embrace comparable cross-platform measurement. Quantify, compare, and evaluate digital and analog media with standardized metrics such as the Viewable Impression, and eventually basing GRPs on a common population number.

Approach measurement with a strategy. Begin by selecting achievable brand objectives, identifying the measurement needs, utilizing a measurement framework, choosing the metrics that matter, partnering with a supplier and, importantly, sharing objectives with the supplier to make sure that the client and supplier are aligned.

Understand and improve delivery. Not all advertising impressions are served to the intended consumer target, in the specified geographies, or on sites that are "brand safe," for example. Accounting for variables like these reduces the number of misdirected impressions, improves targeting accuracy, and may lead to greater advertising effectiveness.

Optimize advertising campaigns in near-real time. Advances in online survey capabilities for measuring attitude and behavioral changes make it possible to adapt and adjust campaigns, media placement, or individual creative executions quickly.

Viewpoints 2:
A More Social Measurement Future

These essays point to the future, pushing our thinking to metrics that incorporate the "social" part of social media and the human within measurement. Their themes constitute an agenda our industry might benefit from debating and working on:

Challenge the need for a cross-platform metric. In contrast with Part 1 writers, these essayists are not certain that comparable cross-media measures are necessary. Re-creating measures designed for the analog era and a mass media model of advertising stifles innovation in the digital realm for brand building and customer experience, constrains media planning and buying to demographics instead of consumer's behavior and other relevant characteristics. *Note: GE's Andy Markowitz made a similar point at ARF's 2013 Re:think Conference. He explained that the company's approach focuses not on evaluating media based on syndicated metrics but on buying media on the basis of an outlet's ability to drive specific consumer behaviors the company deems valuable (reported in Precourt 2013).*

Develop a new model for advertising based on effectiveness, not media exposure. The way many in our industry believe how advertising works is rooted in the 19th century and 75-plus years of mass-media thinking. We need to modernize our understanding of how advertising works and why it works, identify its ultimate goal (e.g., sales or advocacy), and do so in a way that is grounded in contemporary knowledge and empirically supported. Raising our ability to predict outcomes may lead to better practices, better advertising, and better returns.

Incorporate social understanding into the new model of effectiveness. Although several initiatives underway aim to develop and include social data in media currency metrics, such as the 3MS program studying "cumulative social activity" (2012), this book's experts are far more interested in understanding people as people; their situations, actions, behaviors, language, mindsets, and emotions. They seek to know what people do with brand advertising and communications in order to understand effectiveness and to create more effective advertising.

Cross-pollinate. Researchers from different yet complimentary traditions study social behavior and media. Interested in the consumer as citizen, they want to learn how media impacts the actions of people who want to bring about social change in some form. Media engagement is key for them, as it is for us in the commercial sector. Sharing research tools and insights may become one way for us in advertising to expand our knowledge of engagement and apply it in ways that benefits brands and their consumers, and vice versa. ✦

REFERENCES

3MS (2013). FAQs. See: Are social media metrics under development? (http://goo.gl/o3m2Q).

Precourt, Geoffrey (2013). GE's New Digital Marketing Metric: Behavior, Not Numbers. WARC (Available to subscribers. Comments were made during a panel discussion at the conference).

Viewpoints 1:
Perspectives and Practices
in Today's Measurement Landscape

These four essays form a compelling narrative about measurement and measuring today. They take us from the need for cross-platform measurement, through selecting metrics, to measuring campaign delivery and effectiveness

Nielsen's **Megan Clarken** begins by explaining the need for cross-platform measurement and why it is important. Content, Clarken states, is king. For media owners to attract advertising dollars, they need metrics that enable performance comparisons and contrasts across all media types and devices so that each media owner can tell their most convincing story. Ideally, the metrics would come from an independent agency with experience in multi-screen measurement and adheres to standards.

Max Kilger of Experian Marketing Services recognizes that we operate in a world with many metrics, from many different sources. To avoid the "melee of metrics" he mentions, brands and their partners should spend time organizing metrics into a framework (heuristic) so that they can be selected, structured, and related in a way meaningful to the brand. In this era of Big Data, Kilger makes the important point that "more data does not mean better metrics" because of different types of measurement problems. Knowing what the data actually measure and insisting on quality is more important than ever. His discussion of the "privacy paradox" with its critical implications for both data quality and the quality metrics produced should be strongly considered by every organization collecting consumer data.

But which metrics should a brand use? Here GfK's **Florian Kahlert** explains how to relate metrics to the brand—clearly state brand objectives at the outset and agree on them. Then make sure they are achievable, know what you need to measure, select the tools for measuring, decide if you want to rely on your media partner or an independent party, and share your goals with your measurement partner to be on the same page.

Brands running advertising need to know about performance: Is the media plan delivering? Is our advertising effective? On the delivery question comScore's **Gian Fulgoni** explains that Gross Rating Points (GRP) are increasingly being used to plan and measure digital campaigns. He shows that by using viewable impressions and by improving targeting, brands can see that their campaigns are being delivered as intended. (Note: see the entries for viewable impression, GRP and target audience for details.) For effectiveness, Fulgoni points out that consumers' attitudinal and behavioral changes can be measured in near real-time. With this metrical insight and the capabilities of digital advertising technologies, advertisers and agencies are in a position to optimize their campaigns while they are running, increase relevancy of the message, and potentially improve advertising performance. ✦

The Case for Holistic Measurement

BY MEGAN CLARKEN | EVP, GLOBAL PRODUCT LEADERSHIP, NIELSEN

While radios, TVs, and newsprint continue to form part of our personal media choices, we will still have media companies and industries who claim ownership of these consumption platforms and the rules that regulate them. But who owns the Internet, and can the media industry continue to try to lay claim to the devices consumers use to access content?

In the past, concepts of ownership were simple. TV media giants owned the TV set and set the standards for how we rate programs. Newspaper and magazine publishers owned the printed press and set the rules for how we count readership and circulation. Radio companies owned the radio and set the rules for how we measure listenership. The world was reasonably simple and siloed, as media brands competed against each other for the attention of advertisers.

. . . media companies are no longer competing against one another, but against every other form of activity known to man . . .

But roll forward: Who owns the PC, the smartphone, the tablet, and who owns the next screen or device on which we'll consume media? Is ownership of the device even relevant anymore? What is the Online Media Industry? Do they own these devices and how we measure them? What is an online media company anyway?

I've worked in the media industry for several decades now and here's how I see it—a media company is one that uses a medium to communicate to people. In order to sustain their business, they need revenue, and that revenue is primarily generated through advertising. In order to attract advertising, they need to distribute compelling content that attracts their audience. Contemporary audiences demand that content be available anywhere, anytime.

For companies that fulfill these caveats, the single most important element above is compelling content. Not a classified ad, or a storefront, nor a search result, for that matter, but good old-fashioned content.

For media companies today, while some may lay claim to the traditional device that they originated from, none can claim the digital "airwaves" or the device at the other end— they can and should all use digital to their advantage.

So, we're left with a media world that is 100% digitally enabled, aimed at distributing compelling content anywhere, anytime, sustained by advertising revenue.

If you believe this—it is perilous not to—then you also have to believe that in order to attract advertising dollars, the measurement requirements are the same for all media companies regardless of where the content is delivered.

How many people did I reach, how many times did I reach them, did I reach target, did the message resonate, and did it generate the desired reaction?

Regardless of whether the medium is addressable or not, regardless of how the ad was placed, as a media company, to compete against the rest, there needs to be a compelling story—and that story is best told as one set of numbers, regardless of where and how the content was consumed or the ad was delivered.

Evidence shows that those numbers are best sourced through an independent provider who understands multi-screen behavior and how to measure across platforms and who instills advertiser confidence through trust, transparency, and compliance.

Why is this important? Unlike traditional media devices, digital devices introduce "audience leakage." In other words, media companies are no longer competing against one another, but against every other form of activity known to man. Bored with this program I'll just play a game, surf using search, I'll shop—in other words, competition to retain an audience on these devices is fierce. To retain a premium for advertising, companies must tell a premium story— across devices covering the reach, resonance, and reaction to content and advertising I mentioned a moment ago.

What about the other "Online businesses"? Well, they're just businesses that have found a channel and taken advantage of the technology—adapting their business model to be relevant in a digital world. Shopping, searching, matching—they're offline business models that skipped straight past GO and collected $200. They also need measurement, but the KPIs that define their success are different. What I can assure you is that they have them and are refining them by the day to also compete for advertising dollars.

The takeaway for media companies is to focus on what they do best, creating and distributing compelling content over all of the channels that are available to them. Sell the story as a complete and premium story and measure it that way, independently, and comparatively. Finally, be good at it—the competition has just begun and you no longer own the screen. ✦

Putting Big Data and Big Data Metrics in Perspective

BY MAX KILGER, PH.D ▮ CHIEF BEHAVIORAL SCIENTIST, EXPERIAN CONSUMER INSIGHTS

One consequence of Big Data is the plethora of new metrics that are available today, as this book amply demonstrates. In some of the mobile research Experian Simmons has done, I have described the situation as a "melee of metrics." There is such a staggering array of Big Data-generated metrics that researchers have difficulty selecting which ones are really important, as well as deciding what those selected metrics really mean.

Organizing schemes (heuristics) play an important role in overcoming the selection and meaning problem by revealing the structure and relationships among metrics. For example, when faced with a gaggle of more than one hundred mobile metrics, my colleagues and I developed a heuristic in the shape of a pyramid (Figure 1) that clearly outline their purpose and their relationships.

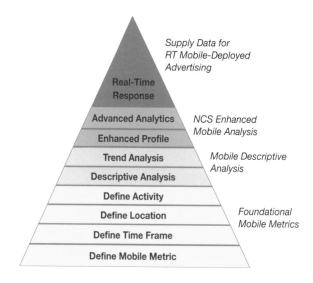

Figure 1. Heuristic Device for Mobile Metrics, Experian Consumer Insights

This step facilitated a much better understanding of the measurement arena for the researchers involved that later guided the development of relevant client-facing metrics dashboards.

More Data Does Not Mean Better Metrics

Big Data's emergence in market research derives in no small part from the deployment of passive measurement applications that run in the background on platforms, such as mobile devices, and record application use, web browsing, and GPS location, for example. However, using passive measurement does not always directly translate into more accurate measurement. Consider the case when someone opens an application on their smartphone, uses it, and then puts the phone away without closing the

application—the "pocketful of measurement problem." Monitoring applications often record the application as open and being used for a long period of time when it fact it is no longer being used by the person. How much time was actually spent with the app? We can't know. Problems like these introduce gross inaccuracies that are capable of generating potentially misleading metrics that lead to bad insights and poor decisions. Disentangling measurement issues such as these are some of the challenges Big Data researchers must grapple with if Big Data promises are to be realized.

The Issue of Privacy and Big Data

Big Data brings privacy to the forefront. Connecting many disparate databases to produce a clearer picture of the consumer elevates privacy concerns. Market researchers need to build a better, more comprehensive understanding of privacy. Phenomena such as the privacy paradox—where individuals express conservative views about personal privacy but then exhibit behaviors that suggest just the opposite—need to be understood. For example, a recent national probability study found that about 37% of the adult US population would be willing to provide some personal information to a company in order to get something they want. How the privacy paradox affects consent rates, return rates, item non-response, and other key response measures is important because, like passive measurement, it affects data quality and ultimately the value of the metrics we produce and the actions we take based on them.

> . . . market researchers need to build a better, more comprehensive understanding of privacy . . .

Summary

In summary, the emergence of Big Data and Big Data metrics heralds a new era that is likely to change market research in ways that will persist for many years. The potential for discovery and advancing our knowledge of consumers and consumer behavior is significant. Despite the hype and magical thinking around Big Data's potentials and benefits, the new metrics we work with must be derived from high quality data sources. Every brand needs to establish or enforce their own data standards—quality in, quality out—and select those metrics that measure what is meaningful for the brand. It is an exciting and a challenging time for researchers; hopefully we will make the best of this new era in marketing to benefit our brands and customers. ✦

Finding the Right Digital Metrics for Brand Marketing

BY FLORIAN KAHLERT ▌ MANAGING DIRECTOR OF DIGITAL MARKET INTELLIGENCE, GFK

In the early days, the allure and promise of digital media were that they were directly measurable—practically Nirvana for people who wanted to understand the value of their advertising.

But with the opportunities came controversies—many of them "teapot tempests," from today's perspective. First we started quibbling about a page impression—should it be defined by a hit or a page load? Then we tried to nail down the ad impression—should it count only when the ad is fully downloaded, or when it is simply requested from the ad server? Clicks came into fashion—but after people started generating automated clicks for campaigns, they fell out of fashion.

> . . . we cannot change the goals to match the most convenient metrics, and we should not pretend that clicks are equal to purchase intent . . .

Things only get more complex when we begin to look at brand advertising. Does a click really represent a changed attitude towards a brand? Is it really more relevant when the user engages with a brand message for ten seconds rather than five? Or 20 seconds rather than 15?

The truth is, we have tried a lot of metrics and approaches—not necessarily because they were the right metrics, but because they seemed easy to collect and to measure reliably. And, for things like direct response advertising, this expedient approach works pretty well.

But the picture is quite different for brands. Brands are often not looking for a conversion (you won't likely be buying cheese slices online); they have goals that are less easily measured. And here I just said the critical word: Goals. A goal can be a change in attitude towards a brand, recall, association, favorability, purchase intent—or, ideally, purchases online or offline. Those goals most often cannot be expressed by easy digital metrics (clicks?); they are more difficult to pin down.

To make matters more complicated, not all brand marketers have the same goals for their campaigns; in fact, a marketer might have two goals for the same campaign. For a new brand, awareness may be the priority; but for toothpaste with 90% awareness, purchase intent will likely take precedence. The challenge is to measure what the campaign was intended to achieve.

To be insightful, then, a metric must be relevant. We cannot change the goals to match the most convenient metrics, and we should not pretend that clicks are equal to purchase intent.

Five Steps to Help Make Your Next Digital Campaign More Effective

➲ Clearly define and communicate the goals of your campaign—not in metrics, but in objectives. "If I achieve a click rate of 0.5%, my campaign is successful" is not a goal. However, "I would like to increase awareness of my brand by at least x%" might well be a goal.

➲ Make sure your goal is achievable, and that the media plan and advertising creative support it. If you have a creative that is designed to drive clicks, but people don't remember why they clicked or what brand the ad was for, you've failed. If you go with the goal of raising awareness, but your goal is impossible to achieve, you are likewise in trouble. For example, raising awareness by 15 percentage points when your base awareness is in the 80% range is probably not doable. Focusing on achievable targets and supporting them with logical steps are key.

➲ Once you have identified what you need to measure (e.g., awareness or purchase intent), select the proper tools to measure. If it is a hard goal (e.g., driving people to a site, or asking them to download information), conversion pixels may be appropriate, allowing you to directly measure how well you're doing. But if your success metric is brick-and-mortar sales increases, things are a bit trickier. Most likely you will have to use an indirect metric (e.g., measure purchase intent as an indicator with a known correlation to purchase).

➲ Decide if you want to rely on your media partner, or an independent third party, to provide these metrics. Often a third party will use the same tools, but usually they can measure your whole plan, not just one site or a few sites. On the other hand, they will charge you for the service, while media partners often include metrics as a value add.

When you select your partner, make sure you understand what they measure, what methodology they use, and what they deliver to you. Some will provide you with data, some with insights and analysis, and the fees they will charge may reflect this. That doesn't mean that more expensive is better, but there are constraints. You shouldn't expect a research company to deliver a full campaign with insights and analysis for the same price as a raw data delivery in a SAAS environment.

➲ Make sure you share your goals with your measurement partner of choice. They can help you decide how to best measure it. It may be a survey that can help you understand why people are making a certain selection, or it may be a passive tracking solution (which tells you what people are doing), or a combination of both.

Summary

Decide on the goals of your digital brand campaign first—then use that knowledge to select your metrics. ✦

Measuring the Delivery and Effectiveness of Digital Media Plans

BY GIAN FULGONI ▮ **EXECUTIVE CHAIRMAN, COMSCORE INC.**

Late in 2011, the 3MS initiative ("Making Measurement Make Sense") was launched by three key trade groups: the IAB, which represents online publishers; the ANA, which represents advertisers; and the 4A's, the ad agency body. One of the key tenets of 3MS was moving digital measurement from a "served" ad impression to a "viewable" standard, which is to say an ad impression that is visible to the end user. In TV parlance, this means "having an opportunity" to be seen.

> . . . Click-Through Rate is fast, inexpensive and easy to compute, but unfortunately it's also a fundamentally misleading measure of digital advertising effectiveness . . .

comScore has now conducted numerous studies around the globe measuring the degree to which digital ad impressions are viewable and the results clearly show that there is much room for improvement. In more than 4,000 studies involving billions of impressions from dozens of leading advertisers such as General Mills, P&G, Ford, and Allstate, we have found that on, average, about 30% of display ads are never visible to the end user, generally because the user doesn't scroll down the page far enough or leaves the page before the ad is fully rendered. Obviously, a non-viewable ad has no possibility of affecting behavior. As a result, publishers are now beginning to guarantee the viewability of their inventory, much to the delight of their advertiser clients. This undoubtedly helps make digital advertising more directly comparable to TV advertising and should help in the formulation of more powerful multi-platform advertising campaigns. It will be most interesting to see the rate at which guaranteed viewable impressions become an industry standard.

An important issue that needs to be mentioned at this point is the relative accuracy of cookie-based targeting. comScore research has shown that while it's generally superior to what can be achieved using traditional media, it often fails to match the hype. Because of cookie deletion (comScore research has shown that about 30% of Internet users delete their ad server cookies in a month at a rate of 5 to 6 times per month) and the fact that a cookie is a unique browser identifier (but not a person identifier), a cookie can often fail to accurately reflect the demographic and behavioral characteristics of the person using the computer at any given point in time.

Here's what comScore has found. Targeting accuracy using cookies (% of impressions delivered accurately):

- ➲ 70% for 1 demo (e.g., women)
- ➲ 48% for 2 demos (e.g., women age 18–34)
- ➲ 11% for 3 demos (e.g., women age 18–34 with kids)
- ➲ 36% for behavioral targeting

On a related topic, digital media is seeing a growing use of online GRPs to plan and measure the delivery of digital campaigns while the plan is still running. When coupled with a viewability measure and a targeting accuracy metric, this can provide a huge step forward in ensuring that an advertiser's media plan is being delivered as intended. This was vividly illustrated recently by Kellogg's (a comScore client), which reported a 5X to 6X increase in financial ROI from their digital campaigns since they began making on-the-fly adjustments to the delivery of their digital media plans. An indication of the growing use of these metrics is that comScore's Campaign Essentials product suite has now been used in more than 5,000 studies by 160 advertisers/agencies across 32 countries, and its use is accelerating rapidly. The value is also clear, with Kellogg's reporting a 5X to 6X increase in financial ROI from their digital campaigns since they began using comScore's service.

Turning to the measurement of the impact of digital campaigns, there are now a variety of ways in which the attitudinal or behavioral impact of online campaigns can be measured—including the ability to measure attitudinal shifts while the campaign is still running (which allows for in-flight adjustments). Because of this, it's especially frustrating to see click-through rates (CTR) still being utilized as an effectiveness metric, even though CTRs average no more than 0.1% (yes, that's only 1 in 1000 ads in a campaign being clicked) and despite the fact that research has shown no relationship between CTRs and campaign effectiveness (see comScore 2009). A recent comScore survey found that fully one third of advertisers, agencies, and publishers routinely use CTR as a performance metric. The reasons are simple: CTR is fast, inexpensive and easy to compute . . . but unfortunately it's also a fundamentally misleading measure of digital advertising effectiveness.

When the correct behavioral effectiveness metrics are used, including the all-important lift in sales, the effectiveness of digital advertising becomes clear. For example, comScore compared the average sales lift from TV advertising for CPG brands (as measured by Information Resources using its BehaviorScan® system) with the lift generated by online advertising as measured by comScore in hundreds of real-world studies comparing ad-exposed consumers to non-exposed control groups. We found that TV generated an average in-store sales lift of 8% over a year, while online advertising generated an average in-store sales lift of 9%, but in a three-month period. Further analysis showed that the faster impact of online advertising occurred because of two factors: 1) a greater use of price and promotion incentives in digital ads compared to TV ads and 2) the more precise targeting that online advertising provides. ✦

Reference: Fulgoni, Gian M and Marie Pauline Mörn (2009). Whither the Click? Journal of Advertising Research, Vol. 49, No. 2, pp. 134–142.

Viewpoints 2:
A More Social Measurement Future

This group of eight essays points to the influence of social media on measurement. These essay writers do not merely focus on the media part of social media, but emphasize its social and human aspects—understanding people as people, and their situations, behaviors, interactions, and emotions. Their essays form an arc, beginning with the incorporation of social into current measurement practices, then changing the advertising model and the metrics used to gauge success, and finally to the value and impact of social media in society.

Yaakov Kimelfeld of Millward Brown Digital starts off by presenting a challenge: Do we need a currency for digital media? His provocative answer—"it's not clear that we do." Well-designed online campaigns "thrive in the absence of a currency." Kimelfeld questions the need for comparable cross-media metrics. While they give us comfort and are simple to understand, they chain us, restraining us from exploiting "online's unique capabilities for brand building and customer experience." Focusing on reach and frequency forces us to serve ads based on demographics, not on relevant audience characteristics such as interactions with the ad, sharing, influence, and other uniquely online behaviors. Kimelfeld outlines the way ahead, urging us "to start facing forward."

UM's **Graeme Hutton** advises that we need to develop a new advertising model, one that is rooted in the 21st century, not the 19th—the time when straight line Awareness-Interest-Desire-Action (AIDA) and purchase funnel models were formulated. Hutton makes the case that we should shift from models of audience delivery—which we still need to measure—to models of advertising effectiveness that are grounded in contemporary science and empirically supported. Hutton sees progress coming from research areas like neuroscience and incorporating online social behavior. Armed with a contemporary model of advertising rooted in effectiveness, advertisers and agencies should be better able to explain why their advertising will work and how it will work, leading to improved planning and purchasing that reduces uncertainty and improves business results.

Advertising's new mental model of effectiveness will likely include context. Media Behavior Institute's **Kevin Moeller** contends that effective targeting in today's complex media system depends on deeply understanding the roles consumers are playing, the situations they are in, and the emotions they are experiencing at the moment that messages reach them. Reaching audiences when they are most receptive to the message often improves response to advertising, resulting in enhanced advertising ROI and increased value to advertisers.

The impact of more relevant messages ends not with a purchase or specific action, but goes further, which is to create advocates who endorse the brand through comments and online interactions. Such endorsements, **David Michaelson**, a member of the Institute for Public Relations Measurement and Evaluation Commission, avers, increase credibility for and trust in brands from consumers—qualities which many business corporations lack (Pew 2011). Michaelson adds that "The challenge for digital and social media is learning how to measure advocacy in a way that is valid, reliable, comparable with other communication efforts and predictive of preferred behaviors. Without this measure, it will be impossible to assess the value, contribution and impact of digital media in any meaningful way." He sees measuring sentiment, the willingness of people to share their experiences and make recommendations, the type and number of recommendations, and comments as a starting point. The typical AIDA measures are secondary.

After Michaelson lays out the rationale for advocacy, **Niels Schillewaert** and **Annelies Verhaeghe** expand on the notion by detailing that the "key performance metrics we need to add to our arsenal for measuring communication effectiveness should really be centered on consumers' online and offline brand-related actions (COBRAs). It is more important to understand what people do for your brand after exposure to marketing initiatives or product and service experiences. COBRAs refer to what consumers do for your brand online as well as offline.

MotiveQuest's **David Rabjohns** then takes it to the next level for brands, demonstrating the relationship of advocacy to sales, arguably one of the "gold standard" measures of return on investment. Rabjohns establishes an empirical case for advocacy, finding that it is the number of people recommending a brand that is most important, and discovering correlations that make advocacy a leading indicator for next-month sales. He instructs us that advocacy does not "necessarily 'cause' increased sales. Instead, advocacy tells us that something is going on in the real world, as well as in online conversations, that is boosting sales or forcing them to plummet."

Google's **Gun Johnson** outlines six reasons underpinning "why measurement must change" and suggests six ways "how it should change." His essay highlights not only the need to recognize and incorporate new consumer behaviors for such things as finding and buying products into measurement, but throughout he echoes many of the points made by others that measurement needs to include—context, the capabilities of social media, its content, and interactions people have within it.

Philip Napoli, a Fordham Professor and researcher for The Norman Lear Center at USC Annenberg, describes a research program underway to study the social impact of media and its social value. Napoli and the Lear Center's Media Impact Project are exploring a different aspect than we normally do as advertising and media industry players—the person as citizen. He spotlights the idea that our shared interest in researching audience engagement provides opportunities for mutual learning and cross-pollination. "[S]ome of the metrics and analytical approaches being deployed in the commercial media sector have the potential to be applied in valuable and productive ways in . . . measuring media's social impact. By the same token . . . methods [such as those for] assessing the impact of social issue documentary films . . . can prove useful within traditional commercial contexts related to brand-building and product marketing." ✦

Reference: Pew Research Center for the People and the Press (2011). Press Widely Criticized, But Trusted More than Other Information Sources: Views of the News Media: 1985–2011 (http://www.people-press.org/2011/09/22/press-widely-criticized-but-trusted-more-than-other-institutions/).

No Currency Needed

BY YAAKOV KIMELFELD, PH.D. ∎ CHIEF RESEARCH OFFICER, MILLWARD BROWN DIGITAL

Back when TV was young, the visionary communications theorist Marshall McLuhan noted: "When faced with a totally new situation, we tend always to attach ourselves to the objects, to the flavor of the most recent past. We look at the present through a rearview mirror. We march backwards into the future."

For an advertiser in today's fragmented media landscape, reach and frequency are such objects; they have a nostalgic value, being the traditional metrics of audience exposure to the advertising. For the past five decades, these metrics and their derivatives, the ratings points, served as media's gold standard. They were the common denominators for evaluating campaign performance across different media channels and schedules. They directed billions of dollars in advertising spending.

> . . . the ratings nostalgia is rooted in the simplicity of the times when GRPs/TRPs were, indeed, a media currency . . .

Conventional wisdom holds that the main reason why online display/video advertising has had trouble increasing its share vs. traditional TV advertising is the lack of a standard metric across the platforms that allows major advertisers to compare the two—a media "euro" of sorts. Without that common currency, major brands have strenuously resisted moving more ad dollars from TV into online display and video advertising.

The industry's experience with cable TV advertising in the 1970s–1980s is often trotted out to show that when an emerging channel has metrics comparable to an older one, budgets quickly follow proportionally. But that argument does not apply to online because the main metric, the Gross Rating Point (GRP) was used by broadcast and cable for planning, buying, optimizing, and evaluating cable TV placements.

Online, however, is not planned or optimized by TV-like metrics. Industry experts convened for a panel at the 2012 ARF Audience Measurement conference extolled the benefits of online GRPs for their potential to shift ad budgets to online ("Now you see, online is just like broadcast!"), but beyond that few could explain why online GRPs were so important. In fact most advertisers on the panel ended up saying that GRPs alone were not sufficient, and that they needed deeper funnel metrics: branding, behavioral, and transactional.

So, GRPs are crucial for TV budgets to come online, but become kind of marginal once the check is cashed? That's not what one wants from a single currency.

When it comes to media ratings, things cease to be completely rational; they are still somewhat of an industry sacred cow. The ratings nostalgia is rooted in the simplicity of the times when GRPs/TRPs were, indeed, a media currency, considered by advertisers and publishers alike to be the best available equivalent of audience value to the advertiser.

The currency, however, is NOT the value; it only stands for value, and only because everyone agrees it does. Just making online GRPs look and feel exactly like TV GRPs won't make them the currency. Even those advertisers whose brands are married to specific demographics became increasingly sophisticated in digging deeper to assess the value of delivered audiences and their impact on the bottom line. Reducing all this to the lowest common denominator with TV just for the sake of cross-media consistency and simplicity keeps us within our comfort zones, but prevents us from grasping and then taking advantage of online's unique capabilities for brand building and consumer experience.

The ratings-points approach is typically detrimental to an online campaign's efficacy. Focusing just on reach and frequency limits a digital campaign's ability to serve ads based on specific audience characteristics other than demographics, such as interactions with the ad, sharing and passing along content, and other online behaviors and transactions.

GRPs certainly have a place as a cross-media campaign metric, but they are unlikely to take root as the universal online currency.

What then would be the currency?

It's not a given that online needs one. With the wealth of data on exchanges, well-designed online campaigns thrive in the absence of currency. Advertisers have learned to apply behavioral tools to fish the muddy waters beyond the premium placements, where the cost of media is defined not by number of eyeballs but by supply and demand. As a result, they discover the untapped potential customers more efficiently. In effect, the US currency becomes the media currency.

Under these circumstances, the best strategy for advertisers would be to assess the relative roles of all available measurements and to create their own internal currencies informed by the unique economies of their specific products and brands.

For example, direct retailers should concentrate on media-attributable visitor traffic, conversions by product type and revenues. CPG advertisers should monitor search behavior, attitudinal response to ads, consumer interactions with their brands' online entities and ads, pass-along behavior, word-of-mouth, and online sentiment.

At the same time, they should match media exposure to purchase behavior (as measured by offline panels or databases) to assess the impact of advertising on sales. For most advertisers, evaluating media investments in the digital world requires working with a number of measurement and tracking vendors and developing proprietary systems to electronically monitor consumer media and purchase behavior.

Of course, no matter what media you're dealing with, it is important to know how many potential customers the campaign has reached. But now it is more important to get a holistic picture of what happens in a media system as a result of advertising. This means recognizing individuals' spontaneous responses to advertising, tracking users' manipulation of ads, and understanding how people influence one another. We're already well into our march into the future. It's time to start facing forward. ✦

The Importance of Why Advertising Works: Measurement's Missing Link

BY GRAEME HUTTON ❙ SVP, GROUP PARTNER, RESEARCH, UM

Over the last decade, the advertising and media research industry has made exceptional strides in understanding how advertising works. Despite these advancements, something big is missing: Our industry has no consensus on how adverting works or how to measure its effectiveness. The plethora of digital metrics documented in this book shows that all too clearly.

Ask the typical ad exec how advertising works and, most likely, she or he will cite a variation on AIDA (Awareness, Interest, Desire, and Action) and the metaphor of the purchase funnel. It was originally coined in 1898 by Elias St. Elmo Lewis of National Cash Register. It assumes the consumer processes marketing information in a sequential and conscious manner, from Awareness to Action. Today, we know the consumer's decision process does not have to be sequential, nor does it have to be a conscious decision. Like or not, AIDA is the archetypal way the industry views how ads work.

> . . . if Nielsen and Twitter can validate the advertising effectiveness of social TV ratings, it could detonate a revolution in how we value and buy TV airtime . . .

We need an industry standard on how advertising works which is openly verifiable and validated:

By verifiable, I mean that at the macro level, such as a market category, there is an array of advertising and marketing inputs, which has been proven to match a known set of sales and consumer response outputs.

By validated, I am suggesting that such a macro model needs to be intuitively understood, by aligning it at the micro level to individual consumer responses seen in studies such as a neuroscience trial.

Identifying the connection between macro effects and micro responses is, arguably, marketing's missing link.

To replace AIDA, or any other industry model of advertising effectiveness, we need both a macro and micro approach. Without both approaches, the missing link will always be apparent and, consequently, doubt will linger about how advertising really works: Quantifying macro effects will allow us to understand brand and category shifts. Econometrics can already do this to an extent, but such studies are only as good as the data that are placed in these models. Such studies can be improved and enhanced by media

and retail sales panels that can track response at the level of the individual consumer. Yet even panels do not reveal an individual's motivations behind their behavior to buy a particular brand on a specific occasion.

Probing individual responses via approaches such as large-scale ethnographic studies or neuroscience trials, etc., alongside quantitative macro data, would allow us to understand why the shifts occurred when they did.

Studies such as fused media-exposure and retail panels via organizations such as TRA and Dunnhumby have highlighted previously unseen insights on price promotions. For example, in the Journal of Advertising Research, September 2012, they showed that simultaneous TV advertising and temporary price reductions drove significantly higher sales than either tactic alone.

While quantitative insights are undoubtedly powerful, and can be transformational in how we architect the MarComs solution, they do not tell us why that architecture is important. What exactly triggered the consumer's mind to cause this behavioral change? And equally as important, was the consumer even aware of this change in his or her behavior?

At the individual motivational level, the industry is making inroads to decrypt this enigma via initiatives such as the ARF's NeuroStandards Collaboration Project. But the importance of creating a validated and verified replacement for AIDA goes beyond just "getting at the truth." It could fundamentally restructure how we view advertising and media research and the resources we put behind it.

If we truly understand how advertising works, at both macro and micro level, we may also appreciate why advertising works. With this insight we could reallocate our advertising and media research resources to best effect with a more confident degree of certainty.

The USA spends $150 billion annually on advertising expenditure. With this level of ad spend, the US has an enviable array of media research resources. For many major media channels, we have two major suppliers. For example, we have GfK MRI and Experian Simmons for print, Nielsen and comScore for digital, and Scarborough and The Media Audit in local media. Notwithstanding the proposed acquisition of Arbitron, we also have Arbitron and Nielsen in radio as well as Triton Digital in online radio. In TV ratings, we do have a dominant supplier, Nielsen, but even here there are alternatives such as Rentrak.

Paradoxically, if we had a new, evidence-based, industry standard for determining how advertising and media work, rather than limit the choice of suppliers, our new knowledge could accelerate the range of potential research partners. One could assess a research partner's capacity to meet and exceed an array of known metrics that determine ad effectiveness for a particular market category. For media companies and media agencies, criteria such as measuring audience reach could be superseded by advertising effectiveness metrics that were known to be related to audience reach; for example, this might be some measure of ad awareness or recall. Media research organizations might be judged not only on service, expertise, etc., but also in their abilities in how best to track and even anticipate advertising and media effectiveness.

A scenario which places ad effectiveness ahead of audience delivery for measuring media vehicles may not be that far away. For example, in the new burgeoning phenomenon of social TV, Nielsen and Twitter have joined forces to launch the Nielsen Twitter TV Ratings (NTTR), slated to be released in Q4 2013. This will take TV audience ratings data into an entirely new realm where, for the first time, we will have true social TV ratings calibrating the number of people talking about shows they watch in real time. These ratings will be based on the full, active universe of Twitter users where each show's ratings are weighted by its demographics as tracked by Nielsen.

If Nielsen and Twitter can validate the advertising effectiveness of social TV ratings, it could detonate a revolution in how we value and buy TV airtime.

Whether social TV ratings fail or succeed, it is only the beginning of a sea change. I foresee many more media research services increasingly focusing on ad effectiveness rather than potential media exposure. Ad effectiveness metrics may transcend media audience metrics in a way that would have been unimaginable just ten years ago. ✦

If Content Is King, Context Is the Power Behind the Throne

BY KEVIN MOELLER

EXECUTIVE DIRECTOR, RESEARCH & ANALYTICS, MEDIA BEHAVIOR INSTITUTE

There are more metrics to quantify audience exposure today than ever before. We have ratings, click-through rate, issue-specific, quarter-hours. One way or another we're pretty good at counting exposures and interactions, even if we do not yet do so equally well across all media—in time we will get there. But what is almost always missing in our understanding of the use of a medium is the systematic evaluation of the context in which all that content is consumed—and that is a critical shortcoming.

> . . . contextual relevance removes the idea that consumption takes place in a bubble and opens the messaging to real-life exposure to real-life consumers . . .

To enhance targeting capabilities by including key contextual factors, media researchers need to augment the prevailing metrics by factoring in the situational variables that influence our ability or willingness to engage with a message at different times. Demographic standards set in place two generations ago may help define a consumer, but used in isolation they dilute and simplify both targeting and measurement to a degree of absurdity. Effective targeting and measurement in the modern media ecosystem is highly dependent on a deeper understanding of the roles consumers are apt to be playing at the moment that messages reach them— the situational or contextual variables.

In the morning I may be a father getting his kids off to school, during the day a C-suite executive dealing with bulls and bears, and a loving husband at night. And on weekends, an affable jokester surrounded by friends and family actively enjoying the outdoor life whenever possible. Contextual relevance removes the idea that consumption takes place in a bubble and opens the messaging to real-life exposure to real-life consumers. With such considerations in mind, the same products and services can be marketed to the same target consumers using slightly different core messages—all of which will resonate in the context of those situational variables.

USA TouchPoints, a syndicated study of American life, uses a smartphone app to survey respondents about their locations, social setting, and media consumption, as well as their moods and emotions. The data provide a landscape of consumers' lives—half-hour by half-hour through their entire waking day over the course of a week. We turn to USA TouchPoints to help us understand the role context plays in how marketers need to expose consumers at the right time, in the right place, with the right message. We learned that while content may drive the consumption of media, the context of consumption has risen in its power to influence message receptivity and response.

Content remains King, but context has become the power behind the throne.

Receptive audiences make for more efficient reach, resulting in better investment of media spend. So while measurement of audience levels is obviously important, the context in which those messages are received is paramount. Plans and campaigns based on this realization create enhanced advertising ROI, resulting in increased value to marketers.

A media plan targeted to young women can use standard metrics to evaluate which media channels have the highest success in delivering reach throughout a day. This may be driven by content that attracts such an audience, and that media plan will no doubt will reach these young women in some degree if standard currency measures are evaluated properly. However, in a case study in which the creative of the campaign was uplifting in its tone, the emotional synergy of emotions and moods of these young women helped improve the effectiveness of that communications plan.

In one such case, a beauty account used USA TouchPoints data to better understand emotional patterns of young women. During the week these women experienced a sudden and consistent emotional dip in the early afternoon. The account team then evaluated the media channels in which these women were exposed during those dips to push their encouraging and uplifting digital advertising creative. The result was a more approachable target receptive to these uplifting messages, yielding an increased affinity towards the brand.

Situational relevance is another form of contextual environment. Research reported in the *Journal of Advertising Research* has shown that one in four consumer conversations about brands involve consumers talking about the content they have seen in paid advertising. These conversations extend the reach of paid messages through the earned media, while increasing engagement with brands and ad content. Marketers have a much greater chance of their content entering consumer discussions if they reach consumers when they are most apt to be in a social context. The work of the word-of-mouth firm Keller Fay has led the way in furthering our understanding of this specific type of social context.

If a movie studio wanted to reach a large audience with their newest blockbuster trailers, TV seems to be an optimal solution. If that movie studio wants to drive attendance through buzz and word of mouth, measuring TV exposure alone wouldn't cut it. The context in which that TV is viewed may be more effective and relevant should the media planner identify programming content in which audiences are more social while viewing. Whether being social is defined as talking or chatting with a spouse, social networking with friends, or interacting via text with family members, those behaviors exhibit a higher degree of contextual relevance to the goal of the studio than simply the gross number of eyeballs.

As media channels evolve and the means and contexts in which we consume content continue to diversify, the media and marketing industries have a choice. We can continue to evaluate and plan against these channels using increasingly "blunt" and aging metrics or advance to a more pertinent measure. The reality is that the optimal choice will be a combination of the two.

Summary

While audiences will continue to choose content and be exposed to marketing messages whether they are Father, Mother, Executive, Husband, Wife, Co-Worker, Friend, or Fan, marketers will need to better understand and leverage the situations in which that consumption takes place so that the power context wields behind the throne of content can also be used to add true power to advertising and marketing today. ✦

The Need to Measure Impact

BY DAVID MICHAELSON, PH.D. I MANAGING DIRECTOR, TENEO STRATEGY

RESEARCH FELLOW, INSTITUTE FOR PUBLIC RELATIONS I MEMBER, COMMISSION ON PUBLIC RELATIONS
MEASUREMENT & EVALUATION I MEMBER, COALITION FOR PUBLIC RELATIONS RESEARCH STANDARDS

Measurement of digital media has been a perpetual bane of communicators. The debate rages over the value of "Likes" on Facebook, the impact of a Tweet, and even what constitutes a valid mention. However, all of this debate misses the fundamental point about the measurement of digital and social media. First and foremost, social media is media, plain and simple. It is a vehicle for the delivery of messages. The only valid measures are those that can demonstrate an impact on the behavior, actions, and attitudes of the target audience who is the intended receiver of the message.

From that perspective, measuring the impact of digital media should not be significantly different than the traditional measures that have been used for decades with print and broadcast media. We still need to understand how exposure to a message impacts the basic measures of:

> . . . in today's media ecology, an action taken by a reader or viewer—buying a product, voting for a candidate, supporting a cause—is no longer the endpoint of communication objectives . . .

⊃ Awareness of the product, brand, or issue
⊃ Correct knowledge about the product, brand, or issue
⊃ Relevance to the target audience
⊃ Intent of the target audience to take a desired action

Each of these measures is based on the reader or viewer having exposure to the intended messages of the communicator.

This does not mean that these four fundamental measures are all that is needed to effectively measure digital or social media.

As with any advancement in technology, there are changes that need to be taken into account due to the unique nature of the medium being measured. This happened with the advent of movable type, continued through the invention of broadcast media, and is now evident with the prominence of digital media.

The most significant addition to these measures is a direct function of the unique social capabilities of digital media. The ability to share thoughts and opinions with other readers/viewers—in essence, credible third-party advocacy—is the primary aspect of digital media that distinguishes it from traditional print and broadcast.

Traditional print and broadcast is a unidirectional form of communication. Messages and information are sent by a media outlet and are received and interpreted by the reader or viewer. Interaction with the media source, if any, is limited to, at most, sharing the article with friends or acquaintances or possibly a letter to the editor.

However, in the emerging world of digital media, these limitations disappear. Readers interact at will with writers and editors. Other readers can follow these interactions and comment on the comments. In this brave new digital world, readers are as much a part of the reporting on story as the writer of the article. In many instances, the most influential aspect of the story is not the story, but the commentary that accompany the original post. Readers are just as interested in what their peers have to say as they are in the original article. They want to know how people just like them feel about what was written. They are looking for support and validation from their peers before they make a decision. They are looking for an advocate who confirms and supports their choices or preferences.

So, what does this mean for the measurement of digital media? In today's media ecology, an action taken by a reader or viewer—buying a product, voting for a candidate, supporting a cause—is no longer the endpoint of communication objectives. A communicator's hope is that a reader will not only buy a product, but will also eventually advocate for the value and benefits of that product and provide an endorsement.

Unlike traditional word-of-mouth advocacy where friends tell friends about what they like, dislike, and recommend, digital media allows virtually everyone to share their experiences and their recommendations with everyone else. Readers can see comments, reviews, and recommendations of others like themselves at will, and many readers rely on these endorsements and reviews when making a purchase decision. This significantly extends the reach of the communicator through independent endorsement that many claim has higher credibility than virtually any other source of information.

The challenge for digital and social media is learning how to measure advocacy in a way that is valid, reliable, comparable with other communication efforts, and predictive of preferred behaviors. These preferred behaviors are almost limitless in their scope and range from an intent to purchase, preference for a political candidate, support for a public affairs issue, and even changes in behavior that affect health and well-being.

To date, scant research has been done to measure advocacy and its impact on these dimensions. As a starting point, measurement of digital media needs to take into consideration the number, type, and sentiment of positive and negative comments as well as softer measures such as willingness to tell others about their experience, types of recommendations, as well as other relevant commentary. These measures are in addition to secondary measures of audience reach, quality of audience, presence or absence of key message, as well as the primary measures of audience impact—awareness, knowledge, relevance, and intent to take desired actions.

The ability to create advocacy is what distinguishes digital media from virtually every other form of communication. Without this measure, it will be impossible to assess the value, contribution, and impact of digital media in any meaningful way. With the decline (dare I say demise) of print media, digital media will become the standard that we measure. Just as we learned to count "eyeballs" when measuring television, we also need to assess advocacy when measuring social media. ✦

Marketing Through Fans, Not to Them

BY

NIELS SCHILLEWAERT, PH.D I MANAGING PARTNER
ANNELIES VERHAEGHE I HEAD OF RESEARCH INNOVATION, MANAGING PARTNER
INSITES CONSULTING

In the nineties, marketers were in control. All eyes were focused on effective targeting via 1-on-1 techniques, direct and database marketing strategies. In this day and age things have changed. Technological innovation has led where marketing attention has followed and consumers obtained a place in the driver's seat more than ever before. Consumer behavior such as participation, information contribution and sharing, social networking, brand liking, product reviewing, user collaboration, and co-creation have become the new normal when it comes to consumer behavior.

> . . . communication developers can and should let creativity rule as long as people get the story behind the campaign such that it triggers people to talk about brands . . .

Marketing anno 2013 has to evolve from a dominantly to consumers approach to a through consumers approach. Gradually, we see marketing move up to work together with consumers, to collaborate with them, to achieve goals through them. The days are gone where we send out a message and want people to react. Today we need consumers to want to participate in our brand activation. Marketers need to rely on consumers doing things for brands because they love to do so. The unilateral call to action no longer works; the call for collaboration is inevitable! This new reality brings up the need to adapt the metrics marketers should consider to assess marketing communication effectiveness.

Advertising effectiveness has traditionally been tested and measured in terms of its impact on recall, likeability (attitude towards the ad), attitude towards the brand, and buying intention. In a recent study of ours (based on 856 different TV commercials evaluated by 29,594 consumers), we found evidence that if TV ads can activate consumers to start conversations about the focal brand then that is more powerful than achieving "advertising likeability" (Schillewaert et al. 2013). Ad likeability is still important and may serve as the stopping power for an ad's effectiveness, but if after seeing an ad, consumers start talking about the commercialized brand, then that is most effective in pushing consumers through the buying cycle. However, when consumers are talking about the ad spot or execution only, the advertisement is ultimately ineffective. Consequently, communication developers can and should let creativity rule as long as people get the story behind the campaign such that it triggers people to talk about brands. Advertising—digital or traditional—should be the start of a good brand conversation (Van Belleghem 2010).

But marketers are still using advertising and digital communication in a predominantly one-dimensional way. They focus on large-scale reach—also online. Generating reach is easy and can be bought, but the real value lies in creating true engagement and brand intimacy with consumers—which preferably grows organically. Many companies only think about building as many fans and likes on Facebook as possible, not about mutual quality connections and conversations.

And while brand identification (or fanship) reinforces repurchase behavior (Lam et al. 2012), that alone is not enough. Today's consumers are empowered and no longer passive receivers. They consume content but also contribute to it by sharing, liking, or further spreading content; some of them even create new content. Consequently, the key performance metrics we need to add to our arsenal for measuring communication effectiveness should really be centered on consumers' online and offline brand-related actions (COBRAs) (based on Muntinga et al. 2011). Next to whether consumers like your communication, it is more important to understand what people do for your brand after exposure to marketing initiatives or product and service experiences. COBRAs refer to what consumers do for your brand online as well as offline and basically boils down to advocacy, word-of-mouth, and word-of-mouse. It can range from consulting a brand's Facebook page or posting a brand Tweet or talking to family and friends about an experience all the way to creating a product review or actively convincing others to (not) buy a specific product. Marketers need to understand which content drives brand identification and specific COBRAs, as well as which consumers undertake such actions, why they do so, and how they do so (see Figure 1).

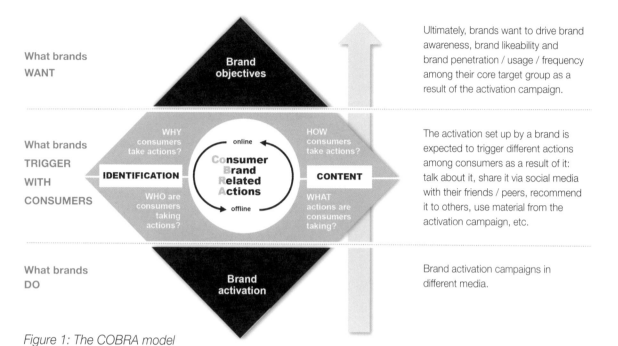

Figure 1: The COBRA model

The text blocks within and around the figure:

What brands WANT

What brands TRIGGER WITH CONSUMERS

What brands DO

Brand objectives

WHY consumers take actions?

IDENTIFICATION

WHO are consumers taking actions?

Consumer Brand Related Actions

online

offline

HOW consumers take actions?

CONTENT

WHAT actions are consumers taking?

Brand activation

Ultimately, brands want to drive brand awareness, brand likeability and brand penetration / usage / frequency among their core target group as a result of the activation campaign.

The activation set up by a brand is expected to trigger different actions among consumers as a result of it: talk about it, share it via social media with their friends / peers, recommend it to others, use material from the activation campaign, etc.

Brand activation campaigns in different media.

Unfortunately, very few companies have yet understood that information and value streams should go through consumers rather than to them. The true value of a brand fan lies in what he/she does for the brand and the impact his/her actions have on others. ✦

References:

Lam, S.K., Ahearne, M. and N. Schillewaert (2012). A Multinational Examination of the Symbolic–Instrumental Framework of Consumer–Brand Identification, Journal of International Business Studies, 43, 306–331.

Muntinga, D., Moorman, M. and E. Smit (2011). Introducing COBRAs: Exploring Motivations for Brand-Related Social Media Use, International Journal of Advertising, 30 (1), 13–46.

Schillewaert, N., Ghys, T. and A. Deceuninck (2013). Ad Conversations: The Forgotten Variable in Advertising Effectiveness, InSites Consulting working paper.

Van Belleghem, S. (2010). The Conversation Company, Lannoo.

Remarkable Implications:
The Correlation Between Online Advocacy and Offline Sales

BY DAVID RABJOHNS | CEO, MOTIVEQUEST

Periodically over the past century, technology has completely altered the way that we live, work, and play; and today we are entering another such transformation.

Over the past ten years, with the explosion of blogs, forums, and social networks, a very powerful force—peer to peer dialogue on a network scale—has been inserted into the buying process.

Shoppers today talk with experts on a specific product or service anywhere in the world. They find reviews of their prospective purchase in just seconds online and rapidly compare features and prices for competing brands.

> . . . people's willingness to advocate for the brand online is a leading indicator (by one month) of the brand's new-customer acquisition . . .

Marketers, and marketing metrics, have been slow to adapt to this reconfigured shopping landscape. Many still pursue the old measuring system that revolves around the core targets of awareness, preference, and purchase or the myriad digital metrics that measure browser actions but which are often difficult to interpret and to derive meaning from. Conventional marketers ask questions in the marketplace and try to align the responses to determine where the market lies on the buying-cycle continuum. This methodology is not only tedious and expensive but also far too slow in producing results for today's trending marketplace. What consumers liked last week may be passé with this week's release of version 5.0—whether it's an iPhone, a restaurant menu, or a video game.

Stop Asking and Start Listening

The best and only valid way to measure what is driving the market is to stop asking questions and start listening to conversations and observing behavior. In this new social environment, we can actually observe the buying behavior of consumers, rather than merely ask them about or infer their behavior. We can measure it, how and why people are talking about a product. Instead of asking them if they would recommend a product (i.e., Net Promoter Score) we can measure the number of times they really recommend it.

It turns out, not surprisingly, that the sorts of things that people talk about around the kitchen table are the same sorts of things they talk about online. Of course, social media conversations are just a sample of all conversations, but online forums enable us to overhear those networked conversations, which were already happening but to which we had no way of listening in on before.

The Most Important Metric

The motivations that drive conversations in social networks are the real treasure to be mined by marketers—they can be a precise and predictable indicator of future sales.

To understand the correlation between social media and sales, we must first determine which aspects of online conversations we should measure. In 2006, MotiveQuest began working with statisticians at Northwestern University to examine all the components of these conversations to attempt to find the most impactful elements.

We looked at correlations and metrics related to such factors as the number of times a brand is mentioned, likeability of the product or service, and the power of influencers.

We uncovered what ultimately became a stunning discovery: The highest correlation—and a direct, measurable correlation—between social-media conversations and offline sales occurred when people online went out of their way to pick a brand and recommend it to a friend. Statements like, "I would recommend the iPhone," rather than, "You might like the iPhone, Samsung, or Nokia brands," led to precise correlations with offline sales in virtually every category. The type of product doesn't matter; in these conversations, only the level of advocacy influences sales.

From this research we developed an Online Promoter Score. The best metric of a brand's health in online conversation, we were able to declare, is advocacy—the number of individuals actively promoting the brand. The Score is an index of the strength of the online community's recommendation of a brand. Further research we did showed, with statistical significance, that people's willingness to advocate for the brand online is a leading indicator (by one month) of the brand's new-customer acquisition. What people say online allows us to predict shifts in consumer behavior offline.

A Canary in the Coal Mine for Market Shifts

The correlation between online advocacy and offline sales does not mean that online advocacy necessarily "causes" increased sales. Advocacy tells us that something is going on in the real world, as well as in online conversations, that is boosting sales or forcing them to plummet.

The power of listening for recommendations produced astonishing results for Sprint, the phone carrier. Sprint was losing a steady stream of customers to rivals AT&T, Verizon, and T-Mobile, but it didn't know why. MotiveQuest built custom linguistic models to understand the essence of the conversation about the company online, categorizing those who posted their opinions in social media as current or former Sprint customers. We then aggregated carrier advocacy conversations—messages in which one brand was being actively recommended over another—to learn what drove recommendations and retention.

We discovered that customers had three primary reasons for staying loyal to a carrier:
➲ Customer Service
➲ Models
➲ Coverage

Sprint trailed competitors in all three areas. The company determined that its best opportunity resided in upgrading its customer service; we discovered that it was the biggest driver of carrier advocacy, ahead of models and coverage. Sprint implemented a number of initiatives to revamp customer service, including the retooling of its programs and rewriting scripts for call centers based on the consumer expectations revealed in our research. Subsequent third-party satisfaction surveys showed Sprint rated very highly and, most important, Sprint pulled in 644,000 net subscribers in a single quarter, an astonishing turnaround from its loss of 565,000 during the same period the previous year. Six months later, it added 1.1 million net new customers in a quarter.

The Secret of Boosting Online Advocacy

Above all, create products and services that are remarkable; inherently, that's the best way to ensure people remark on them to each other. Social networks turbo-charge this process, accelerating good products to the forefront and quickly killing off products that are disappointments.

For a product to become remarkable, attach it to a core passion or movement in the marketplace—it is a three-step process:
➲ First, identify what your best customers are most passionate about.
➲ Then, figure out how you can be useful around that passion—how you become part of the movement.
➲ Finally, create buzz-worthy products and services that help serve the passion. For instance, Apple created MacWorld, a conference that is little short of a religion for its advocates. MacWorld is a movement.

Connecting your brand to a passion creates the foundation for advocacy that can lead to higher sales offline and improved market share.

So as you step back and think about the changes that are happening in your business, it is important to also step back and examine what you think about the metrics you are using. While there are hundreds of new metrics out there, do you know which matter most to you? ✦

Why Measurement Needs To Change and How It Should Change

BY GUNNARD JOHNSON I ADVERTISING RESEARCH DIRECTOR, GOOGLE

There are six reasons why measurement needs to change and six ways it should:

➲ *Audience measurement has to change because the audience we are trying to measure has changed.*
From 2000 to 2010, the population growth in the United States was driven almost exclusively by racial and ethnic minorities. A recent estimate released by the US Census Bureau showed that as of July 1, 2011, 50.4 percent of our nation's population younger than age 1 were minorities. Although the US has always had a diverse population, the last election was just one demonstration of the impact of that shift. How we recruit for panels and how we project the results from research is now that much more important and more difficult.

> . . . we are going to need better ways to measure cross-channel frequency and multi-channel simultaneous usage . . .

➲ *Audience measurement needs to change because we can know so much more about our consumers than before.*
Consumers are so much more than just their age and gender, which never were very good proxies for purchase anyway. They are the interests they pursue online, the in-market signals they send out when searching for information in a product category, the brands they discuss on blogs and forums, the products they actually buy online, and the TV shows they now watch online.

And that information can be utilized—all while maintaining their anonymity.

Measurement needs to be able to combine all the available information into a usable format for efficient targeting.

➲ *Media measurement has to change because the way consumers shop has changed.*
People no longer walk into a car showroom to find out more information. They come in to transact—and they come armed with more pricing information than ever before.

For everything smaller than a car, e-commerce has allowed consumers to shop anytime from anywhere. It has turned physical stores into showrooms for online stores. 2012 was a record year, with $186.2 billion in retail e-commerce sales. That growth represents the twelfth consecutive quarter of year-over-year growth for e-commerce spending, as well as the eighth consecutive quarter of double-digit growth, according to comScore.

There are so many opportunities now for measurement to include the impact on sales.

Word-of-mouth recommendations are no longer limited to the backyard fence. They happen across the world's largest social media sites and play a critical role in how consumers create their consideration set.

Measurement needs to not only include the effect of earned media but also help us understand how paid and earned media can complement each other. Measurement also needs to help us identify the best ways to react to viral videos, both positive and negative.

➲ *Media measurement has to change because the media we are trying to measure has changed.*
Yes, it is probably true that people are watching more TV than ever. The heaviest quintile of TV viewers watches 623 minutes of TV per day while just five years ago they were watching only 583 minutes a day. But that doesn't mean they are watching the same way. Consumers are watching TV on demand, on their computer, on their smartphone, and on their tablet. They are watching TV while checking their email or tweeting their reactions. And it is not just TV. Print as well is becoming more digital.

We are going to need better ways to measure cross-channel frequency and multi-channel simultaneous usage.

➲ *Media measurement has to change because the way media is bought has changed.*
Why buy millions of impressions against broad demographics and lock yourself in months in advance when you can buy individual impressions as needed against a much richer target definition. Measurement needs to learn to deal with frequency caps, frequency floors, cost per performance buys, propensity-to-purchase models, context relevance, etc.

➲ *Measurement has to change because advertisers and publishers all feel that the world is rapidly changing and measurement has not kept pace.*
This doesn't mean we have to throw away our current set of metrics, i.e., clicks and click-through rates, interaction rates, time spent, site composition, and even GRPs. It is important to be able to continue monitoring historical trends. But it also doesn't mean we should continue using a metric just because we've always used it. It's all too easy for a line in the sand to become a metric etched in stone that can stand in the way of advancing in today's digital world. ✦

The Evolution and Use of Digital Metrics:
A Social Value and Impact Perspective

BY PHILIP M. NAPOLI, PH.D | GRADUATE SCHOOL OF BUSINESS, FORDHAM UNIVERSITY

It is well-understood, at this point, how the ongoing digital transformation taking place in the media sector has brought both challenges and opportunities to the processes of measuring and valuing the behavior of media audiences. On the one hand, increased audience fragmentation and the diffusion of new platforms make many traditional measurement approaches much more challenging, and much more expensive, to effectively implement. On the other hand, the interactive nature of many of these new platforms creates new sources of data on wide-ranging dimensions of audience behavior that extend well beyond the fairly limited criteria that have characterized the measurement of legacy media. The end result is perhaps unprecedented disruption, uncertainty, and innovation in how advertisers, content providers, and measurement firms assess and value media audiences (see Napoli 2011).

For the commercial sector, one obvious question that arises from this scenario is how best to develop and employ digital media metrics to measure audiences, and to assess media and message effectiveness in reaching consumers and affecting their brand perceptions and product purchasing behaviors. This book is helping to address those concerns.

Thinking more broadly, the metrics question also arises for the creators, distributors, and funders of media and journalism aimed at inspiring audiences to make individual and social change. Here the primary concern is whether media content is having a measurable social impact; the key questions revolve around how the social value of the enterprise can be effectively measured. This is something that is of growing importance to the many charitable organizations—such as the Bill & Melinda Gates Foundation and the Knight Foundation—that devote substantial resources each year to supporting media campaigns and enterprises whose mission is social change. These concerns are the focal point of the Norman Lear Center's newly launched Media Impact Project, which is focusing on bringing greater clarity, rigor, and accountability to the process of assessing media impact (Cieply 2013).

While this may sound like a very different—and perhaps completely unrelated—analytical context relative to the core concerns of the ARF and its stakeholders, the Lear Center believes that some of the metrics and analytical approaches being deployed in the commercial media sector have the potential to be applied in valuable and productive ways in this realm of measuring media's social impact. And, by the same token, the Lear Center thinks that methods of,

say, assessing the impact of social issue documentary films (see, e.g., "Films that Make a Difference," 2012) can prove useful within traditional commercial contexts related to brand-building and product marketing. This kind of cross-pollination of analytical perspectives and priorities is essential to making the most of the growing array of data sources and analytical tools available to assess how audiences engage with media, and how this engagement translates into meaningful effects on knowledge, attitudes, behaviors, and social conditions.

Indeed, one of the key points of intersection that has already become clear involves the notion of audience engagement. Audience engagement has been a focal point of debate, discussion, and measurement experimentation not only in the commercial media sector (Kaplan 2012), where advertisers and content providers are seeking to unearth the economic value that lies beyond basic exposure, but also in the public interest media sector where engagement lies at the core of concerns about better understanding "how storytelling connects people and inspires action" (Green & Patel 2013).

> . . . in the digital measurement space as a whole, there tends to be something of a tail-wagging-the-dog mentality, in which those things that can be easily and comprehensively measured are measured and utilized, with the tough questions about their genuine value only being addressed later . . .

In order to dig deeply into the questions of if and how media have a meaningful social impact and create genuine social value, we will need to draw from—and integrate—new digital analytical tools (such as social media analytics) and innovative analytical approaches derived from more traditional social scientific methodologies (such as employing propensity score matching to survey data). This is, of course, a complex and rapidly evolving terrain to navigate, with one of the key challenges today being effectively distinguishing between data and analytical approaches that represent meaningful, reliable, and actionable assessment criteria that can effectively inform decision-making, and those that are more superficial manifestations of the ongoing explosion of data streams that are a byproduct of our increasingly interactive media environment (Gannes 2012). This point is a reflection of the fact that, in the digital measurement space as a whole, there tends to be something of a tail-wagging-the-dog mentality, in which those things that can be easily and comprehensively measured are measured and utilized, with the tough questions about their genuine value only being addressed later (see, e.g., Napoli 2012).

It might also be the case that, in the media measurement realm, some important dimensions of media impact have gone unmeasured due to the potential implications of the findings. Some histories of audience measurement have suggested, for instance, that media research became increasingly focused on measuring audiences' media exposure in part to avoid raising the more complex concerns that could arise from measuring criteria like appreciation and impact (see Napoli 2011).

More comprehensive measurement of the social impact of media can potentially produce findings that may reflect both positively and negatively on content providers, with political and economic repercussions that could be wide-ranging. For instance, although the Media Impact Project is focused on media with a social change mission, the open source measurement tools that it develops may encourage advocates of corporate social responsibility to develop and apply impact metrics to profit-driven media companies. Such activities would provide both challenges and opportunities for the media sector, perhaps similar to the impacts that sustainability is exerting on brands' environmental and social practices and on consumer preferences. Certainly, media organizations themselves have also always been mindful of their impact, and perceived impact, on society (see, e.g., MediaCSRForum 2013); and the Media Impact Project could prove to be a useful tool in this regard.

The Media Impact Project is in its very earliest stages, and so has produced far more questions than answers at this point. And even with the increase in available data and analytical tools, assessing media impact will never be an exact science. Nonetheless, there is a tremendous opportunity for a well-resourced, collaborative, research-driven initiative involving USC's Annenberg School to produce a body of knowledge and best practices that will represent significant steps forward in our understanding of how media has an impact on the public, and how this impact can be effectively measured. ✦

Note: Dr. Napoli is conducting a critical review of academic and professional literature on promising media engagement strategies for the Lear Center Media Impact Project.

References:

"Films that Make a Difference" (2012). Panel discussion at the Seattle International Film Festival. Transcript retrieved May 10, 2013, from: http://www.learcenter.org/images/event_uploads/seattlefilmfest.pdf.

Cieply, M. (2013, April 28). Center will offer new tools for measuring the impact of media beyond numbers. New York Times. Retrieved May 10, 2013, from: http://www.nytimes.com/2013/04/29/business/media/center-to-offer-tools-for-gauging-impact-of-media.html?_r=1&.

Gannes, L. (December 17, 2012). Andreessen and Mixpanel call for an end to "bullshit metrics." AllThingsD. Retrieved May 10, 2013, from: http://allthingsd.com/20121217/andreessen-and-mixpanel-call-for-an-end-to-bullshit-metrics/.

Green, D., & Patel, M. (April 29, 2013). Retrieved May 10, 2014, from: http://www.impatientoptimists.org/Posts/2013/04/Gates-and-Knight-Foundations-Fund-New-Project-to-Improve-Measuring-Media-Impact.

Green, D., & Patel, M. (April 29, 2013). Retrieved May 10, 2014, from: http://www.impatientoptimists.org/Posts/2013/04/Gates-and-Knight-Foundations-Fund-New-Project-to-Improve-Measuring-Media-Impact.

Kaplan, M. (March 6, 2012). From attention to engagement: The transformation of the content industry. Presentation at the Barcelona Media Center. Retrieved May 10, 2013, from: http://www.learcenter.org/pdf/Barcelona2012.pdf.

Kaplan, M. (March 6, 2012). From attention to engagement: The transformation of the content industry. Presentation at the Barcelona Media Center. Retrieved May 10, 2013, from: http://www.learcenter.org/pdf/Barcelona2012.pdf.

MediaCSRForum (2013). http://mediacsrforum.org/home.php. (Retrieved May 14, 2013).

Napoli, P.M. (2011). Audience evolution: New technologies and the transformation of media audiences. New York: Columbia University Press.

Napoli, P.M. (2011). Audience evolution: New technologies and the transformation of media audiences. New York: Columbia University Press.

Napoli, P.M. (2012). Program value in the evolving television audience marketplace. New York: Time Warner Research Program on Digital Communications. Retrieved May 10, 2013, from: http://www.twcresearchprogram.com/pdf/TWC_Napoli.pdf.

Napoli, P.M. (2012). Program value in the evolving television audience marketplace. New York: Time Warner Research Program on Digital Communications. Retrieved May 10, 2013, from: http://www.twcresearchprogram.com/pdf/TWC_Napoli.pdf.

Summing Up:
What We Have Learned from 197 Metrics, 150 Studies, and 12 Essays

ooking across the 197 metrics that made it into the Field Guide, the 30+ authoritative metrics sources consulted, the nearly 150 research studies and reports cited, and the 12 essays contributed by recognized industry experts, the natural question is: " What did we learn that helps practitioners and their brands use metrics wisely?"

Quite a lot.

Some learning centered on practices. Other learning shed light on our industry's mental models towards what we measure and why. Still more learning provided views on measurement futures. Hopefully the discussions, debates, and actions that the lessons learned inspire will enable all brands to maximize their use of metrics and through them achieve higher levels of brand performance. Now, onto the lessons:

DON'T BITE THE APPLE OF VANITY METRICS, Experian's Chief Data Scientist Max Kilger warns us: "Far too often metrics are selected because they … may look good, but may not mean much of anything." (See his essay in Viewpoints 1.) Reports crossing your desk most likely list one or more brand objectives, such as "generate 10% increase in sales leads over the next 90 days," or "raise brand awareness from 20% to 50% among mothers with children under 18 in 1 year." Charts or tables within the reports announce that "unique visitors doubled over last month," "page views are up 50%," "time on site increased from 15 seconds to 1 minute and 45 seconds," and "likes increased by 30%"—all resulting from the digital group's brilliant new strategy or marketing adjustment. Numbers like these make people feel good while giving the impression that digital marketing efforts are performing. But the pertinent questions of why these metrics were reported, how they relate to an objective, and what resulted, remain unanswered. Brands need to answer these questions; frameworks can help.

IMPOSE A FRAMEWORK ON MEASUREMENT METRICS, GfK's Florian Kahlert advises (see his essay in Viewpoints 1). He emphasizes that all parties working towards achieving an objective—the brand organization, agencies, media outlets, and measurement partners—must agree on the objective and agree on the measures used to gauge progress. Without that shared understanding, each party may well select and report those metrics that reflect their efforts in the best light, but when brought together the metrics may not throw light on the brand's objective.

Frameworks provide the logic for selecting and reporting metrics: They are conceptual structures that support a specific approach to achieving a business objective. Kraft Foods Group's Paul Banas showcased an excellent example regarding social media measurement that ably illustrates this point. Banas's November 2010 presentation to the ARF Social Media Forum outlined the framework employed to achieve the goal of "increasing consumer involvement with the Oscar Mayer brand." For Banas's team, Involvement captures what people are doing with the brand, the time they are spending with it, and the social capital they are expending on it. Their "social involvement" framework is progressive, taking the form of a four-level pyramid, with each level precisely defined. Awareness (consumers passively receiving brand messages) forms the pyramid's base and lowest social involvement level. Social involvement increases with Participation (simple efforts to interact with the brand), then Engagement (greater or more frequent interaction with the brand and sharing), and culminates with Advocacy (unsolicited speaking for the brand to other consumers). The brand aims to move people from awareness to advocacy.

Banas and his colleagues evaluated many metrics. Guided by the four pyramid levels and their definitions, the group eventually selected a core group of 12 measures, about three per level. Taking two examples at the extremes shows how the metrics and levels fit together: The low-involving, passive Awareness metrics included impressions, reach, and brand mentions; whereas Advocacy metrics focused on positive user-generated content created on the brand's behalf, the number of social recommendations, and net promoter score.

Standardizing on a set of metrics tied to their framework and brand objective enabled the Oscar Mayer team to measure their marketing's effectiveness on moving people towards their goal of advocacy. By doing so, the Oscar Mayer team streamlined the metrics tracked and assigned a clear and distinct role to each one. They also increased their analytic power, achieved consistency in their reporting, and enhanced their ability to share insightful stories about the consumer journey from awareness to advocacy with co-workers and partners. (For perspectives on advocacy, see the essays by Michaelson, Rabjohns, and Schillewaert/ Verhaeghe in Viewpoints 2).

Brands with frameworks avoid the problems of vanity metrics, falling for sexy numbers, and wondering what they all mean. Frameworks provide discipline, rigor, guidance, and confidence. Locate the frameworks used by your brand and use them to guide metrics selection, analysis, and reporting. No framework handy? Invest in developing one.

OPTIMIZE TO BRAND OBJECTIVES, NOT PLATFORM METRICS. Many of the digital metrics available to brands come from the platform providing them, such as Facebook, Twitter, or YouTube. (Technically, these are "endometrics"—measures that come from within the system being measured.) It is vitally important to recognize that the metrics supplied by platforms are derived from their business philosophies and business models, and that these morph as their business priorities change. Facebook, for example, is gradually becoming a source of public information regarding brands in order to compete with other ratings services and to attract more advertising revenue, as its adoption of brand page star ratings implies. A social network that talks up the philosophy of engagement, word-of-mouth (WOM), Liking, implied endorsements from friends, contacts or connections, or sharing as drivers of advertising effectiveness, for example, will capture data and report metrics along those lines. When their philosophies are promoted as "how advertising works on their platform" by themselves or others, brands quite naturally seek to optimize one or more of the metrics available for that platform to improve their chances for success. Consider the ubiquitous "Like." How many times have you heard someone say: "We have to get more Likes!" But what is the business reason why?

Optimizing to platform metrics benefits brands when it helps brands achieve their specific objectives. Take the brand targeting greater growth by reaching light-users, brand switchers, and non-users. Some research shows that people who Like a brand are disproportionately the brand's "heavy users" or deal-seekers (Nelson-Field 2012, UPS 2013). They are not necessarily a diverse group of people with warm feelings towards a particular brand, as often assumed. Given this finding, a strategy designed to increase Likes unintentionally risks transforming a growth play into a volume and promotion play. Undoubtedly it will achieve results, but probably not the growth outcomes sought. Conversely, the brand aiming for volume gains or offering a sales promotion may find increasing Likes the right way to go. Reflexively optimizing to platform philosophies and metrics puts the cart before the horse. Move that horse in front: Leverage your brand's framework, fit relevant vendor metrics to it, and optimize those. When using third-party research like that cited, evaluate it thoroughly, then test the findings to determine if, how, and when they apply to your brand.

LET METRICS BE THE ACTORS THAT TELL A BRAND'S STORY. Digital media plans frequently employ combinations of digital media channels and providers. It is routine for brands to deal with disparate and multiple data sources for email, social media, websites, and mobile. Yet, all too often these sources are pitched into data silos like bales of hay. Keep in mind that the data used for metrics, and the metrics themselves, reflect the actions and behaviors customers or prospects take as they interact with brands, advertising, and one another. Integrating multiple data sources is to the brand's advantage, especially when that integration describes patterns of consumer behavior and engagement across media channels and touchpoints. Going the next step—synthesizing data and generating insight— allows brands to gain windows into people and craft compelling stories about users' digital experiences told from their point-of-view—such as stories about the experiences people had when they clicked links in emails that they viewed on a smartphone, then traveled to sites where their journeys continued, the problems they faced or the enjoyment they had, and about the results the brand obtained. Telling and sharing such stories through metrics helps brands enhance brand experiences and betters the odds of achieving brand objectives.

GIVE YOUR METRICS "CHARACTERS" A "PERSONALITY." Because metrics represent people, understanding their richness, what makes them unique, or what they hold in common, becomes a path to even deeper consumer insight. All too commonly, however, reported metrics lump people into totals or averages that yield the equivalent of stereotypes. Merely knowing a trend in Total Unique Visitors or Time Spent on Site does not insight give.

Just as we appreciate and differentiate our friends, family, and others by their qualities, characteristics, and interests, segmentation enables us to appreciate aspects of metrics. A segment is a subgroup of a larger group. Gender, for example, is segmented into male and female. Age may be segmented any number of ways to suit a particular research purpose and analytic requirement, such as by decade, generation, or marketing target (e.g., men 18–49). Each segment narrows our attention and gives more details about whom we are interested in. The same holds true for digital metrics: They are generally segmented by demographics, behavior, technology, and user profiles. Brands' abilities to segment vary according to their data sources, data processing capabilities, and analytic resources. Segmentation tools are becoming more sophisticated and powerful.

Segmentation helps brands analyze progress towards achieving a business objective in ways that evaluating a total metric by itself often cannot. Assume that a brand's business objective is to build its website traffic 35% per month. Assume further that the brand's framework for building its user base (as distinct from just "getting more traffic") is to attract new users and retain prior visitors, and that the brand implements a strategy based on the framework. One month later the brand manager gets a fresh metrics report showing that Unique Visitors climbed 25%. Can the success of the brand's strategy be properly evaluated with that number?

Of course not. (But it sure sounds good).

The brand needs data about what types of visitors came. It needs data segmented by visitor type to properly evaluate the strategy's ability to attract new and prior visitors.

Most analytic packages segment Unique Visitors in three ways: New Visitors (first-timers in a reporting period), Repeat Visitors (people who come two or more times in one reporting period), and Returning Visitors (people who come two or more times across reporting periods). By looking at changes in the numbers for the three segments, the brand can better judge how that strategy is working than it can by using the total alone. Drilling down even further by creating sub-segments for media type and device, for example, adds descriptive precision about the visitors' context that can be used to fine-tune strategy. To illustrate, recognizing that most New Visitors access the site via mobile media using an iPhone whereas Returning Visitors use a laptop or desktop, furnishes guidance for optimizing each type of visitors' experience that may well contribute to more effective strategy.

Although this brief example used Unique Visitors, one of the most common digital metrics and one chosen for its familiarity, it highlights the merit of relying less on one-size-fits-all stereotypes and choosing to understand people and their "personalities" in ways that brands can leverage. However, this example barely scratched the surface of the analytic insight available to brands when they take advantage of standard, "out-of-the-box" segments and custom segments created for specific brand purposes. Segments supply more granular analysis, more penetrating business insight, and ultimately better storytelling. Explore them.

EMBRACE MEASUREMENT'S PARADIGM SHIFT. Experts contributing to the *Field Guide*'s Viewpoints section describe a shift from metrics rooted in a paradigm centered on media exposure—"what is our advertising doing to people?"—to metrics grounded in social activity—"what are people doing with our advertising?" The movement is towards "humetrics"—understanding people as people, their situations, behaviors, connections, interactions, influences, subconscious processes, and emotions in order to grasp why people do what they do, and then apply that learning to create more effective advertising, marketing, and media strategy.

The advent of social TV ratings heralds the beginnings of valuing and incorporating social data into metrics. Certainly they are in the vanguard of measuring what has been called the "engagement age" or "participation era." We, however, have much more to understand so that our industry continues on its path of updating its mental models, from the widely held ones grounded in mass media thinking to newer ones accommodating digital, interactive, and social concepts of communications effectiveness. (The Advertising 2020 initiative at the Wharton Future of Advertising Program is at the forefront of discovering, researching, testing, and validating new mental models.)

Advances in measurement will follow changes in mental models that become adopted. With new metrics for guidance and management that are tuned to the age we live in, whatever it is called, the prospects for brands to prosper become brighter. ✦

Appendices

Appendix I
Authorities for Metrics Definitions

Coalition for Public Relations Research Standards (2012). Standards for Engagement and Conversation (http://goo.gl/jli4H).

comScore (2012). Digital Analytix Metrics and Dimension Guide.

Digital Analytics Association (2007). Web Analytics Definitions—Version 4.

Digital Analytics Association (2013). Proposed Social Media Standard Definitions for Reach and Impressions, from the Digital Analytics Association (http://goo.gl/FQugv).

Dynamic Logic and IAB (2001). Ad Unit Effectiveness Study (Note: Dynamic Logic was incorporated into Millward Brown Digital in 2013).

Experian Marketing Services (2013). Appendix I. Metrics Definitions.

Facebook (2012, 2013, 2014). Page Insights (online), Insights Data Export, and Graph API v2.1

Farris, Paul W. et al. (2006). Marketing Metrics: 50+ Metrics Every Executive Should Master. Wharton School Publishing.

Google (2012, 2013). Google Analytics (http://goo.gl/ktRQ).

IAB (2013). Glossary of Interactive Advertising Terms v2.

IAB (2012). IAB Wiki entry for "Ad Impression" (http://goo.gl/YbW2Rz).

IAB (2009). Click Measurement Guidelines, Version 1.0—Final Release.

IAB (2008). Audience Reach Measurement Guidelines, Version 1.0.

IAB (undated). Email Campaign Performance Metrics Definitions (http://goo.gl/5rY46h).

IAB (2007). Rich Media Measurement Guidelines.

IAB (2009). Social Media Ad Metrics Definitions.

IAB (2004). Interactive Audience Measurement and Advertising Campaign Reporting and Audit Guidelines (http://goo.gl/kd8KEP).

IAB & MMA (2011). Mobile Web Advertising Measurement Guidelines, Version 1.0 Final Release. Adapted from IAB (US) AD Impression Measurement Guidelines.

IAB, MMA and MRC (2013). Mobile Web Advertising Measurement Guidelines, Version 2.0 Final Release July 2013. Adapted from IAB (US) AD Impression Measurement Guidelines (http://goo.gl/qKJAU3).

IAB, MMA, and MRC (2013). Mobile Application Advertising Measurement Guidelines, Version 1.0 Final Release July 2013 (http://goo.gl/2w9zOZ).

Institute for Public Relations (IPR). Dictionary of Public Relations Measurement and Research, 3rd Edition. Don W. Stacks and Shannon A. Bowen, Editors. Institute for Public Relations Measurement Commission. July 2013 (http://goo.gl/oxle5F).

Kaushik, Avinash (2010). Web Analytics 2.0. Sybex.

LinkedIn (2013). Company Pages: Frequently Asked Questions (http://goo.gl/1P1FM).

LinkedIn (2013). Follower and Page Insights for Company Pages (http://goo.gl/Lqx2l).

Microsoft (2013). Microsoft Advertising PubCenter (http://goo.gl/ug319N).

Mobile Marketing Association (2008). Mobile Marketing Industry Glossary.

Mortensen, Dennis R. (2009). Yahoo! Web Analytics. Sybex.

Nielsen (2012). Online Publications Glossary.

Patel, Hemen and Laurent Flores, Ph.D. (2010). Digital Marketing Performance Evaluation: Key Metrics, 1st Edition.

Pinterest Analytics (2014). Pinterest Analytics (http://goo.gl/xVLESG)

Social Media Measurement Standards (2013). Standard Definitions for Conversation and Engagement (http://goo.gl/6N9sv).

TubeInsiders (2013). A YouTube Analytics Guide for Beginners (http://goo.gl/LxXomB).

Twitter (2014). The Twitter Glossary (http://goo.gl/Y1Rxi)

Twitter (2014). REST APIs (http://goo.gl/QVRN8y)

Yahoo! (2012, 2013). Web Analytics Resource Center. Yahoo! Help (http://goo.gl/SW4nSa).

YouTube Analytics (2012, 2013). Analytics available on YouTube account page.

WOMMA (2013). Influencer Guidebook 2013 (http://goo.gl/Zrfr5).

33 Across (2013). Content Sharing Motivated Primarily by Ego (http://goo.gl/kdJqS).

3MS (2013). FAQs (http://goo.gl/o3m2Q).

Aaker, David (1991). Managing Brand Equity: Capitalizing on the Value of a Brand Name. New York: The Free Press.

Abraham, Linda et al. (2012). Changing How the World Sees Digital Advertising. comScore (http://goo.gl/vld9h, free to download, registration required).

Adobe (2013). Click Here: The State of Online Advertising (http://goo.gl/e75Z2).

Adotas (2013). Wired To Share: New Research From ShareThis and Digitas Reveals Important Insights Into Digital Sharing Behavior of Moms (http://goo.gl/z8uTK).

Agarwal, Ashish and Kartik Hosanager (2012). Social Advertising: Does Social Influence Work? (http://goo.gl/UqkMo).

Allen, Larry (2012). We Need a New Way to Define Ad Impressions. The Business Insider, February 14. (http://goo.gl/dlK8d).

AllThingsD (2012). Facebook Actions Could Be Unveiled as Soon as Tomorrow (http://goo.gl/s68od).

ARF (2012). Digital/Social Media in the Purchase Decision Process (White Paper available from ARF. Fee for non-members).

ARF Neurostandards Collaboration Project (2012) (Available from ARF, fee for non-members).

Baekdal, Thomas (2012). Facebook Insights: Debunking Friends of Fans (http://goo.gl/aSfS5).

Banas, Paul (2012). Social Media Measurement: From Awareness to Advocacy. Presentation given to ARF Social Media Forum November, 2010 (Available to ARF members).

Baron, Roger and Jack Sissors (2010). Advertising Media Planning, 7th Edition. McGraw-Hill.

Batra, Anil (2007). Understanding the "Time Spent on the Site" Metrics—Web Analytics, Behavioral Targeting and Optimization (http://goo.gl/EHjf8).

Belkin, Matt (2008). Measuring Visitor Engagement Take Two: Unique Visitors and Page Views. Adobe Digital Marketing Blog (http://goo.gl/sDRFx).

Belsky, Gary (2012). Why Product Reviews May Be The Next Big Thing for Investors (http://goo.gl/jRXgy).

Bentley, Alex, et al. (2011). I'll Have What She's Having: Mapping Social Behavior. Cambridge: MIT Press.

bzzAgent (2011). A Field Guide to Brand Advocates: Insights for Marketers (http://goo.gl/yQN5U).

Chacos, Brad (2012). Facebook: For Ads, Clicks Aren't All That Counts (http://goo.gl/t78q5).

Charlton, Graham (2013). Companies Struggling with Mobile Optimisation: Report (http://goo.gl/FJjrB).

Coalition for Public Relations Research Standards (2012). Standards for Engagement and Conversation (http://goo.gl/jli4H) .

Cohen, Terry (2014). Personal communication.

Compendium (2010). Corporate Blogging and Social Media Trends Survey. Reported by MarketingProfs.com (http://goo.gl/d5VWN).

comScore (2011). The Impact of Cookie Deletion on Site-Server and Ad-Server Metrics in Australia: An Empirical comScore Study (http://goo.gl/t1D6d).

comScore (2011). The Power of Like: How Brands Reach and Influence Fans Through Social Marketing. (http://goo.gl/Mi46Y).

comScore (2012). For Display Ads, Being Seen Matters More Than Being Clicked (http://goo.gl/vycS4).

comScore (2012). The Power of Like 2: How Social Marketing Works (http://goo.gl/eY4Os).

comScore (2012). The Power of Like CPG (http://goo.gl/gCbnZ).

comScore (2012). The Power of Like Europe: How Social Marketing Works for Retail Brands (http://goo.gl/awndP).

Cutroni, J. (2007). Event Tracking Pt. 1: Overview & Data Model (http://goo.gl/oPZYi).

Dainow, Brandt (2005). Defining Unique Visitors (http://goo.gl/qxvSu).

Digital Analytic Association (2013). Proposed Social Media Standard Definitions for Reach and Impressions, from the Digital Analytics Association (http://goo.gl/FQugv).

DoubleClick (2009). The Brand Value of Rich Media and Video Ads (http://goo.gl/OoSQN).

Earls, Mark (2009). Herd: How to Change Mass Behaviour by Harnessing Our True Nature. Hoboken: John Wiley & Sons.

EdgeRank Checker (2012). Did Facebook Decrease Page's Reach? (http://goo.gl/V2Clg).

Eisenberg, Brian (2003). 20 Tips to Minimize Shopping Cart Abandonment, Part 1 (http://goo.gl/WToZ3).

Eisenberg, Brian (2003) 20 Tips to Minimize Shopping Cart Abandonment, Part 2 (http://goo.gl/bmGoW).

Email Experience Council (2012). Five Ways to Improve Email Deliverability with Gmail (http://goo.gl/HVeEV).

Etherington, Darrell (2013). A Like Is Not Enough: Facebook Tests Star Ratings Displayed On Pages (http://goo.gl/w09wnG).

eMarketer (2010). Propelling the Pepsi Spirit with Mobile Apps (http://goo.gl/D0lW6).

eMarketer (2010). Best Practices: Mobile Marketing & App Strategies for Food Brands (http://goo.gl/Wb7PC).

eMarketer (2011). Mobile Ads Outperform Standard Banners (http://goo.gl/5JF7G).

eMarketer (2012). Brand Advocates Are Here to Help (http://goo.gl/QtlaZ).

ExactTarget (2012). Best Practices: Understand Your Deliverability (http://goo.gl/i6Pz7).

Experian Marketing Services (2012a). It's All in the Wording: A Guide to Optimizing Your Email Subject Lines (http://goo.gl/UTzUi).

Experian Marketing Services (2012b). Three Pillars of Successful Email Deliverability: Ensuring Safe Arrival and Optimum Placement in the Inbox (http://goo.gl/KuehF).

Experian Marketing Services (2013). Email Plus Mobile Interactions (http://goo.gl/w23Kla).

Facebook (2013). Updating Page Insights (http://goo.gl/X5f29E).

Facebook (2013). Like (definition) (http://goo.gl/guISi).

Facebook Business (2013). What Increased Content Sharing Means for Businesses (http://goo.gl/XRZokL).

Facebook for Business (2014). Organic Reach on Facebook: Your Questions Answered (http://goo.gl/sGblSG)

Facebook Developers (2012). Define Actions (http://goo.gl/LOnwh).

Farris, Paul W. et al. (2006). Marketing Metrics, pp. 289–290. Hoboken: John Wiley & Sons.

Feinen, Michael (2011). The Idiot's Guide to Event Tracking (http://goo.gl/TDWLP).

Feldman, Konrad (2013). Display Ad Clickers Are Not Your Customers. (http://goo.gl/vE02y)

Fulgoni, Gian (2013). Personal communication.

Fulgoni, Gian M. and Marie Pauline Mörn (2009). Whither the Click? Journal of Advertising Research, Vol. 49, No. 2, pp. 134–142.

Gluck, Marissa (2011). The State of Mobile Measurement: Prepared for the Mobile Marketing Center of Excellence of the Interactive Advertising Bureau (http://goo.gl/O00vRc).

Google Analytics (2013). Bounce Rate (http://goo.gl/CI5Y1)

Google Analytics (2012). Conversions: About Goals (http://goo.gl/koOSA).

Google Analytics(2013). Direct Traffic (http://goo.gl/NS7gL).

Google (2013). The Customer Journey to Online Purchase (http://goo.gl/rxICA).

Google Developers (2013). Registering with Google (http://goo.gl/0Ak98).

Google (2012). The New Multi-Screen World: Understanding Cross Platform Consumer Behavior (http://goo.gl/vbrEu).

Grappone, Jennifer and Gradiva Couzin (2011). Search Engine Optimization: An Hour a Day. 3rd Edition. Sybex.

Grimes, Seth (2012). Social Media Sentiment: Competing on Accuracy. Getting to the Truth on Measuring Sentiment in Online Conversations (http://goo.gl/lNCcO4).

Group M and comScore (2011). The Virtuous Circle: The Role of Search and Social Media in the Purchase Pathway (http://www.wpp.com/~/media/sharedwpp/readingroom/digital/groupm_search_the_virtuous_circle_feb11.pdf).

Ha, Anthony (2012). Facebook's Brad Smallwood Offers More Data on Ad Effectiveness, Says Datalogix Partnership Isn't a Privacy Risk (http://goo.gl/Qm3UU).

Ha, Anthony (2014). Facebook Relaunches Atlas Ad Platform With Cross-Device Targeting And Offline Sales Tracking (http://goo.gl/3JrozQ).

Haring, Arjin (2013). Why Marketers Should Focus on Persuadables (http://goo.gl/lLgw9).

Heath, Robert (2009). Emotional Engagement: How Television Builds Big Brands at Low Attention, Journal of Advertising Research, Vol. 49, No. 1, March 2009, pp. 62–73.

Heath, Robert (1999). The Low-Involvement Processing Theory (Admap, March Issue).

Hemann, Chuck and Ken Burbary (2013). Digital Marketing Analytics: Making Sense of Consumer Data in a Digital World. Indianapolis: QUE.

Hess, Mike and Tristan Gaiser (2013). Frequency: Don't Overlook It as Part of Digital's Toolkit. Nielsen (available from author Mike Hess at Nielsen).

Howto.Gov (2013). Digital Metrics for Federal Agencies (http://goo.gl/04OTA).

IAB (2007). Rich Media Measurement Guidelines (http://goo.gl/KN84S).

IAB (2011). Best Practices for Conducting Online Ad Effectiveness Research (http://goo.gl/2RTJP).

IAB (2011). 3MS Initiative Releases 5-Part Digital Marketing Measurement Solution. September 19 (http://goo.gl/xQHuz).

IAB (2012). Mobile Rich Media Ad Interface Definitions (MRAID) (http://www.iab.net/mraid).

IAB and MMA (2011). Mobile Web Advertising Measurement Guidelines: Adapted from IAB (US) Ad Impression Measurement Guidelines (http://goo.gl/d942B).

Jennings, Jeane (2011). The Value of Calculating Revenue per Email (http://goo.gl/JxuZO).

Kanter, Beth (2013). How to Use Negative Feedback on Facebook to Improve Your Content Strategy. (http://goo.gl/vk05E).

Katona, Zsolt. Competing for Influencers in a Social Network (July 1, 2013) (Available at SSRN: http://goo.gl/qcYih1).

Katz, E and Paul Felix Lazarsfeld (1955), Personal Influence: The Part Played by People in the Flow of Mass Communications. New York: Free Press.

Kaushik, Avinash, (2007). Web Analytics Demystified (http://goo.gl/eVjqJ).

Kaushik, Avinash (2007a). Web Metrics Demystified (http://goo.gl/LLXIP).

Kaushik, Avinash (2008). Standard Metrics Revisited: #4: Time on Page & Time on Site (http://goo.gl/bbVLp).

Kaushik, Avinash (2009) *Standard Metrics Revisited: #6: Daily, Weekly, Monthly Unique Visitors* (http://goo.gl/0Pvlq).

Kaushik, Avinash (2010). *Web Analytics 2.0. The Art of Online Accountability & Science of Customer Centricity.* Sybex.

Kaushik, Avinash (2011). *Email Marketing: Campaign Analysis, Metrics, Best Practices* (http://goo.gl/LLSlc).

Kaushik, Avinash (2012). *Facebook Advertising/Marketing: Best Metrics, ROI, Business Value* (http://goo.gl/dgPjV).

Keller, E. and Brad Fay (2012). *The Face-to-Face Book: Why Real Relationships Rule in a Digital Marketplace.* New York: Free Press.

Kemp, Patrick (2013). *Personal communication.*

KissMetrics (2012). *How Loading Time Affects Your Bottom Line* (http://goo.gl/hvGDl).

Koegel, Kathryn (2012). *Is an Online Ad Still an Ad If Nobody Saw It? Advertising Age,* April 9 (http://goo.gl/CEdk1).

La France, Adrian (2012). *Coming in the Side Door: The Value of Homepages Is Shifting from Traffic-Driver to Brand* (http://goo.gl/IEVsN).

Laubenstein, Christine (2010). *What Is Cost Per Action Advertising? WordStream Blog* (http://goo.gl/Ohhtv).

Linhorst, Michael (2013). *Five Tips for Reducing Email Spam Complaints* (http://goo.gl/QzkCf).

Lipsman, Andrew (2012). *For Display Ads, Being Seen Matters More Than Being Clicked* (http://goo.gl/OHXgY).

Lipsman, Andrew (2013). *Personal communication.*

Litmus (2013). *Emails Opened on Mobile? Start Designing for Fingers and Thumbs* (http://goo.gl/tFL02).

Plummer, Joseph et al. (2007). *The Online Advertising Playbook.* Hoboken: John Wiley & Sons.

Mallon and Bruner, 2009, *Can Rich Media Metrics Predict Branding Impact?* (http://goo.gl/hpsXH).

MailChimp (2012). *Email Marketing Benchmarks* (http://goo.gl/0E4ZP).

Mane, Sherrill (2012). *Clear Guidance. Mediapost Metrics Insider* (http://goo.gl/IQwSs).

Mane, Sherrill (2013). *Better Safe Than Sorry* (http://goo.gl/z14qX).

Martin, Ben (2013). *Do Brands Understand What Motivates Sharing?* (http://goo.gl/xyZ3E).

Mashable (2012). *Former Twitter CEO Says Network Needs a Better Metric Than Follower Count.* (http://goo.gl/bhFZV).

Mastronardi, David (2012). *Six Brand Advocate Archetypes* (http://goo.gl/2ccYL).

Media Ratings Council (2014). *Viewable Ad Impressions Measuremnt Guidelines, Version 1.0 (Final).* June 30 (http://goo.gl/1sLBdl).

McDermott, John (2013). *Are You Wasting your Money on Mobile Ads? AdAge.com* (http://goo.gl/Rgh68S).

MediaPoondi (2013). *SMG and ShareThis Announce 'Social Quality Index' Integration Into comScore Media Metrix Interface* (http://goo.gl/Yt4G0).

Microsoft Advertising (2010). *Dwell on Branding* (http://goo.gl/MlN7Z).

Mobile Advertising Association Mobile Analytics Committee (2012). *The MMA Primer on Mobile Analytics: Mobile Marketing Update September 2012* (http://goo.gl/vfsPnc).

Moses, Lucia (2013). *What's the Best Time of Day to Send an Email? Adweek.com* (http://goo.gl/UcwqT).

Nail, J. and J. Chapman (2008). *Social Media Analysis for Consumer Insight: Validating and Enhancing Traditional Market Research Findings* (ARF WebEx presentation).

Moth, David (2013). *Seven User Shortcuts That Will Help Reduce Checkout Abandonment* (http://goo.gl/bE2sw).

Nelson-Field, Karen et al., (2012). *What's Not to "Like?" Can a Facebook Fan Base Give a Brand the Advertising Reach It Needs? Journal of Advertising Research,* Vol. 52, No. 2, pp. 262–269.

Nestivity (2013. *The Most Followed Brands on Twitter Are Not the Most Engaged: A Study of Top Brands on Twitter* (http://goo.gl/n5bb5).

Nguyen, Joe (2011). *Cookie Deletion: Why It Should Matter to Advertisers and Publishers* (http://goo.gl/VhCkW).

Nielsen (2010). *Nielsen/Facebook Report: The Value of Social Media Ad Impressions* (http://goo.gl/rzEV).

Nielsen and Facebook (2010). *Advertising Effectiveness: Understanding the Value of a Social Media Impression* (http://goo.gl/BJ5P6).

Parr, Ben (2009). *Clickstreams: What They Are and Why You Should Track Them. Mashable* (http://goo.gl/IW2Tb).

Paine, K.D. (2009). *Towards a Definition of Engagement. The Measurement Standard* (http://goo.gl/3fNXb).

Paine, K. D. (2013). *Now What: From Good Metrics to Best Practices, How to Design a Framework That Makes Sense to Senior Management, and Also Makes Your Programs More Effective* (personal communication)

PC World (2010). *Facebook 'Like Button' Replaces 'Become a Fan'* (http://goo.gl/HTNo).

Performics (2013). *Retailer Has 62% Increased CTR for On-the-Go Boosts Smartphone Orders* (http://goo.gl/iCR6Y).

Piech, Dan (2013). *Personal communication.*

Plummer, Joseph et al.(2007). *The Online Advertising Playbook.* Hoboken: John Wiley & Sons.

PointRoll (2011). *PointRoll Mobile Research Reflects Differences in Consumer Behavior by Device, Driving Ad Engagement; Interaction Rates Increase on iPhone, Brand Time Grows on iPad* (http://goo.gl/r4TV7).

Polich, Adrienne et al (2012). *Understanding paid and earned reach on Facebook* (http://goo.gl/HLrCe).

Quantcast (2013). Beyond Last Touch: Understanding Campaign Effectiveness (available from http://goo.gl/0JPBb).

Rabjohns, D. (2013). Personal communication.

Rappaport, Stephen D. (2011). Listen First! Turning Social Media Conversations into Business Advantage. Hoboken: John Wiley & Sons.

Rickson, E. (2010). Top Metrics for Mobile Apps: Measure What Matters (http://goo.gl/n6NfV).

Romaniuk, Jenni et al. (2004. Brand and Advertising Awareness: A Replication and Extension of a Known Empirical Generalisation, Australasian Marketing Journal 12 (3), 2004 (http://goo.gl/67FcD).

Rutenberg, Jim (2013). Data You Can Believe In: The Obama Campaign's Digital Masterminds Cash In. (http://goo.gl/YwudG).

Ryan, Tim (2011). Article Metrics and Discoverability, blogs.wiley.com (http://goo.gl/E9313).

Smallwood, Brad (2012, Oct 1). Making Digital Brand Campaigns Better. (http://goo.gl/yuy12).

Socius, 2012. 6 Key Customer-Engagement Metrics for Improving Online-Community ROI (http://goo.gl/0sBiP).

TechCrunch (2012). Facebook Unleashes Powerful Marketing Tool: Page Post Targeting by Age, Gender, Likes, and More (http://goo.gl/ERh3J).

UPS (2013). UPS Pulse of the Online Shopper (http://goo.gl/CkW6X). Registration required for download.

Venture Beat (2012). Facebook's Biggest Change Yet: Actions Are Here (http://goo.gl/kpEyv).

Vertical Response (2005). Acceptable Bounce and Unsubscribe Rates (http://goo.gl/5GOsS).

Video Brewery (2012). 18 Big Video Marketing Statistics and What They Mean for Your Business (http://goo.gl/xDLJE).

Vizu-A Nielsen Company (2013). Online Advertising Performance Outlook 2013. Available from Nielsen site, registration may be required (http://goo.gl/VoT0D).

Vizu-A Nielsen Company (2013). Paid Social Media Advertising. Industry Update and Best Practices 2013. (http://goo.gl/W9aL4c).

Vollman, Andrea (2013). Personal communication.

Wagner, Kurt (2014). Facebook Set to Eliminate Sponsored Stories in April (http://goo.gl/jjFZDi).

Wall Street Journal Online (2013). ESPN, Twitter Expand Tie-up (http://goo.gl/yWFI1).

Wang, Alan (2011). Digital Ad Engagement: Perceived Interactivity as a Driver of Advertising Effectiveness (http://goo.gl/Ew3Hk).

Watts, Duncan (2007). Who Are the Influentials? What Are They Good For? (paper presented at ARF Word of Mouth Session).

Webtrends 2014. "What is Direct Traffic?" (http://goo.gl/zClzC6.)

Wikipedia (2013). Social Media (http://goo.gl/B23cX4).

YesMail (2013). Study: Almost Half of All Brand Emails Opened on Mobile Devices (http://goo.gl/0EYC1v).

Zuberance (2009). Zuberance, the Leading Word of Mouth Company, Wins Prestigious Social Media Award (http://goo.gl/6LbfU, reported in SmartBrief).